Life, Education, Discovery

Life, Education, Discovery

A Memoir and Essays
by W. Roy Niblett

With a Foreword
by Sir William Taylor

Pomegranate
BOOKS

First published in 2001 by Pomegranate Books

© 2001 W. Roy Niblett

Printed in Great Britain
by Antony Rowe Ltd, Chippenham
All rights reserved

ISBN 1-84289-002-6

Pomegranate Books
3 Brynland Avenue, Bristol BS7 9DR, England
www.pomegranatebooks.co.uk

Contents

Foreword

Professor W.R. ("Roy") Niblett's life spans nine decades. He was born at a time when the reign of Queen Victoria and the South African war had only recently ended, motor cars were rare, tonsil operations could be conducted without anaesthetics, and secondary education was not for all but for the few.

Between a degree course at Bristol undertaken with the aid of a teacher training grant and a post-graduate course at Oxford, he worked as a trainee teacher with classes of more than sixty. After teaching English in schools in the North of England in the mid-1930s he began a career in university-based teacher education which led to professorial appointments at Hull and Leeds, the Deanship of the University of London Institute of Education, and the first chair of Higher Education to be established in a British University.

Part I of this book is made up of vignettes of his life in these times. It is not the whole story. It is short on events and on contributions of which others would have made much, but which typically he has chosen to understate.

One such was the role he played during his spell as Registrar at the University of Durham during the Second World War in arranging for books to be supplied to British prisoners of war in German camps, thus enabling many to begin or to continue their higher education studies.

Another was his role in helping to set up the Society for Research in Higher Education. Roy's appointment as its life Vice-President in honour of his contribution, was and remains unique. He has been an active force in other organisations whose work has been consistent with his values and beliefs, from the Student Christian Movement to the Higher Education Foundation.

Roy Niblett was a staunch advocate of strengthening the academic and intellectual base of teacher education through the links with universities that Institutes of Education facilitated. His co-authored book *The University Connection* is an unique source of carefully documented evidence about the origins and development of the Institutes, which can be seen as precursors of the subsequent broadening of the role of universities in society.

The value of an education in the humanities and the importance of both individual and collective religious experience run through the whole of Roy Niblett's life and writing, and unite the two parts of this book. He nominally retired nearly thirty years ago. In fact, he has never stopped working. The first of his publications on educational and religious topics is dated 1933. The most recent, 2001. Others are in press. Part II of this book comprises a selection of these writings.

To enjoy the opportunities for growth our lives offer us and to fulfil our human potential requires us to remain open to the new and the unexpected. Such openness has been central to Roy Niblett's writing as much as to his life. In his own words:

"One of the key duties of homes and schools and universities is to keep selves open to experience, open to insight, open to faith and belief, open to love, open to hope, open to knowledge."

This is unfashionable language in education today. Some, mistakenly, might regard it as old-fashioned, irrelevant to a curriculum focused upon information acquisition and skill development, achievement and accountability, the reconciliation of equality with excellence. Sharply critical of many features of contemporary life and the education that sustains it, Roy Niblett is also alert to the social, economic, technological and political factors that shape the physical and the mental worlds we inhabit and the transformations they have wrought.

Throughout his long career in education, he has remained consistent in his beliefs about the characteristics of a worthwhile education and the importance of a spiritual dimension to life, whilst always being receptive to new ideas and practices. Thus he writes sympathetically of the impact of philosophical movements such as existentialism and post-modernism, but makes the important point that:

> ... the assumption of post-modernism that we must do without appeals to authority, do without all certainties, is not something it quite believes itself ... concealed in the very quest for freedom –

freedom from imprisonment in an objective world alone, freedom from being confined to formal dress and formal manners, freedom to be informal in speech and behaviour, freedom even from having to have definable, unchanging beliefs – is there not somewhere concealed … a conviction that genuineness matters, that pretentiousness is out? Such conviction is in itself, in a subtle way, a kind of certainty."

Roy Niblett does not deny the oft-repeated maxim that education today must include preparation for a life of uncertainty. But he makes the case that some level of certainty is necessary to sustain our humanity and to give meaning to our existence. The addiction to *things* that capitalist market forces encourages helps us little when facing the crises of our lives. Education must do more than equip individuals with skills and competences as means to worldly success.

None of us can know what new challenges the twenty-first century will pose for humanity. But some certainties remain.

Men and women will need to continue to form mutually fulfilling relationships with other individuals and to work hard at the task of living peacefully together in groups. They will continue to be faced with difficult choices and decisions. They will need courage and integrity rooted in giving and receiving love. They will be called upon to transcend immediate self-interest for the sake of their own happiness and survival and that of their descendants and fellow beings. And they will go on having to confront their own and others' weaknesses and failures, illnesses, incapacities and eventually deaths.

These endeavours will require attention to the fundamentals of education with which Roy Niblett has long been concerned. His own education began soon after the end of the nineteenth century. He continues in this penetrating, thoughtful and entertaining book to contribute to our thinking about the education and the values appropriate to the twenty-first. His argument is rooted in a faith that does not claim to have all the answers, that "…is not a rigid, complete or completed system of doctrines to be held on to". Instead, he invites us to recognise the limitations of our own knowledge of ourselves and of the world – for despite all the discoveries of science, our ignorance is still profound – and seriously to engage with the idea that: A faith that is much beyond human limitations of mind and sense, beyond human knowledge, will help to bring us hope; to bring stability and confidence into our lives – and into the life of twenty-first century Britain.

William Taylor

Preface

Some who glance through this book are likely perhaps to be more interested in one of its two Parts than its companion. Each can in fact be read in pretty complete independence from the other. But some readers who approach the whole as a memoir may find that the Parts, though disparate, do throw light each upon each.

The book would not have come into existence at all but for the prompting, confidence and maintained encouragement of my friend and former colleague, Sheila McCullagh. I owe a very great debt to her for her unfailing support. I want to thank also Anne Mallitte and Elspeth Gray for the secretarial services with which they have provided me so devotedly in connection with it.

And my appreciation of William Taylor's kindness in reading the text and contributing so personal a Foreword to it is real and deep.

W. Roy Niblett
August 2001

On Not Being Sent Empty Away

An inward life there is, whose scope
Is generative; it yields a flowing stream
Of trust, and power, and hope,
Of confidence that changing we are we.

Without such inward life, we're lost,
Must feed on substitutes – success and thrills;
A life deprived of meaning but not cost:
Unnourished by our barren questionings.

Introduction to Part I

In the womb we are part of another human being and once we are individualised our growth still depends on her – and increasingly on others – not only for nourishment physically but emotionally and culturally. From the very start we need to be valued, loved and believed in – a need that is lifelong.

But we also for our safe development require a stability for the protection of the life within our minds and bodies – a stability given us by having people, or at any rate one person, in touch with us whom we can trust intimately. Our outward environment may or may not be a stable one. What matters more still is that – whatever the dangers, disasters, threats, quarrels among people we encounter – there will be at very least someone who believes in us whom we can deeply trust.

Our development as human beings is many-dimensional, at many levels. What the French so aptly call our formation is only in part a matter of the education provided in school or college – utterly essential though schools and universities are.

As we grow up through childhood and adolescence, we feel ourselves into our environment, learning gradually what to take for granted in the society we live in. This is an immensely wide-ranging process, affecting both the subconscious and the more deeply unconscious parts of our minds. Though we may become aware of some of our preconceptions and limitations we shall never become conscious of all of them. Capacity for experience involves ability to observe our world objectively, to observe not merely things but people, and ourselves too, with increasing introspection. But a feeling-into element is also much involved.

So, not to be sent empty away from life calls for trust; for being believed in; for capacity gradually to feel ourselves more and more into a culture; and also for power to observe our environment as sensitively and objectively as we can. Whether or not religious belief or religion is involved in this process of development, what seems certain is that an adequate religion will welcome and reckon with all the elements I have listed, emptiness being its negation.

A Village Childhood

Keynsham, in July 1906, when I was born, was a large village between Bristol and Bath very contentedly separated from both. It had character and characters lived in it.

It was from our small, terrace house in West View Road – the sort that house agents call cosy – that, soon after I was three, I started to go to the village infant school, some two-thirds of a mile from home. In 1909 we used large sand-trays in the classroom, with real sand in them. We were taught gently and warmly by what many would think were methods introduced much later in the century. I delighted in school from the earliest days there – and from the beginning they were whole days, not half days. The headmistress lived in a large house higher up the same road as the one we lived in, and on rare, special mornings, she or I caught up with one another and I trotted along by her side. Several of the teachers cycled to school from villages some miles away.

Among my recollections in early school days was seeing a cow which had fallen down and died on a hillside just opposite the school. So great living things could die!

On Sundays I used to go with my mother to the evening service at the Baptist Chapel in the main street of the village, but it was to a Wesleyan Sunday School that I was sent, largely because the Wesleyan Chapel was on the safe side of the main road, though opposite the Baptist. Each Sunday we had Bible cards given us with vivid pictures, texts and far more written material on the back than would any longer be acceptable or even thinkable.

Keynsham was a quiet place in those days. The four bells of Queen Charlton church wafted their sound on Sunday evenings slow and melancholy over the fields to emphasise the quietude. But from Monday to Saturday the main street of the village and its shops were busy – George E. Chappell's grocery store opposite the Parish church (later, much later, labelled International Stores); the grocery shop of Chappell Brothers near the Post Office, opposite the Wesleyan Chapel; Mrs Beer's sweet shop with its bars of Fry's Five Boys Chocolate with the

Five Boys on the label at various stages of blissfully eating it. There was the Constitutional Club, which, I gathered, was very exclusive and snobbish; the chemist with four enormous pear-shaped glass vessels in his window, each filled with a bright coloured liquid, one red, one heliotrope, one green, one yellow.

What family quarrel was it that caused George E. to separate from Chappell Brothers and how many brothers were there once? Inside George E. Chappell's shop there were tins of biscuits arrayed, mostly with rather dull patterns on the sides of the tins to indicate the species of biscuits they contained – Marie, Garibaldi, Oval Rich Tea and so on. But there was one tin whose sides magnificently represented a tropical blue sea with a sandy bay. The biscuits were called *Bourbon* and they seemed to me delicious and of superb quality – a quality far higher, I must believe, than those tame descendants of theirs which now have the same title so undeservedly given. George E. Chappell also stocked *Bear Brand* tinned fruits, with a fascinating label showing a comfy sort of bear sitting down and looking at himself in a mirror holding a tin of *Bear Brand* apricots, whose label also portrayed a comfy-looking bear holding a tin of apricots and looking in a mirror – and so on, fascinatingly, apparently *ad infinitum*.

In between this shop, with its large two-window front, and the Parish church was a large triangular space along which traffic passed, but which was the venue of exciting events. At intervals, there was a military band, said to be a German band of itinerant players, who made blaring music in return for coppers dropped into hats. More exciting still was a bear attached by a chain to its keeper. The bear performed some antics at command, as coppers were industriously collected from spectators. The Town Crier also used this venue as one of several points in the village from which he proclaimed public events which were to take place in Keynsham in the next few days. He preceded his sing-song utterances by ringing a bell loudly and then calling out what sounded to me like "O Yes! O Yes! O Yes!" It was only much later that I was given to understand that this was a corrupted form of the Old French "Oyez! Oyez! Oyez!"

Then there was Bert Dorey's greengrocery shop with his horse and two-wheeled cart often outside, waiting to go the rounds of the district delivering goods from house to house. When I was six I used to be allowed sometimes to go with Bert on such a delivery expedition – being left, fearfully, in charge of horse and reins as he made deliveries. There was at least one occasion when the horse made for some grass on the other side of the road, disobedient to such feeble pull on the rains as I could manage, so that before Bert could return to restore normality there was an irate driver of some other cart brought up sharply in the road that Bert's was impeding.

Further along the High Street was the Post Office, whose hours of business were long and included even an hour and a half's opening from 9 to 10.30 a.m. on Sundays. We had at least three postal deliveries a day, the last in the late afternoon or early evening. It was certainly possible then to post a letter to Bristol early in the morning and, if your correspondent wrote a reply at once, and posted it, to receive that reply by the evening delivery on the same day.

The shop I knew best of all was the Sticklers' shoe shop. The Sticklers had been our next-door neighbours when we lived in Station Road; the Stickler children, including my contemporary Winnie, were a friendly lot, and George Stickler, their father, a superb craftsman at his cobbling trade. He would expertly drive small nails in a pattern around the sole made of leather which he was fastening to a shoe. One by one the small nails would come out of his mouth, where he kept a supply of maybe 20, as he hammered each in turn into the precise spot called for. He was a shrewd man, with intelligent comments on all sorts of matters to be overhead by a small boy in his workshop.

I can recollect various social distinctions which were real to me as I grew up in the village, though I would not of course have thought of them in those terms. The doctor who had helped to bring me into the world was named Peach Taylor and he had three daughters whom I regarded as undoubtedly superior beings. When the time came for them to go to school, they did not go to the local Church of England school, and when they were old enough they went day by day to schools in Bristol. There was a certain subtle superiority about being C of E (Roman Catholics were either unknown in the village or utterly cut off from the society I mixed with: they were not regarded with much approval anyway.) I never knew the vicar of Keynsham but I often penetrated into the kitchens of the rambling vicarage where there were two servants – one a cook, a homely person named Edie and one, I suppose, a housemaid, Susie. The vicarage was large and its stables housed a horse and trap.

I cannot have been more than five when, following the fashion of the day, Dr. Taylor decided that to prevent the constant succession of colds I developed in the winter – one of which developed into "bronchial pneumonia" – I should have my tonsils removed. This had to be done in Bristol General Hospital, some five miles from our village, and necessitated going to the hospital and waiting with other small boys and girls for the operation to be carried out. I was taken by my mother one morning to the hospital. We went by bus and walked from the bus route to the hospital – not more than, I suppose, a quarter of a mile. There was a long, long, wait in the waiting-room before I was summoned into the room where the operation itself was done. It was done without anaesthetic and I can remember the surgeon inserting an instrument to keep my mouth wide open and another to catch the tonsils when they had been cut out, so that they did not escape into lower regions. Afterwards I was kept in another room sitting down until the bleeding had eased and then we were discharged. But it was too late in the day then to catch the bus which would take us back all the way to Keynsham. We could get a tram back to the edge of Bristol and then had to walk the remaining two miles or so home. It was certainly after midnight when we arrived home and I cannot imagine today such an early discharge of a small patient in the condition I was. But I survived!

Much of the imagery I have used all my life in placing situations read about in novels or poems has come from those familiar village streets and from house interiors I encountered before the age of eight. I imagine that many people must draw in their dreams and in their reading upon the pictorial stores laid down for them in childhood.

My own father I saw chiefly at weekends, for during the week he was employed with his own small grocery business away in Bristol on the heights of Kingsdown. There were no early-closing hours then compelled by law. From Mondays to Thursdays the shop was open from 7 a.m. to 10 p.m., on Fridays till 11 p.m. and on Saturdays sometimes until midnight (though after the Shops Act of 1912 it was closed from 2 p.m. onwards on Wednesday afternoons). On Saturday nights my father cycled the seven miles or so to Keynsham where he stayed until early Monday morning, setting off in time to take down the shutters of the shop at 6.45 a.m. Sometimes he would come home for a Wednesday night during the week, cycling both ways. Later on, I got to know his shop much better and to realise what a disciplined, orderly, taking-no-risks, kind of shop-keeper he was. But in fact, he was only a shop-keeper by combination of circumstances.

He had left school at 11 or so and early in his teens had been apprenticed as an engineer for seven years. During his apprentice years he had worked hard and by his early twenties he was bringing some new ideas to the firm's notice. For a number of years he spent all his spare time in designing a new form of lathe chuck, which at the age of 28 he patented. Since he had no financial resources of his own, he was dependent upon someone recognising the potentialities of his invention and eventually the patent was sold, giving him a small capital for investment. Others were to make much money from incorporating the new Niblett chuck into the lathes they made. By this time, however, there was no connection with my father. He always described himself on forms requiring him to state his profession, as "engineer" and this was what by rights he should have been all his life. He continued to take almost every week the periodical called *The Engineer* which had contained a long and technical account, with illustrations, of his invention when in 1887 it had been made public. How long it must have taken in those days to work out the complexities of its mathematics I do not know, but trial and error is a process demanding incredible patience; with little mathematics and no computers, one only discovers the right answer at long last, after the achievement of many wrong ones.

On Sundays, in childhood, he used to take me for walks in the country around – in particular to see one Georgie, a swan, who moved with such dignity and grace on the gleaming waters of the River Chew two miles or so from our house, even on the fast-moving sliding waters, above the weir.

But it was with my mother that I went to Chapel on Sunday evenings and it was with her that I passed most of the out-of-school hours week by week. She, like my father, was the youngest of a large family, and some of her brothers and sisters and members of their families I came to know as childhood went on.

My mother was an attentive and excellent cook and before her marriage had for a good many years been a dressmaker – the making of dresses in those days being a highly complex business, with their flounces and complicated decoration. She still in Keynsham days "took in dressmaking" and made a little money from the craft, about 14 shillings in the average week if I remember rightly. This was an important and necessary addition to the family funds, as the profits made on a small grocery business were few.

But this did not prevent some interesting expeditions from time to time. One which had its fascination came at pretty regular intervals: going to a cookery demonstration at Keynsham Drill Hall where an assembly of mothers, some accompanied by children as mine was, saw a young woman, aided by a gas cooker, magically producing cakes, pies, buns and tarts. "Take 6 ozs. of Brown and Polson's self-raising flour; add 4 ozs. of Brown and Polson's plain flour and mix together in a basin with a little milk (like this) ..." and so on. At home a variety of chairs served me for ovens, their seats forming the top and their legs the sides.

Further afield, there were trips to Bristol and Bath. I much preferred Bristol. The dignity of Bath was too overwhelming. Its buildings frowned on small children. And though it was intriguing to be able to sip "the water" from the metal cup-on-a-chain attached to a public fountain, its taste was peculiar. But Bristol was different: it was full of life and variety. Once or twice we visited Clifton Zoo, the roars of the lions audible sometimes before we entered the gates – and there they were brushing the bars of their cage as they paced undulatingly to and fro waiting with flashing eyes for their meat, hours before it was pushed by a keeper with his long-handled fork between the bars. The reptile house with its boa constrictor was horribly fascinating and to see it fed, with the bulge formed by (was it a rabbit?) travelling on down its huge tubular body, revolted me. The stench of the animal houses was offputting, too. But the elephant rides and the camel rides were delights, even if at moments of ascent and descent a trifle nerve-racking. It must have been in 1911 that I watched, with my mother, Edward VII on a Royal visit to the City – or was it the newly crowned George V paying his first visit to the West? I remember the crowds, and the vivid hush preceding the arrival of the royal carriage, but not the occupants.

Occasionally, maybe twice a year, my mother visited an old friend, Annie Blackler. We went by bus to Bitton and then walked to Warmley where she lived in a house which had a workshop attached, for Charles, her husband, was a tailor who employed three or four women workers to help him. They could be dropped in upon by a small boy: and Charles himself could be seen as he sat with legs crossed sewing, or stooped over a long table cutting the cloth for a pair of trousers. The attractions of a visit had to be paid for, but the credits on the whole outran the debits. I had two teas! – one, at 4 p.m. in the best room of the house, was partaken of by Mrs Blackler and my mother – with myself bidden to drink the china tea from a delicate cup and eat pieces of bread, spread with butter, jam and lovely clotted cream. But on condition that no crumbs were dropped! The seat of each chair was protected from dust by a tight cover, and there were antimacassars to guard the tops of the armchairs. The piano was similarly decorated. I was bidden to sit upright ("Don't lean back") and to remain silent save when spoken to ("Little boys should be seen but not heard"). And in replying I must not refer to my mother as "she" ("she's the cat's mother"). This I found extremely difficult not to do and still wonder what the required recipe was. Yes, afternoon tea was a terrifying ordeal and the compensation of the clotted cream was not enough. But there was always 6 o'clock tea to look forward to relaxedly. This was a meal I could share with Charlie and Norah and the other workers. There were meaty sandwiches and no prohibitions about sitting or making crumbs. But then it wasn't served in the best room. Afterwards the workers cycled off to the villages in which they lived and which had such intriguing names: Doynton, Pucklechurch, Wick.

In between the meals I could go out for a walk on Goose Green, which stretched between the house and the railway embankment, a quarter of a mile away, along which the Midland Railway trains ran between Bath and Gloucester or Bath and Bristol – with an occasional through express, from Birmingham to Bournemouth perhaps, excitingly double-headed. The hazards included the population of geese on the green: clearly they lay in wait for small boys and could recognise me. They could hiss menacingly through long lowering necks and run surprisingly fast towards me, I discovered. Their wings they could use as evilly powerful weapons. On one side of the Green there were disused brickworks, with old rails partly grass-covered connecting one part with another. This was splendid territory for exploring.

But in Keynsham itself there was plenty to interest me, some provided by the changing seasons of the year and by its festivals. "One a penny, hot cross buns; one a penny, two a penny all hot buns," sang the lilting boy, with his swinging basket, its handle within his elbow. You got seven of the smaller ones for thruppence, seven of the larger for sixpence. And each had its currants and its glossy top. On Easter Day there were round yellow Easter cakes with serrated edges, but I preferred the Simnel cakes topped with their "hundreds and thousands" of tiny sweets which had marked Mothering Sunday weeks before. Late in the year Fireworks Day on November 5th meant adjournments from garden to garden as friends set their bonfires alight in agreed sequence. Each young guest could, if he liked, bring a few sparklers or crackers of his own. And at Christmas (I was never required to believe in Father Christmas; such deception was rather frowned on by both my parents) there was joy unconfined – at waking to find and explore the stockings (one of mother's added to one of mine) hanging down near the brass knob at the foot of the bedstead. Stirring of the pudding, weeks earlier in the large basin before it was cooked, and wishing ("You mustn't tell your wish or it won't come true") added anticipation to the delight of tasting it at Christmas dinner. We never had a "bought pudding", openly scorned as the inferior article it undoubtedly was compared with the ones my mother made.

Emigration was a normal part of the life of the village. The sons of one of the large families who lived near us, named Clark, when they left school, one by one went off to Canada. One of my mother's friends had gone with her husband and all her family to Alberta, where they bought a plot of land, and throughout my childhood we had letters from time to time postmarked "Grassy Lake" and telling of their toil and pleasures and gradually increasing prosperity.

My first seven years in Keynsham seem, looking back, to have brought with them a quite remarkable amount of leisure and of sunshine. I remember the sunny days, I hardly remember the rainy ones. There were many walks we went, notably one through the fields below the main railway track to the Humpty Dumps and by the river – the River Avon, whose serpentine course was bordered by fields lush in the early summer with cowslips, later with buttercups. In the autumn there were moon daisies growing in profusion along the borders of lanes and peopling the railway cutting. Near the bridge over that cutting I looked with increasing intensity of interest at the expresses on their way between Bristol and London and London and Bristol, with their superb (and well polished) engines, many of them named. They made a magnificent noise as they dashed by at 60 m.p.h. in an ecstasy of steam and speed. Later on I collected engine names and numbers like 10,000 other small boys. But the collecting instinct and the aesthetic pleasure were two distinct things, not coincident, even if simultaneous.

It was because one of my mother's sisters – the one indeed she knew best – lived in Oxford that several childhood holidays were spent in Oxford Augusts. I first remember Oxford in 1912 with horse trams running up and down St. Giles' with a terminus near Balliol. My Aunt Edith had been a schoolmistress, trained at Battersea College, and her disciplinary abilities were apparent to any small boy welcomed into her home.

My mother herself had been brought up as a member of the Brethren sect – though a broad-minded one. Her mother was Welsh and had been born in Swansea; whereas my father came from a solidly English Gloucestershire family, on both sides, his own father having been a daily carrier from Stroud to Gloucester in Victorian times. It was because of these Cotswold connections that I came to spend several childhood holidays later on at Dudbridge not far from my father's birthplace.

In 1913 much family discussion took place on what was to happen about a secondary education for me – an intention which my father had had firmly in mind before I had reached the age of one. If we remained Keynsham residents, the chances were much less of my having a secondary education at all than if we emigrated to Bristol. Moreover, even if one obtained one of the few secondary school places Somerset allowed, this would mean a daily journey into Bristol throughout secondary schooldays. It was decided that, to obtain the necessary residential qualification for me, we should move to Bristol soon after my eighth birthday, thus enabling me to study for various scholarships when the time came. But, at seven, I was of age to leave the infants school and for a year I went to the Church of England "big" school in Keynsham, that is, the school to which the 8s to 13s went, for 13 was then still the statutory leaving age. One of the memorable things for me about that year was being "withdrawn" from religious education under the Cowper-Temple clause. My mother felt that for me to be taught the catechism and the Anglican creed was against her religious principles – and anyway educationally undesirable. In fact, what happened was that I was given a seat at the back of the room, with some arithmetic to do, while the other boys and girls in my class were taught the formularies in the syllabus. This meant that I came to learn the catechism and the Creed on the side while doing, or pretending to do, my arithmetic. So that, maybe, everyone benefited!

Our move to Bristol, exciting in prospect for me and much looked forward to, was timed for September, 1914. I can vividly remember the newspaper placards which appeared in Keynsham streets on the night of August 3rd that year. One of those placards leant against the churchyard wall. It said simply, "MIDNIGHT DECIDES". And duly, on August 4th, the Great War was declared and when we moved to Bristol that war was already a month old with its threats of unknowns to come.

Reflections I

There are dangers of course in reminiscing, let alone deducing conclusions from what one remembers. The last time Mark Twain was asked to give a talk he replied: "I'd love to. The trouble is that I can only remember the things that never happened." Recollecting has its hazards.

To live an interesting life is not as intimately related to one's income or the extent of one's leisure, or to one's possession of social and athletic skills, as is sometimes thought. But interest matters. It may just be that for some children a little more love shown them at home, a little more belief in them shown at school would do more for their numeracy and literacy than an extra half an hour a day spent instructing them in those very necessary acquirements. And acceptance matters too. For me reading, writing and "sums" were part of the order of things; and when in due course we moved to a big city, Bristol, and I found myself in what was then called an elementary school in a part of the town which was going downhill faster than my parents had any idea of, I accepted it as natural to be one of a class of 52, natural that there should be no girls in it, natural that I should need to work and, if I did, go on to a grammar school. One of the foundation principles governing both education and life is the enormous importance – and influence – of what we take for granted. Leaders, whether of schools or nations, are those who can change a little what their followers assume to be right and natural. This is what leaders do for us in good – or very far from good – directions.

For young children our own time has much in common with the years when Margaret McMillan was fighting for them with a lot of her strength. But its pressures are more subtle and inescapable than those of a century ago. The England of the early 21st century is in some ways – especially in physical ways – a healthier and better country for children to live in than it was. There are fewer slums than in 1910. Streets are better lighted after dark. There are far more amenities and comforts in the homes of working people, there are supermarkets, leisure centres, mobile phones. But in a hundred other ways, many of them not physical, life threatens young children at least as much as it did. A higher proportion live in large cities; roads everywhere have grown more blackly dangerous with traffic. And all the time that imaginary epitaph on Henry Ford becomes more apt: "Here lies a man who made everybody want to be somewhere else." It is easy to mistake acceleration for progress. Life is much noisier than it was, more propagandist, piercing the nervous quick, stretching the elastic of sensitiveness. Television, radio, computers, the internet, discos are very much with us. The circulation of popular dailies and sex-filled weeklies is enormous. Many more things happen to young children that are exciting but which have little depth of meaning to child or to parent. For parents, like children, can be "distracted from distraction by distraction"[1].

Fundamentally education is not a detached teaching of facts and skills. It is a leading of the child into a whole inheritance of belonging. The child has to learn with heart as well as head: indeed it is very difficult to separate one from the other, especially in young childhood.

One of the things that mattered immensely to me from early childhood and throughout school days was being able to take it quite for granted that a loving God existed who took an interest in us. But for that, experiences would have come in differently and in a different hierarchy.

It seems to me impossible for children to see or understand the world objectively. I don't really know in fact what that could quite mean for any of us at any stage. One just has to have a faith and see many things through it – at a simple level a faith, though it is of course underwritten by evidence, that day will follow night infallibly; a faith when we are children that grown-ups know better about some matters than we do; that when we are older we shall understand – and also be able to do – many things better than we can now. We may have a certain range of choice in the faith or faiths we hold but not about the condition of faith itself.

At a less simple but no more conscious level we need when we are still children to begin to glimpse that there are rules about existence that we just can't gainsay and facts to be learned that have to be accepted, rational procedures which yield results that are not to be disputed: 2 x 3 always equals 6, to go from London to Edinburgh by the shortest route will mean travelling north the same number of miles every time and so on. And there are moral principles as well as rational ones and these one learns, in the first place, by *feeling* into them; it is, for instance, wrong to tell a lie, right to forgive someone who has accidentally trodden on our foot. An introduction to moral rules which is merely antiseptic, which consists chiefly of warnings, prohibitions, instructions to toe the line, is not likely to be very effective.

Throughout the years of the First Great War my mother and I went to a Congregational church, my father not going to any. When I was 15 or so its Sunday school, to which I belonged, put on a Christmas entertainment. Part of a Mummer's play and a section of *The School for Scandal* were bits of it but so also was the Magnificat. I had never heard this before, and had no idea that it was part of the Church of England liturgy, but it appealed to me and opened new doors into beauty for me. One of the advantages maybe of not being brought up as an Anglican is that its heritage can pour itself in as a reviving current!

At about this time I propounded to the astonished minister of my church the idea that when Jesus said, "Other sheep have I that are not of this fold", he must have been referring to people God had created on planets other than the earth. He promised to think about it.

But it was his more scholarly successor, a graduate of Yale, who gave me devoted tuition in the Scripture syllabus for the School Certificate (i.e. G.C.S.E. level) exam – that subject not being one on offer at my school. Week by week he prepared a lesson especially for me which he taught me at his home. I passed the examination all right, but could not understand one of the questions which referred mysteriously to "Holy Week", a term not then used in Free Church circles and which I had never heard. Ah me, those Anglican examiners! – for I had prepared an answer to such a question rather thoroughly. At school sometimes a Collect was used at Morning Assembly – antiseptically read sometimes by our agnostic second master, Gammy Borland. But I had no idea that it was from the Book of Common Prayer that it came.

A fair proportion of our friends – though by no means all – took for granted the viewpoints of our Free Church Christianity. But there was little denominational mixing because it no more seemed called for than did making a deliberate attempt to mix with any intimacy with people from a different social class. The war certainly and often pretty vividly had given to many a sense of the fragility of life, its unfairness, the nearness of the brutal to us all; and the peace which the Armistice of 1918 brought with it by no means caused everyone in the early or indeed later 1920s to recollect adequately what they and their nation had been through.

A City Schooling in Wartime (1914-18)

The house in Bristol we went to live in was at the western end of a terrace – the upper terrace of two parallel ones on a steep hillside. From the windows at the back there was a magnificent view of the spreading city, with its church spires and towers, its factories and office buildings. Much of the far horizon was bounded by the southern ridges of the Cotswolds. These ended to the east with Kelston Tump, topped with its clump of trees, clearly visible except on misty days.

The hill which descended steeply by the side of our house was every winter the scene of accidents. For in icy weather horses followed (and pushed) by the heavy two-wheeled carts to whose shafts they were harnessed slipped and slithered – and two or three times each winter fell miserably, with a load of coal on top of them. Rescuing them was not an easy or undramatic job. On occasion a horse had to be shot – its leg or back broken. More usually though, with much heaving and struggling the fallen beast was raised to its feet again, the cart righted and the coal or goods shovelled painfully back on to it.

The school to which I went daily down the hill was called "North Street Wesleyan". It once had been a far more select school than it had become by 1914, and my parents in sending me to it no doubt had its past rather than its present in mind. But some other parents, too, sent their children to it from "better" suburbs than those in the St. Paul's area from which the majority now came. The boys were taught upstairs well separated from the girls and the asphalted playground accommodated the two sexes at different times for the mid-morning break. "My" class, at first made up of some 50 nine and ten year olds was taught without undue strain over several years by the same teacher, Mr Turner, for all subjects; few of the boys attended with concentrated interest to what they were supposed to be learning (for some a bit of quiet masturbation sitting at one's desk did occasionally relieve things a bit). But quietness was normal, hardly anyone actively rebelled. At North Street remarkably little noise penetrated from one classroom to another in spite of the thin, partially glass-windowed, walls which separated them. Serious offenders were sent to Mr Sheldon, the grave and alert head teacher, to be caned on both hands – but the numbers queuing for such correction on any day were really quite small.

By tradition at Christmas-time each year the whole school gathered to listen to the deputy head teacher – another Mr Turner – reading Dickens's *A Christmas Carol* in vivid instalments spread over several days. A collection of pennies for some charity followed. An unusual amenity in 1915 was the availability of lessons in out-of-school hours in shorthand and typewriting on the school's solid Empire machine.

During the interval between morning and afternoon school no food or drink was provided by the authorities and most of us went home for "dinner". But there was a corner shop in the street nearby which sold sweets and lemonade and locust beans – of which for a halfpenny you could get a large helping in a triangular, blue paper bag. They were sickly sweet but very filling. Potato Crisps and KitKat biscuits were unknown, but you could get slim bars of milk chocolate (a more aristocratic comestible that most of us could afford). Those on offer included Fry's "Five Boys" chocolate bars made in Bristol, whose wrappers depicted a boy in five expressive stages sampling it – from "Anticipation" through "Realisation" to "Delectation" itself – far more intellectual words than would have been employed later in the century.

I was at North Street for most of World War I and in those years many an elder brother of the boys I knew was killed in Flanders or the Middle East. Occasionally great airships flew spectacularly over the city including once a Zeppelin but no bombs were dropped. We keenly backed the Allied cause detesting and hating the Kaiser and all he stood for. We knew and sang with fervour the national anthems of our allies or at least their first verses – from France to Russia (though in English of course). And when we went to Saturday matinées at the cinema every performance would begin with "God Save our Gracious King" and we stood in silence. A *sine qua non* at each show was an episode from a "serial". *The Exploits of Elaine* in 14 episodes was one of the most memorable. It featured Douglas Fairbanks and Mary Pickford and every episode ended suddenly – at an almost unbearably exciting point – with the hero or heroine in terrifying danger, the "clutching hand" about to seize hold of the villain or to push the frail, beautiful Elaine over a cliff. Then "TO BE CONTINUED NEXT WEEK" would flash on the screen and we had to depart in agonised suspense. The pictures were of course in black and white and there was no sound except for the accompaniment provided by a rather tinny piano (played by a local, not particularly skilled, pianist). Besides the serial films there was the "News", usually the *Pathé Gazette*, and one or more comedies. The young Charlie Chaplin was the darling of us all. We sang

> The sun shines bright on Charlie Chaplin,
> His boots are cracking
> For want of blacking;
> And his baggy trousers they want mending
> Before we send him
> To the Dardenelles."

It cost each of us a halfpenny, sometimes a whole penny, to get in to these crowded shows – but what sheer joy one got for the money!

On Sundays I went with my mother to the Evening Service at Brunswick Chapel with its loyal congregation. When I first went it had an articulate minister aged 30 or so, who rejoiced in the name of Dr. Roderick Michael, though I fear the doctorate was not one he earned. From the age of 12 or so I was roped in occasionally to "blow the organ", for electricity had not yet taken the job over. One had to raise and lower a long handle which protruded from the back of the organ and was attached to invisible bellows somewhere inside it. If the organ was played quietly it was easy to cope and to keep the bobble high which told the amount of wind from moment to moment in the bellows. But if the organ was played vigorously (as perhaps for the last verse of a hymn or for a loud closing voluntary) I puffed and blowed and hoped against hope that the organ wouldn't run out of wind before I did.

The trams in Bristol in those days had open tops – the driver, too, was pretty exposed to the weather – with an ingenious arrangement by which the wooden seats on the upper deck had a double base, one part of which could be rotated so as to present a dry surface on which to sit if the other surface had been rained on. I sampled the whole widespread tramway system and with the aid of the mangle at home drove many imaginary trams through all its suburbs. For with the help of the levers on top of it which controlled the degree of closeness of the rollers to one another I could be the tram driver myself. In time I came to be able to imagine each bump in the rails on some routes and the speed, too, at which every curve had to be taken, so that a "journey" by mangle from A to B would take exactly as long as the genuine article.

In early adolescence I was bitten with the craze of collecting engine names and numbers. Temple Meads Station, which in those days was busy with both Great Western and Midland Railway engines and trains, attracted other boys in considerable numbers. What glorious engines there were to look at and listen to! On the Great Western there were four-cylinder monsters like Rising Star, two-cylinder ones like Saint Agatha; graceful 4-4-0s such as City of Truro and (a rare visitor) The Great Bear itself, an enormous 4-6-2 of unique vintage. All were green and proud and polished. On the Midland lines the engines were red and the more important trains they pulled north, to Birmingham and even York, were often double-headed when they left Temple Meads, for the gradient north-east through Fishponds and Mangotsfield was severe and had to be climbed very soon, giving little chance beforehand to get up speed. Sometimes the pilot engine was an old-fashioned "single driver" (a 2-2-0) not really suitable for the task which confronted it and often there was much splendid slipping to start with. What clouds of steam, what noise, what excitement for the small boys (for there were never any girls)!

Where I spent my summer holidays was largely determined by the fact that my mother had a sister who lived in Oxford and a brother who lived in Bournemouth. So that for a happy fortnight my mother and I would go together either to Bournemouth or to Oxford. When I was 12 I went to Oxford for the first time by myself and being of an exploratory turn of mind started to visit on my own each of the Colleges. But of that more later – as of my first visits to the Cotswolds where I was to stay at the home of one of my father's sisters at Dudbridge near Stroud.

During the years 1914-18 England was an anxious, sober country. Rationing was severe though well ordered and as a child I never really suffered from the shortages. Indeed the shortages of sugar and butter may have been good for me. With no elder brothers or close relatives drafted off to France or the Middle East I was saved from the threats of personal loss which deeply wounded so many hearts. I can remember through most of the war years going to collect at fortnightly intervals two strange but unrationed items of diet for an old lady who lived in a largish house opposite our own. These items, her chief means of subsistence, were "Toy Cracknell" biscuits and champagne. It must have been quite an expensive regime.

But the great object of our moving in 1914 from Keynsham to Bristol was so that I could at the appropriate time take the "scholarship" exam which, if I passed it, would entitle me to a place in a grammar school – an exam later to be called the 11+.

Bristol: The Grammar School Effect (1918-24)

The last few months of a war, devastating, impoverishing, that by now had gone on for more than four years, wasn't the ideal time at which to begin one's secondary schooling. But there were so many beckoning unknowns ahead that I was hardly conscious of the nation's tiredness. And anyway there was a fast-growing hope that peace would soon come and with it a country fit for heroes to live in. The school I was to enter had been founded in Bristol by its Merchant Venturers Society and called by their honoured name. It was not far from the city centre and I found myself journeying to it by tram morning after morning – including Saturdays – from September 1918 for the next two years.

The printed school timetable of which each of us had a copy was impressive – listing every period and the teacher responsible for teaching it for every form, including the Sixth. The bias was emphatically towards "modern" subjects. No Latin or Greek was offered, but Maths, Chemistry and Physics, English and French were given generous allowances of time – History too, and before long, German again. For on November 11, 1918 – only two months after I had started at the school – the Armistice was signed amid rapturous rejoicings, with immense relief predominating. The war had crippled, almost starved, England, robbing her of most of a whole generation of her young men and much of her wealth. But hope shone through: to make the country into one really fit for heroes to live in was a challenge. We imagined innocently that there would always be an Empire with those bright red patches spread out world-wide on the map – an Empire upon whose size, power, loyalty and resources too, we could depend with confidence. And there certainly would never be another conflict: for had we not just fought victoriously the war to end all wars?

Most of us worked quite hard at our lessons. Two hours' homework a night was expected from both boys and girls in secondary schools then, except at weekends, and a good proportion toed the line, however reluctantly. After I had been at the school for two years, the Merchant Venturers in their wisdom decided that the school they had created in 1854 should be taken over by the Bristol LEA and re-established well away from the city centre, on higher ground in Cotham. There gardens and lawns separated the main part of the school – at first housed in temporary buildings – and Tower House, where the Sixth Form, the school offices and the headmaster's quarters were sited. It was called Tower House because, standing on the summit of its front lawn, and leaning at a slightly perilous angle, was a stone-built cylindrical tower. Cotham School was our school's new name. Astonishingly little protest seems to have been raised at the dramatic transition – from endowed to maintained status, with change of school colours, change of school cap and badge, etc., etc.. We had the same masters – a new head though, to stride along the paths with gown billowing, possessing three Christian names and much majestic determination. Qualified in Mathematics, he was endowed by nature with many a managerial gift and instinct.

Certainly Mathematics was not one of my own favourite subjects; but now we had a Yorkshireman of character to teach it to us – Arthur Pickering, a member of the staff since 1903. He would put up with no excuses about homework left undone: "I'm not calling you a liar boy, but I don't believe you." On Saturdays in local Club cricket he had scored century after century, but when the invitation had come to him to play for Gloucestershire, as it did on four occasions, his top score amounted to a sorry 15.

"Bunny" Rahtz, our English master, was so nicknamed because one of the muscles of his nose twitched from time to time. But that made no difference to his steady sobriety as a teacher or his enthusiasm for the teaching of grammar. He had written a whole series of books about it: *Preliminary English*, *Junior English* and *Higher English* among them. They were extraordinarily thorough textbooks and they sold over many years in such numbers as to make the name Rahtz a household word all over the country. There were also volumes on *English Composition* and four covering English literature. My own copy of *Junior English* was marked Thirtieth Edition and that of *Higher English* Twenty-First. If you really knew your Rahtz you were splendidly furnished with knowledge of the English tongue

– to the extent indeed, by the time you were in the Fifth, of knowing not merely what onomatopoeia meant but synecdoche, litotes, oxymoron and pleonasm. Nor would you dare to use an unrelated participle. The general view when we were in the Fourth form, was that Bunny Rahtz was very old as well as very learned. Actually when I was in the Fourth in 1920 he was 49. Which just shows!

So thorough, hard-working and perceptive as a teacher of English was Bunny that when in 1936 I became Chief Examiner in English to the University of Durham School Examinations Board, I invited him to become an Examiner for us; and so reliable was he that he went on and on for years as one of the team. His papers were always marked to time – indeed he was often the first to send in his results. And his judgement could rarely be faulted: when others checked the marks he had awarded in this tricky case or that, he had usually hit the target plumb.

We were taught French in a disciplined, thorough, way by a highly intelligent Swiss graduate of Geneva University, C.A.L. Dirac, father of Paul who was later to become a Nobel Prize winner and the school's most famous old boy. I had overlapped with Paul when I was in my first year at the MV and he a rather odd-looking prefect. Dirac père taught French with verve and skill but can hardly have been accused of using a direct method to excess.

What of the other subjects I took in those long middle school years? Chemistry was certainly one of those upon which I was keenest, and I was usually top of the form in it, whereas in English (my other favourite subject) I was never even near the peak because I could never remember crisply the poetry set for homework – and many marks were given for perfection in repeating it. For at least two years at this time I had had a home laboratory, its equipment built up by slow accretion and expenditure of pocket-money – a multitude of jars of chemicals and bottles of reagents, and a dark- room in which I slowly developed photographs. Did I not possess, in fearful secrecy, a supply of potassium cyanide, and put on a few more or less colourful experiments for such of my friends who could be persuaded to look? But my Maths was not good enough for me to risk taking

Chemistry in the Sixth Form. And, anyway, I was developing a growing taste for English Lit.

A great problem for me was that the school had no Arts Sixth. The thing, therefore, was to see if it could be made to create one. Were there others who would join it, if it came into existence? Yes, at least two, maybe three. But my credit with the Head had been reduced by my failure to join the School Cadet Corps, his pride. My parents were adamant that I should not join it; and I had no wish to do so myself, though my motives for objecting were as mixed (albeit in different proportions) as theirs. A consequence, however, was that I was not made a prefect. How could I influence a Headmaster I had offended in this way so as to get him to create a Sixth Form? I must have had allies among the staff, and maybe the Head himself thought that a small Arts Sixth might bring credit to the school. Whatever the reason, it was decided in July that a Sixth which offered English Literature, Modern History and French should start up in September 1922; and, with three other boys, I joined it, thereby beginning my higher education – for higher education begins for most people when they go on to the Sixth at about 16, not when they enter a university or college.

One of the new masters at Cotham School that September was Rupert Jackson, then 24. He taught us History more excitingly but more rigorously, too, than any of us had known any subject could be taught. He was ambitious, keenly so, but for us as well as himself and his wide interests fertilised ours. He expected us to work hard, even though not as fiercely hard as he worked himself. One of his gambits was to introduce us to a book he was commending by giving us a personal account of the author. Pollard's *Factors in Modern History*, for example, was introduced something like this: "A week before term began, I was working in the British Museum and there – five seats away – was old Pollard himself. He seemed to be referring to one book after another as if he was collating what they had to say. ("Collating; what does that mean?") What a curious, lively face he had ..." and so on.

History was being written, scholars were people, life itself was young! And so R.J.'s other interests too began to matter to us –

painting, architecture, contemporary politics, the Oxford unattainable to him (he had won a scholarship to Oriel but, bitterly, had been unable to afford to take it up – and he had not been to a university: his degree was a London External one). The essays we did fortnightly for him for homework and those also written fortnightly in the classroom in a timed three-quarters of an hour were all marked for style and for content separately. It was very hard in the early terms to get more than 3/10 or 4/10 for either; but his comments written in red ink and rapid, small handwriting at the end of each essay could cover half an exercise book page. Nothing showed more clearly that an intelligent audience mattered, or that if one showed intelligence, grasp or wit oneself, it was appreciated.

And so there was a carry-over to my literary studies. What I wanted more than anything, then, was to be able to develop into a sound and understanding critic with wide range of concern, not too confined by period or limited by narrowness of taste.

It was her own trust in Rupert Jackson and his commendation more than anything else that finally overcame my mother's suspicion of the theatre – enough at any rate to allow me to go to a performance of *The Mikado*, a memorable first experience at 16 both of opera-going and of the theatre. Seeing Wolfit's company in a variety of Shakespeare's plays followed, in many of which Donald Wolfit himself tempestuously appeared. And later I started to go on my own initiative to organ recitals fortnightly in entrancing St. Mary Redcliffe church.

But it was not until 1923 that I went for the first time to London. I travelled with my father on a long day trip; we had planned our itinerary with meticulous care so as to cover as many of the main sights as possible in 16 hours. But how to spend the time after all the public buildings were shut, it was dark, and when we had no money (or inclination) to go to an entertainment? It was a great waste to return by any earlier train than the latest the ticket would permit. The answer was simple and joyous: we visited all the great railway termini we could fit in between 8.30 p.m. and 11.30. So I had that day my first sight of Euston, St. Pancras, King's Cross, Cannon Street, Waterloo and Victoria, and I'm not sure that we didn't somehow take in Holborn Viaduct *en route.*

Holiday visits to my Oxford aunt's house continued and one by one on my list I ticked off as "seen from the inside" the chapel, dining hall and library of all the 21 colleges which then existed. This is not as straightforward a pursuit as might appear. Some were but rarely open to visitors; others at awkward times or only on certain days; or not at all.

With my father I went on my bike into Gloucestershire a number of times, visiting his "childhood's haunts" as he called them and his sister Sarah Stephens who kept The Railway Inn at Dudbridge, near Stroud. Later I went by myself to stay with her and explored some of that magic Cotswold country for the first time.

Summer holidays during my middle teens normally meant a fortnight or so spent with mother at the seaside – an increasing radius from Bristol being gradually brought within our range. To travel was becoming a key interest but cash was scarce. We experimented with Southsea and Portsmouth; we suffered the mosquitoes of Hayling Island; there was an unforgettable experience at Ramsgate. Unprecedentedly we had answered an advertisement in one of the London dailies – "our" paper was the *Western Daily Press* – offering accommodation in The Plains of Waterloo at Ramsgate. We were intrigued by the romantic sound of the address and the very reasonable price asked. When we arrived we were more doubtful. Were the bedrooms, were the beds, clean? That night, in separate rooms, we found ourselves each coming out in lumps, each chasing mysterious insect creatures I had never seen before and never since. Though we endured one more night it was impossible to sleep, impossible to contemplate staying longer. We had had, however, to pay for a fortnight's board and lodging in advance and the landlady was up in arms to hear any criticism whatever of the accommodation she provided – which had, we were given to understand, been blissfully occupied by scores of people before us ... "and no complaint". So our holiday ended miserably and we used our return halves of our tickets to go back home, the delights of Ramsgate hardly sampled and now left disappointingly behind.

But holidays were interludes, of course. The major concentration for me was my work at school. Of my French set books I found Pascal's *Pensées* particularly appealing. There are excellent arguments though for introducing Philosophy to some boys and girls at the Sixth Form stage. In English, Shakespeare only slowly came to seem for me the equal of Milton or Wordsworth. History was the subject which mattered most to my two chief Sixth Form rivals and both of them later got Open Scholarships to Cambridge in the subject. English remained my own first love, though R.W.J. became keen that I, too, should try for a Cambridge History scholarship when Higher School Certificate was over. The examination for that was in the summer of 1924 and I was surprised to find myself with Distinctions in English and History, though not my Pass in French.

A battle ensued with my father whether I could be allowed to stay on to try for a Cambridge (or Oxford) scholarship. This would mean a year's delay in entering a university and he felt strongly that one of the older universities was anyway beyond our station. It would also have meant my leaving home and a greater drain on the family resources – and was not Bristol University a very fine one? I found it hard to reconcile myself to this verdict and relationships with my father henceforward for a long time had a distance and a coolness they had not suffered before.

The University Effect (1924-28)

Bristol University, which I now entered with the help of a four-year teacher training grant – for neither my parents nor I doubted that teaching was the right profession to aim at – was from the start a welcoming place and one whose Honours School of English had standards and individuality too. These qualities it owed in part no doubt to the traditions it had already established; but they were maintained by the imaginative young Professor now at its head. J.E.V. Crofts had been appointed to the Winterstoke Chair of English at the age of 29. Four years later when I became a member of his Honours Class he was at his vigorous best – left wing in sympathy but independent of mind, he was personally interested in his students – or at any rate in some of them. Shakespeare, the 17th century character writers, Blake,

Wordsworth, Vachel Lindsay, were among his many enthusiasms – each of which came accompanied by an acuity of insight and robustness of comment that made him a personality. He was an excellent *teacher*, especially when he knew he might have two or three perceptive and sympathetic people in his audience; and he marked the essays we did for him with memorable and pithy comments.

Philosophy was my subsidiary subject in the First Year and gave me an introduction to Plato for which I've been grateful ever since. At the end of the year I was top of the class of some 35 or so in this and it was with reluctance that I signed on to continue with Anglo-Saxon instead of "going over" to Joint Honours in English Literature and Philosophy. I am sure that it was mistaken advice to me that I should opt for the conventional Language and Literature course, "as more useful for someone who is going to be a schoolmaster". Rubbish!

The lecture rooms and library we frequented were in the light and graceful New Building whose Gothic Tower and Great Hall were in the autumn of 1924 still unfinished. In 1925 the whole was opened by King George amid great jollifications and I had a seat (accompanied by my mother) on the terrace stands erected between Library Wing and the Tower and a fine view of what was going on.

Fellow students in my Honours year in the School of English included Alex Evans, then a runner at some speed over the mile and half mile, as well as poet, dramatist and scholar; Reg Jones, at whose home I heard Beethoven's *Moonlight Sonata* (played by him) for the first time; the able Maureen McGrath and Vera Pheysey, full of intelligence and humanity, soon to be joint President of the University Union with her husband-to-be, Philip Parrott. There were more women than men taking English for Honours and I enjoyed that, however shy I might be at dances or social events.

At the end of my First Year I had a fortnight's holiday in Romford, in Essex, at the home of Stanley Laws and his family. He was the youngest of Aunt Edith's three sons – the oldest was Graham, a bright and keen schoolmaster; then came Douglas, manager of Boots main shop at Bournemouth; and finally Stanley, who worked in an architect's office.

On most mornings that fortnight I went by myself into London, in trains incredibly crowded then as now. On one occasion, 25 others with me were packed into one compartment: I counted them! Each day I explored, with curiosity and enthusiasm, parts of the City and West End. But one was given up to a first visit to Cambridge, memorable not only because of its sights but the diarrhoea which afflicted me throughout.

My aunt's house at 44 Aston Street, Oxford, was still a place to which both my mother and I went to stay from time to time. A great delight was an occasional trip we made by Salter's steamer on the Thames – whether starting from Oxford or going to Henley or Reading by train so as to board the boat there. Day's Lock, Shillingford Bridge, Cliveden Woods and the buttercupped meadows of Berkshire in the sunshine are memories still.

There is no doubt that one of the constantly formative influences on me throughout childhood and into adolescence was my mother's Christian faith. In my later teens, when I argued with her that no one could *prove* the existence of God she was greatly upset, in spite of my insistence that logical proof was not what we depended on in the matter. But in general we understood one another pretty well and could make allowances.

I cannot remember when it was that I started to go to the 7 p.m. Sunday Nave service at Bristol Cathedral when the Dean (E.A. Burroughs) was preaching. One had to queue outside, unless one was lucky, for though his sermons were those of an intellectual and lasted 25 minutes or more he could communicate his thoughts and feelings in a very personal way, especially to the young. And there was one special occasion (not a Sunday evening) when my father surprisingly took me to the Cathedral to hear someone named Carpenter speak who was one of his heroes.

But then he did from time to time reveal facets of personality which would not normally have been guessed at. He was a steady but energetic cyclist and on one of our expeditions to mid-Gloucestershire took me to a Roman Catholic service at Woodchester Priory church. Why he did this I cannot remember, but it was a new experience to add to my widening store.

My own church membership was transferred, soon after I entered Bristol University, to Highbury Congregational chapel among whose prominent members were the Franks family – Dr. Robert Sleightholme Franks, Principal of Western Theological College, and his wife with her close Quaker connections, and their two sons and two daughters. The elder son Oliver (later Lord Franks) had been captain of Bristol Grammar School during one of my last years at Cotham. He was often one of those taking the collection – with suitable dignity – at Highbury chapel.

1926 brought with it the redecoration and re-opening of the Theatre Royal in Bristol after a closure which had lasted for many years. Among the events inaugurating this was a remarkable season of opera sponsored by Napier Miles, a local philanthropist, for which students could buy series tickets at a bargain price. So I saw Mozart's *Cosi Fan Tutte* in the first production it had had in England for a number of decades, Vaughan Williams's *Shepherd of the Delectable Mountains* and Ethel Smyth's *The Wreckers* (conducted, of course, by upright herself). What a curious selection of operatic performances to go to! Apart from a little Gilbert and Sullivan these were among the first serious operas I saw and heard.

My increasing interest in music, however technically ignorant I stayed, and the supposition that I might be administratively trustworthy put the idea into people's minds that I might be an appropriate first secretary of a new Bristol University Music Society which would have Meyrick Carré, my former lecturer in Philosophy, as its chairman. In 1926 I found myself, therefore, going to see the Vice Chancellor in his study to ask if he would give his blessing to the formation of the Society. It was the first time I had spoken to so exalted a being. Soon a series of concerts, chiefly of chamber and piano music, had been arranged and during the sessions 1926-8 the panelled Reception Room was their venue – as it was for many years afterwards.

The Honours English course meant more and more to me as it continued – Crofts's deep reading voice, his scholarship, his irreverence, all leaving their mark. But the final examination in June 1927 was an ordeal nevertheless, though I had prepared myself hard – Jackson's recipe of questions, self-set, and answered to a strict time schedule serving me well. I lost some 6 lbs. in weight during the examination period of just over a week in which we, the candidates, had to sit ten three-hour papers, and I was resigned to the achievement of a Third Class degree.

My viva with the External Examiner – a formidable Scot named Dewar, the Professor of English at Reading – vivid of phrase and given to expletives – did not raise my spirits. He was encouraging and friendly enough, but by then I had decided that my cause was hopeless. So that it was with astonishment, maybe a week later, when I went to look at the Pass Lists on the Notice Board, that I found that I'd been classified among the few Firsts. I was quite sure that this was a mistake in the list; and some time elapsed before I even came to accept that if there was one it was on the part of the Examiners, not of the administration. In due course, however, it became clear that the list had to be acknowledged, and moreover that I was to share with Alex Evans the Albert Fry Prize, awarded to the graduate in Arts who had done best in any subject in the year.

The idea now began to bubble up that after I had taken a year's Education course I should have two years at Oxford probably reading for a B.Litt. Getting the money with which to do this was the problem, but the University of Bristol in making available to me the John Locke Scholarship for the two years 1928-30 generously agreed that this could be held at Oxford instead of Bristol. Later a letter to the Merchant Venturers' Society, saying that I was an Old Boy of their former school, produced a further sizeable sum. I was interviewed for the grant in Merchants Hall near the quayside – among Bristol's most handsome buildings and one of her greatest losses in the bombing of the early 1940s. I was also awarded by the City of Bristol a special grant – and this added to the others gave me enough to survive for two whole years if I could eke things out by fees for examining or by loans.

John Crofts himself offered me a loan saying that I could repay it or not – and when, if ever, that was convenient; but I did not need to

call on his munificence. The question of which College to try to
enter was one that gave both my parents and me quite a bit of concern. Crofts advised applying to St. Edmund Hall on the ground
that it was a small College and that I was less likely to be cold-shoul-
dered there than at one more dominated by former Public School-
boys. He had himself been at Magdalen and, I gathered, did not
regard that as at all likely to fill the bill suitably. So I wrote off to
Teddy Hall and without much difficulty secured a place though, to
my disappointment, they could offer no hope of residence to someone who was to be a research student. While the application was "in"
Meyrick Carré, a Balliol man, heard for the first time that I was in-
tending to go to Oxford and urged me to let him back me for a place
at Balliol but it was by then too late. "Might be worth quids to you to
go to Balliol!" commented Crofts. But the chance of happiness was
greater at Teddy Hall, he thought, and was not happiness more important than quids?

Meanwhile I had my "Education Year" to do and, in September
1927, a preliminary period of teaching practice to put in at a South
Bristol elementary school where at least one of the classes I minis-
tered to had 62 children in it. The Department of Education was
housed in the Royal Fort, a fine 18th century house with magnificent stuccoed patterns on the walls of its wide, balustraded staircase.
Our Professor of Education was the still young Helen Wodehouse,
fresh from her time as Principal of Bingley Training College, a mathematician and a progressive, enlightened, left wing in political views
and an excellent teacher. She lectured during the first term on Educational Psychology but left it to her students' decision whether from
then onwards she should continue with a lecture course or arrange a
weekly seminar, attendance obligatory only upon those who opted to
join it. The vote (rather to my disappointment) was for the seminar. I
enjoyed the subsequent discussions but missed the clarity of her lectures. She also, however, gave a course in the Teaching of Religious
Knowledge, robust and individual in its combination of the philosophic, the psychological and the practical.

The Master of Method, who was also my "tutor", was an oddity named T.S. Foster. It was rumoured that he had formerly been a master at Marlborough and that he had eight children: both rumours probably being true. He imposed a regular regimen of essays and then saw his group one at a time, in the Oxford manner, to discuss what had been written. The fact that I had to read my essay aloud more often than not did not convince me that he had necessarily looked at it himself beforehand. He would pronounce in an arcane but authoritative way what shape he saw it as being – a triangle, a spiral or parallel lines which somehow tapered to a point. But one left little the wiser for his counselling, intelligent though he appeared, and seemingly thought himself, to be. He had, we were given to understand, been "passed over" for the chair when Helen Wodehouse was appointed and was to be passed over again when she went on, in 1931, to be Mistress of Girton.

My "long practice" lasting for the spring Term of 1928 was spent at Colston's Boys School at Stapleton near Bristol – a boarding-school to which a cousin of mine had gone during the war years, and where I found plenty of kindness and help available. I remember teaching my "examination lesson" in the presence of John Pilley, then a Lecturer in the Bristol Department and subsequently Professor of Education at Edinburgh. At this time he had recently completed *The Oxford Book of Electricity*, but his lecture course was on educational administration and his keenest interests music and philosophy. It was only later that I came to know him and J.H. Nicholson whose course on *Education and Society* was an alternative to Tony Foster's on *The History of Education* which I felt it incumbent upon me to go to since T.S.F. was my tutor and anyway I was potentially interested in this subject. Unfortunately we never, during the two terms the course lasted, got beyond prehistoric man, Foster resolutely maintaining that this was the key to an understanding of almost all subsequent developments in educational history and anyway necessitating that we cover the textbook on Prehistoric Man written by himself, which we were all required to buy.

There was no written examination (apart from one paper in Hygiene which hardly counted) at the end of the year, for Helen

Wodehouse was the first Head of an Education Department in Britain to inaugurate a system of "continuous assessment" of essays done during the year, and this formed the basis for our final classification. This, surprising as it might seem today, was into three divisions. I was included in the First division and given a distinction in Theory of Education. A happy year, and one which, with Oxford still to come, was forward-looking. I expected to be a schoolmaster in two years' time and was sorry in a way that I couldn't go out now at once to earn my keep. Meanwhile an interlude!

These four years at Bristol University were formative ones – I was extraordinarily fortunate in having someone almost always who *cared* about the students they taught. Most of my teachers were very human beings. My late development showed itself still in a whole variety of ways, but some kinds of confidence were growing and some kinds of self-reliance being firmed up.

Oxford Years, (1928-30)

In the USA tablets are often put up to commemorate some past event: a battle won, a treaty signed, a writer born, a statesman dead. For nations need a history which helps to make their inhabitants into a community, giving them ancestors and bestowing a past upon them. An older nation may take its past more for granted – too much for granted maybe – perhaps because so many of the consequences of that past whether for good or ill have sunk entirely into the unconscious. Granted, however, that the legacies which may make a community feel that it is really one may at the same time breed in it a false notion that it is a chosen people, quite superior to the rest.

When from my undergraduate years at Bristol I went on to study at Oxford for a further degree I knew of course that I was, as knowingly as Wordsworth had been when he had gone up to Cambridge 150 years before, now to be endowed with new ancestors. What I had not yet realised was how vital a part in an Oxford education the College to which a student belongs can play. Nor had I realised that in 1928 the College of which I was to be a member, St. Edmund Hall, differentiated so little between those coming to it straight from school and the few who were already graduates of some other university. All were warmly welcomed into the friendliest of societies, each on more or less equal terms. So that most of my new companions were four or five years younger than I.

In some ways this was good for me. It restored my youth; it enabled me to give a certain amount of leadership quietly to others; it could foster both humility and confidence. At meals in Hall I sat with those who had matriculated with me, though outside College it was with my contemporaries on the B.Litt. course in English that I chiefly associated. And among those were some whose names were later to become well known: C.S. Lewis, for example, Bergen Evans of *The Natural History of Nonsense* fame, Allen Walker Read – the last two Rhodes Scholars (they could not bear each other, but both became my friends).

Oxford indeed I found a wonderfully cosmopolitan place. Later in life far more of those with whom I remained closely in touch were people I had met there than people I'd met in the years at Bristol. This was, I am sure, in part due to the collegiate system itself – still now in the 21st century so essentially a part of both Oxford and Cambridge. It creates relationships and nourishes loyalties – produces networks too. Part also was due perhaps to the very separateness of university from city – a university much of it housed in buildings centuries old, most of whose members are in the town for only half the year, are of limited age range and mix little with the city's more permanent inhabitants.

Though my own course was one which demanded a lot of work and close attendance at a number of classes – they included such comparatively recondite subjects as Elizabethan handwriting, the history and resources of the Bodleian and printing by hand press – I found time to sample quite a few lectures in a range of subjects well outside my English/Education concentration. I went for example to hear the young Oliver Franks lecturing with vivid lucidity on Descartes – his student listeners crowding Queen's dining hall, sitting on window sills and floor; and R.G. Collingwood giving the course which formed the basis of his classic *Speculum Mentis*. Like Franks,

Collingwood lectured to an audience which overflowed the seats available in a large dining hall. Part of the attraction was his opposition to the realist school of philosphers then so powerful in Oxford. As he wrote a little later in his *Autobiography* (1939), "The "realist" said to his pupils, if it interests you to study this, do so; but don't think it will be of any use to you. Remember the great principle of realism, that nothing is affected by being known. That is as true of human action as of anything else. Moral philosophy is only the theory of moral action: it can't therefore make any difference to the practice of moral action. People can act just as morally without it as with it!" So, argued Collingwood, students were given no ideals to live for or principles to live by. And many of his audience *wanted* ideals to live for and principles to live by.

Other lecturers I sampled were G.D.H. Cole on Economics and E.F. Carritt on Aesthetics and I also went to some seminars on Psychology and Metaphysics. In general the standard of lecturing did not seem to me to be particularly high. There were indeed a few lecturers in a highly specialised field who appeared deliberately to lecture dully to the small audience of students they attracted. This may have started by numbering 12 or 15 but rapidly reduced itself to seven or eight and soon to two or three, so that the lecturer could now pleasantly declare that since there seemed to be no demand for the course he would be ceasing to give it. And this apparently without offending his own conscience.

I was rather disappointed that Teddy Hall could find no bedroom to enable me to live in College even for a term – and though I had a characterful landlady for a year (whose generous lunches on Sundays could not be missed without gross offence and whose agnostic husband sang beautifully in the Cathedral choir), this was not really a compensation for the experience of living in College I should have liked to have. My own Sunday mornings often found me going to the service at Mansfield chapel, with the Principal – W.B. Selbie – giving a discourse wonderfully suited to the large congregation of students sitting before him and with its eloquent conclusion timed to the minute. But there were other distinguished preachers too, among them C.H. Dodd, C.J. Cadoux, J. Wheeler Robinson – each a scholar of parts.

My time at St. Edmund Hall saw the beginning of the great Principalship of A.B. Emden – historian, leader and manager of men, who gave to the College something of his own vision and energy. He concealed immense scholarship under a facade of urbanity, as did under a curtain of scintillating wit, Canon J.N.D. Kelly, world authority on the Creeds, soon to become in turn its Chaplain, Vice-Principal and, later, Principal.

I have already spoken of the friendliness of Oxford. The friendships I made there included one which has been a support to me throughout a long life. When first I came to know Geoffrey Nuttall, later a distinguished church historian and an FBA, he was reading Mods and Greats at Balliol; others I came to know closely in those years were at Wadham, Exeter, University College and Christ Church, and from the Hall itself. The link sometimes was the membership of the SCM we had in common; but some of my friends had no religious interests. Several were scientists, one a historian, one a mathematician.

The fact is that, in those days certainly and even to a great extent now with the subtle changes (still hardly analysed) brought about by almost every College becoming co-ed, much of the inwardness of an Oxbridge education comes from the closeness with which highly selected, intelligent young people, brought together while young in a beautiful place and an atmosphere which respects knowledge highly, learn from one another. Awareness that this University and its Colleges occupy a special slot in the national life is also a factor; as is a sub-consciousness that now (in spite, it may be, of working hard) you have leisure, whether deservedly or not, the gift of an interval in a fleeting life.

In the late twenties research was still a post-graduate ploy and of far, far more peripheral import to many Colleges than it is today. No respectable Arts don hoping to teach in the University would have wished then even for a moment to graduate as a D.Phil. Though C.S. Lewis did all the work for a B.Litt. degree, he drew the line at having it conferred. For it was a plain MA which had the prestige and was the right degree for a gentleman to have.

At Oxford in those days one had a sense of belonging to a university with a status that had come unsought (much like a hereditary peerage). There were no great fund-raising campaigns, glossy brochures, personal appeals down the telephone. There were, no doubt, other places calling themselves universities of which Oxbridge had heard, but dons with even a London doctorate would not normally expect to find themselves credited with it in official Oxford University publications.

Authorised lodgings for undergraduates still had to be within two and a half miles of Carfax (and school examination papers for Oxford Locals still had to be marked within that same magic inner circle). Cars belonging to the still fairly few well-off students who had them were required to carry a little green light to show the fact; but anyway jaunts to London or elsewhere in term time could only be made legitimately by car or any other form of transport if special permission was obtained. A faint sense of the Public School pervaded most of the Colleges – to both their advantage and disadvantage. There were certainly some odd characters of uncertain age still to be seen wearing gowns and tottering down the High. A loveable and quite unforgettable place this of which to be a part for three years or so, and then to find oneself belonging to, without further effort, for the rest of one's life.

Looking back, it strikes me as significant that I had to fight very hard to get the topic approved at all on which I wanted to write my thesis for B.Litt. It was considered too vague, too interdisciplinary, for research as orthodoxy understood it – and still, indeed, understands it. For I wanted to think about the function of literary criticism and though I was entirely willing to consider this in special relation to one particular author I did not want to confine most of my attention to him or her. In practice there had, of course, to be compromise and after I had spent some of my efforts in what for me were highly profitable fields, sociological and philosophical, I devoted the rest to a study of William Hazlitt as a critic who exemplified the theories I had adumbrated.

Today one consequence of much (though not all) research work undertaken for degree purposes is to prevent the students from thinking broadly and compel them to concentrate narrowly, though of course rigorously, too, upon the main chance. If they are to ponder or indulge in cross-disciplinary adventures they must usually do so elsewhere than in the work for the higher degree they may need for their professional advancement.

The cost of my being at Oxford was covered from a variety of sources: the Bristol Education Committee helped, a grant from the Merchant Venturers Society helped more, the fees I was paid as a young examiner for School Certificate English for Oxford Locals helped most. The job involved a hectic three weeks' work each summer in Oxford, where the whole team of examiners had to undertake to live till the scripts were marked – so that discussions between the chief examiner and any of his assistants on points of difficulty could happen whenever required. (Admittedly the chief examiner sometimes finished his batch of scripts a bit sooner than his assistants and then escaped.) Every year to begin with we all (some 14) sat round a table and, after an introductory talk by the Chief, each marked independently some scripts, passing them on without comment to our neighbour as we finished. A grand inquest followed: hazards were identified and temptations to differ analysed. During the three weeks each of us would mark 1,000 or more scripts.

Until well into the thirties I returned to Oxford every summer for those three weeks of hard labour. Soon I began also to examine (at home) for the Oxford and Cambridge Board and in due course came to act as Chief Examiner for the Durham and Bristol ones. But I never forgot the lessons the Oxford Local experience had driven in or ceased to respect the efforts made by that Board to ensure that justice was done (as far as was possible) to every candidate.

Introduction to Teaching: Doncaster (1930-34)

The first half of a journey by train between Sheffield and Doncaster at the beginning of the thirties was a grim business. Beside the line factories and steelworks belched smoke and flames; any grass to be seen was covered in dirt; stretching away on both sides were landscapes which oozed filth; every stream and stagnant pool was mud begrimed; desecration everywhere one looked. I had never been as far north before. Was this what it was like? But Doncaster itself seemed almost a return to the England I knew and the buildings of the Grammar School, with its Gothic cloisters and Great Hall approached up a tree-lined avenue, a renewed promise of civilisation.

In fact, in accepting the offer of the Senior English Mastership there I found I had done absolutely the right thing; my four years at D.G.S. were to be among the most fruitful I have had. The School, run on pretty traditional lines, had never had a Senior English Master before. For the patriotic Senior Classics Master (Captain S.E. Evans) had taken upon himself the ordering of English teaching as a minor responsibility, with the Senior History Master (Captain P. G. Bales) taking an appropriately conscientious interest also. This meant that from the start I had splendid opportunities for pioneering and experimenting – always providing that I could retain the friendship of the traditionalists and not propose alterations which seemed too outlandish.

The boys in the School – there were some 600 altogether – came predominantly from miners' homes, for coal mines ringed Doncaster, and were from families no member of which previously had had any secondary education. But they were many of them intelligent, ready to learn, willing to work. I was given a form of my own (2B) of first year boys and a time-table which gave me predominantly Sixth Form and Second Form teaching with some Fifth Form (School Certificate) work: an almost ideal arrangement, though in fact I rarely had any disciplinary troubles to cope with in a school that was by custom well ordered and well behaved. It was proud of its past – one which went back for centuries, proud too, of being one of the ten or so northern schools eligible to enter candidates for Hastings Scholarships to Queen's College, Oxford.

Life for me in Doncaster was immensely brightened by blossoming friendships with other young teachers at the School – enthusiastic and enterprising newcomers who brought vitality with them. They included

Hugh Walker who taught Chemistry and Bertram Lucia who taught Maths. There were others on the staff who encouraged us, notably Jock Anderson, a humane no-nonsense Scottish mathematician. And the Head, nearing retirement, who kept a large glass- fronted hive of bees in his study, was benign enough too. We were all regaled from time to time by neatly written little notes headed "With the compliments of P.G. Bales" which requested, for example, that at the end of the period a certain boy we were teaching should be sent to him for this undefined purpose or that.

One of the die-hards on the staff was Irving, the Senior Classics Master, aged perhaps 40. He continued to run his farm, often coming to school in the morning in muddy wellington boots after having delivered a load of vegetables or other farm produce at the Doncaster Market. He was a fierce and fearless disciplinarian who terrified many of his pupils, upon whom he used the cane freely. It was not an enviable job to take a form which had just emerged from one of Irving's periods. But the school's exam results in Latin were excellent! When there was a general inspection of the school, Irving did not change his methods one iota, proceeding to cane boys in the normal way in front of the visiting HMI. He was of course reprimanded and told to mend his ways before the Inspector came to see him again later in the week. No change occurred, more caning took place, the Inspector being told very firmly that it was Irving who knew how to teach Latin and that he had every intention to go on doing so in a time-honoured way. Caning was good for boys anyhow!

Among Hugh Walker's enthusiasms was dramatics and before long he had inaugurated a tradition by which some worthwhile play should be performed by the School each year. Shaw's *Androcles and the Lion* was an early choice. And Hugh insisted that all programmes and printed propaganda for the play should be printed in type faces he approved and with the right positioning on the page. His zeal for good typography educated us all.

But it was Bertram Lucia, not Hugh, who became a member of the Education Committee of the so-called Auxiliary Movement of the S.C.M. which met in London during the early thirties and which

I chaired. Membership of the Movement was largely made up of men and women who in their University or College days had belonged to the S.C.M. but were now in the early stages of professional careers. Many of them were teachers or lecturers. Its Education Committee included among its members Kenneth Muir, once at Teddy Hall with me, now a Lecturer in English at St. John's College, York, and later to be King Alfred Professor of English at Liverpool; Marjorie Reeves, Lecturer in History at St. Gabriel's College and soon to become an Oxford don; and John Drewett, Vicar of a City church in London. The railway line from Doncaster to London was a link for me with a wider world than that represented by the staff, however varied and characterful, of a provincial Grammar School.

Among the new experiments I tried in my teaching was the initiation of a cyclostyled journal we called *Venture* and which came out several times a year. It was made up of lively articles and poems contributed by the boys – many of them pieces they had written as stories or essays or verses for homework or even work in class. Another experiment was founding a Discussion Society for Sixth Formers which we called the Carlyle Society. It held a number of meetings during the year, one of them an Annual Dinner held at a hotel followed by a talk. We were encouraged by capturing the Archdeacon of Durham to speak at the first of these. Membership of the Society was limited, to belong to it was a privilege.

From the start we benefited enormously by having George Woods – a brilliant scholar and teacher – as a keen supporter. He had become an unorthodox curate at Doncaster Parish Church. To my delight he offered his services as a leader of discussions for D.G.S. Sixth Formers on religious topics of current interest. Before long he was coaching a set of boys for the Archbishop's Certificate in Religious Studies – all of them having joined the course voluntarily and been willing to give up time for it out of school hours. The friendship of George Woods meant much to me in Doncaster days, and indeed in the years to come.

My first trip abroad had taken place immediately before I joined the staff: it had been with friend, Jesse Stickler, to Belgium and Germany.

Our first memorable, but noisy, nights were spent at the home in Malines of some of his family's friends who had been refugees in Keynsham during the 1914-18 war – a home just opposite the tower which housed the famous carillon in the central square of the town. A festival was going on and the bells played merry tunes – no more conducive to sleep than the singing crowds regaling themselves on beer and ice cream outside. We visited Antwerp before going on to Cologne and seeing a little of the Rhine.

In my third year at the school a new Headmaster took up office. Then aged 33, Randal Carter Unmack was determined to develop it on more Public School lines than those to which we had become accustomed. Soccer was replaced by Rugby ("Wugga" as he called it), the school cap and colours were replaced by brighter ones. The head dropped in to classes to see what was going on. Since he seemed to approve of my own efforts, I got on quite well with him but numerous Old Boys and some of my colleagues found the new regime objectionable. It has to be said though that the vigorous new broom did sweep up some dust and that now there was clear leadership from the top – even if one might object to the direction in which one was being led.

In 1931 at my suggestion my parents gave up life in Bristol and emigrated to Doncaster – to a part of the country they had never even visited, let alone lived in. Why should I have bought a house in this temporarily adopted town of mine in which both they and I could live? My father was now 73 and his shop, according to my reckoning, was now yielding an annual profit of a miserable £38 as a reward for incredibly long hours of devotion to it week after week. Besides this sum, they had only small annuities and an old age pension to live on. Neither did they find one another's company particularly satisfying. Surprisingly enough, however, they adapted to their new life rapidly. My father explored his new environment with interest, my mother joined the church to which I belonged and made new acquaintances. Yorkshire is a welcoming county!

Our house at 12 St. Mary's Road soon became a meeting place for a little Education Society which drew its members from a number of sources in addition to friends at D.G.S. Among them was the Secretary of the Pilgrim Trust who at that time lived in Sheffield – our nearest big city, which we visited ourselves from time to time.

My skills as a teacher of English were certainly honed by a course run in Oxford by HMI in the Easter vacation of 1932. So stimulating did a number of us find it that we got together afterwards and arranged to meet again the following January at Harrow School, where one of our members taught, for further exchanges. Before long we found we had established a little Society for Teachers of English, the initial nucleus being one of some ten members, all under 30 who were teaching in grammar and public schools in different parts of the country. The first rules we solemnly drew up (all of them to be broken before long) stated that no member could be over 35, or a woman, or a headmaster. Each of us took a vow not to refuse to let any member of the Society watch him teach. Soon we began to think of ways in which we could spread our gospel of good English teaching – particularly by an approach to the teaching of poetry which broke both with convention and the doctrines then being preached in Cambridge circles by I.A. Richards. So in the mid-thirties the Oxford Press published two little STE books, *Teaching Poetry* and *Poetry in the Sixth Form*. By that time, however, I had left Doncaster (though certainly not the STE) and become a lecturer in the Education Department at Armstrong College, Newcastle-upon-Tyne.

Strangely enough I was invited in 1934 to sit with a Committee made up of Councillors from the Doncaster LEA which had the job of choosing who should be my successor as Senior English Master. I remember two of the questions addressed by someone on the Committee to George Whitfield[2] who was later that day to be appointed to the post. One of the questions was "What would you do if a boy threw an inkpot at you?" and the other (what an amazingly wide remit an English teacher seemed expected to fulfil!) "How would you teach good handwriting?" George faced the barrage with great aplomb – among other things pointing out that the Gregg system of teaching handwriting in his experience yielded good results, involving as it did the right deployment of the muscles of the forearm, not merely those of the fingers and hand. He got the job – but not of course simply because of his answers to such questions as those.

University Community: Newcastle (1934-40)

When I was appointed to that Lectureship at Newcastle, I looked forward to spending much of my time in helping those who wanted to teach English to find and practise good ways of doing so – though I was already interested in wider aspects of the educational scene, particularly the purposes of schooling in a society which had become so unsure of itself. But I wondered whether I should be as happy and accepted in a university community as I had been in those four spring-like years at Doncaster.

I need not have doubted. From the start I found Armstrong College welcoming and its Education Department, then housed centrally within it, very much part of the place. Morale was high, enterprise yielded dividends, there were vivid characters on a staff which nevertheless felt itself a unity. And Newcastle as a city had vitality too. Its nearness to the sea, its freedom from fog, the youth in its air appealed to me – in spite of a certain harshness in its winters and the lack of interval between winter and summer in those north-easterly parts.

My years at Newcastle, among the most sparkling I have lived, included those of my marriage to Sheila in 1938 and the birth of our daughter Rosalind in 1939 and of our son Roland in 1942. Sheila was teaching English at the Duchess's School, Alnwick, when I first got to know her, for though we had overlapped as students at Oxford I only remember catching a fleeting sight of her cycling along the High. How well I got to know the section of the A1 which links Newcastle and Alnwick! I had learnt to drive a car early in Doncaster days. And the roads were rather empty in the mid-thirties. It was still possible to drive on almost any day from Newcastle to Carter Bar on the Scottish border and not pass more than three cars on the way. Those journeys to and from Alnwick were in a BSA with flywheel and automatic gear change. The same car took me to and from Harrogate where Sheila taught – not too contentedly – for a year at Queen Ethelburgh's

School before we were married.

It was Alan Richardson, then Vicar of Cambo in Northumberland, who married us. I had come to know him from the interest in the SCM we had in common and from his being one of the two secretaries of the Newcastle Theological Society, of which I had become a member soon after going to live in Newcastle. The wedding, though, in the August of 1938, took place at St. Philip and St. James' Church in Cheltenham – for Sheila's brother Philip, in charge of the Music at the boys' College there, could play the organ for us and Cheltenham, too, had happy associations for Sheila from her schooldays at C.L.C.

My parents had of course moved from Doncaster with me. They and I shared a house in West Avenue, Gosforth, during the years at Newcastle before our marriage. After it, my parents and Sheila's mother and our two selves went to live at 81 Osborne Road, Jesmond, in a double-fronted house large enough to provide quarters for all which were nevertheless separate enough for viability. And in June 1939, at a nursing home in Newcastle our daughter Rosalind was born and welcomed joyously.

With the outbreak of war that autumn, Sheila and the baby went for a time to stay in a farmhouse at Powburn, in sight of the Cheviots, with me spending occasional nights there. At the time we fully expected Newcastle, with its munition factories temptingly lining parts of the Tyne, to be bombed. In fact throughout the whole of the war Newcastle was hardly raided but Sunderland and Hull suffered heavily.

Newcastle in the middle and later thirties had a confidence about it, a sense that it was a provincial capital. And indeed it was – and still is – one of the few cities in Britain more than 90 miles from the nearest town larger than itself. Armstrong College in October 1934, when I first began to know it, was small, coherent and vital. Its 800 full-time students came overwhelmingly from Tyneside and the three northernmost counties of England, and among them were many of high promise. For it was only a minority of those who might in later years have applied for places at Oxford, Cambridge – and other universities south of the border between Northumbria and Yorkshire – who thought of doing so.

The Department of Education when I joined it had a full-time staff of only five, including the Professor, John Nicholson. Lopsided of gait, keen of glance, liberal of mind, he had come to Armstrong from the University of Bristol Department where he had been responsible for a wide-ranging option which considered the impact of education on society. Nicholson's lectures at Newcastle were highly conscious of the nation's social problems and his devotion to the cause of the W.E.A. (of which he later became the National President) fitted in well with his democratic hopes. In 1935 he went off to become Principal of University College, Hull, and was followed in the Chair, after an interval of a couple of terms, by Brian Stanley, then only in his late twenties, kind-hearted, clever, not afraid of making mistakes, individual alike in sense of humour and stubbly hair style. Looking back now it strikes me that we were all somewhat amateur in our approach to the study of Education as a subject. We were not professionals and specialists in the contemporary sense, though we had respect for and understanding of scholarship. But we had in some cases a lot of enthusiasm and adaptability and we certainly all shared an interest in children and schools, and in our students as people. But the ground earlier prepared by Professors Godfrey Thomson (1920-25) and Frank Smith (1925-33) to ensure that Newcastle should blossom as a centre where higher degrees in Education could be taken by increasing numbers of students lay for the most part fallow during the years 1934-40, largely because the concerns of their successors in the Chair and of the members of staff took them in other directions.

One of these concerns was undoubtedly to encourage the initial training Diploma course itself to be one which broadened and humanised those who took it. Lecturers were given what would now be regarded as a surprising amount of freedom to cover areas of educational relevance which interested them personally, even if they included territory not normally cultivated in Departments of Education. Thus I can remember suggesting to John Nicholson that I should include a series of lectures on the training of taste and being encouraged to give an illustrated course lasting for an hour a week for most of a term. The overall title of my lecture course "The Principles of Education" was interpreted generously enough for them to be fitted in. The Professor himself came to an occasional one of the series.

The students taking the Diploma course in the 1930s included many of outstanding ability. Among those taking their Diploma year to whom I lectured in the six sessions between 1934 and 1940, were eight or nine who later became University Professors in a wide variety of subjects; there was a future Principal of the University of London, a future Head of its Institute of United States Studies and two distinguished poets, in addition to the many who became able teachers, heads of schools and educational administrators both in Britain and overseas. The liveliness and intelligence of the group in my own time year after year was marked and the proportion with First Class Honours degrees was greater, I fancy, than at any later period in any postgraduate Education year anywhere in England. Yet the students were surprisingly local in the range of their travel. I took a census of those doing their postgraduate Education year *circa* 1937-38 – some 120 altogether – and found that, at the age of 21 or more, less than a third of them had ever been to London and only the tiniest sprinkling had stepped on continental soil.

Armstrong College was for the whole of its history part of the University of Durham, the examination at the end of the Diploma year being a University examination with the papers set jointly by members of staff of both the Newcastle and the Durham Departments. Meetings were normally held in Durham and Newcastle alternately; they were friendly, supportive, non-disputatious affairs. But occasionally some intriguing problem presented itself, of which I will give two illustrations.

As well as being taken by students at the two English ends of the University, the Diploma in Education examination catered for students at Fourah Bay College, Sierra Leone, an affiliated part of the University of Durham for the whole period 1876 to 1967. The papers written by the students there were marked in Newcastle and Durham by the same examiners as the candidates in England, and on the whole those from

Sierra Leone acquitted themselves satisfactorily – except in the Hygiene paper. Why was this? How was it that intelligent candidates year after year made such a mess of it and in consequence failed to achieve their Diploma? Inquiries were set on foot, prompted by the results one summer when the outcome had been particularly disastrous. The survey showed such factors as these: one of the questions had been on the design of school classrooms and their ventilation. In Fourah Bay there were no problems of ventilation, only of protection from the heat coming in from the open sides of the classrooms. Another question had been on infectious diseases and their recognition – measles, scarlet fever, chicken pox, etc. In Fourah Bay these were all but unknown, though tropical fevers and infections were rampant. Another question dealt with food and drink, the value of fresh milk, pure water, etc. In Fourah Bay no milk was available or drunk and the staple articles of diet were entirely different from ones familiar in England. And so on. We recommended strongly that a different Hygiene paper should be set by people in Fourah Bay and marked by them before being sent to England. But no: such a solution was entirely unacceptable. The candidates from Fourah Bay must take the genuine Durham examination. No special exceptions whatever were desired or to be allowed – and no favouritism!

One of the trickiest problems with which the Examiners were ever confronted was in connection with the choice of the candidate one particular year for the Mark Wright prize. The prize was awarded to the Diploma student from either end of the University who presented what the examiners decided was the best long essay that summer. The agreement of the External Examiner to the verdict of the internal examiners had, however, to be obtained. On the occasion I refer to, the internal examiners sent to the External (who shall be nameless) a complete set of the essays which had been submitted, together with the list in the order of merit assigned by the internal team. When the package was returned, the External Examiner said that he entirely agreed with the order suggested on the list and nominated the bottom candidate! The general assumption in universities is that when there is an irreconcilable difference of judgement between Internal and External

Examiners, the verdict of the External is the one which must be accepted. As may be imagined a somewhat hectic 'phone call ensued, with the External remarking, "Oh, I thought your list was in ascending order of merit." But he capitulated eventually. Nor was he re-appointed.

One of the pleasures of being a member of staff of the Education Department in the thirties was the sense it brought that one had become *ipso facto* very much a member of the staff of the College as a whole. The Senior Common Room was near at hand; the Principal's rooms and those of the administration underneath on the ground floor. Departmentalism generally was in those days not the isolating factor it has tended in universities to become: the "characters" among the Professors were characters of a large academic village as it were: Cuthbert Girdlestone, the Professor of French – whose book on Mozart's Piano Concertos introduced many in England and Europe to them for the first time – played the flute in the staff-student orchestra; Thomas (later Sir Thomas) Havelock, Sidney Newman, Harold Orton, the dialect pioneer, were not merely experts in their subject but highly individual beings. The Medical School was pretty separate from Armstrong College and regarded itself as an independent part of the University of Durham. But on its staff was perhaps the most famous paediatrician in the country, Sir James Spence, the Professor of Child Health, and a member of the UGC.

During the years 1935 and 1936 a Royal Commission was at work drawing up a by then very necessary new constitution for the University of Durham as one whole. On the acceptance of its recommendations, the University was from 1937 formally constituted in two divisions, one at Durham under a Warden, the other at Newcastle, with the name King's College, under a Rector, with the Durham College of Medicine, henceforward to be called the Medical School, as an integral part of King's. Warden and Rector were to alternate for two-year periods, as Vice-Chancellors of the University as a whole.

The transition of 1937, by which Armstrong College, as the Newcastle division of the University, became King's under its new chieftain, Lord Eustace Percy, increased rather than diminished the

College's corporate sense. For Percy, as its Rector, was determined to ensure that a forward-looking unity should be a dominant characteristic of the institution. Coming to King's after a period as an exceptionally able President of the Board of Education, he brought to the College new consciousness that we belonged to the country as a whole. He also contributed an eager and prophetic sense that there was a future to inherit.

Among the advantages of being a lecturer in the Education Department in those days were the opportunities it brought of being in pretty close contact with schools and of knowing a number of their best teachers personally. The experience taught me things not only about schools but about politics too. In those days appointments to school staffs in Durham county tended on occasion to be rather subject to bias. Canvassing was permitted; that fact indeed was publicised in every press advertisement for a post: it was certainly expected that some of the better candidates would call at the homes of the governors before any formal interview took place (an uncomfortable situation at times both for the candidate and the governor). In the mid-thirties Jarrow Secondary School had on its staff an outstanding teacher of Mathematics (continuing a tradition from the time of George Goldsbrough who later became a Professor of Mathematics at King's). Open Scholarships to Oxford and Cambridge in that subject (but no other) were won every year or two. The time came when this master handed in his resignation to take a post at another school. There was a large field of candidates who applied to become his successor, several of them with a First Class Honours degree and highly relevant teaching experience. But among the applicants was a young man from another school in County Durham who had a Pass B.Sc., one of whose three subjects was Mathematics. He had never taught in a Grammar school, but he was a cousin of the Chairman of the governors. To my surprise as one of the governors myself, his name appeared on the short list. He was duly interviewed, was asked if he had ever taught Mathematics at the Sixth Form stage and replied that he had not but was very willing to try and would do his best to tackle any problems. At the private discussion which followed, the Chairman commented that he seemed a very nice, modest and willing young man and proposed that he should be appointed. In vain did several of us argue the outstanding merits of a number of the other candidates; in vain did the Headmaster (who had no vote) plead almost from his knees that this man should not be chosen, as this would mean a certain end to the tradition of scholarship winning. I remember vividly the classic final retort of the Chairman to the Headmaster, now almost in tears, "And how do you think you got your job, Mr Headmaster?" The young man was appointed by a majority vote.

In the thirties there existed in Newcastle a remarkable example of a private Education Society, at whose meetings challenging discussions of the aims and practice of education regularly took place. This was the Education Society of the Newcastle Royal Grammar School, the membership of which was confined to the 42 people on its staff, though I was allowed to attend and, if I wanted (or dared), allowed to take part in its discussions. The quality and intellectuality of the papers contributed to its meetings and the clashing debates which eventuated almost every time owed much to the enthusiasm of two quite outstanding young participants: Michael Roberts, then Senior Physics Master of RGS, poet, literary critic, mountaineer, regular contributor to *The Listener* and later principal of the College of St. Mark and St. John, Chelsea, and Max Black, who taught Mathematics and later was for many years distinguished Professor of Philosophy at Cornell.

During my early days at Newcastle I became more and more sure that concepts of Education as a subject which confined its field to schools and colleges and to the curriculum and methods of teaching, was limiting in quite fundamental ways – indispensable though it was, and is, to study such matters. But too exclusive an attention paid to them, I came to think, can easily lead to a gross under estimate of the educative influence of society itself upon both the conscious and the unconscious mind – an influence incarnated in the family, the media, advertisements, in the assumptions and beliefs which permeate the traditions we inherit.

Russian Interlude (1936)

Sixty years ago the people of the Ukraine were not, I suspect, essentially different from what they are today. How did I get to know any of them?

It was like this. In 1936 as one of a party of 17 from England curious to discover what was afoot in Russian schools, I spent an intensive three April weeks in visiting educational establishments of assorted kinds in Leningrad, Moscow, Kharkhov and finally Kiev. On the very last day of the trip I came out in bright red spots. Scarlet fever it was and soon I was waited upon by three white-robed attendants, who conducted me solemnly down to a waiting ambulance and off we went to a hospital, housed in the remarkable buildings of the famous Lavra Monastery (no monks there any more), not far from the broad, sweeping river Dnieper. I didn't feel particularly ill but was certainly puzzled about what was going to happen to me – left on my own in Kiev while the other 16 members of our party made their cheerful way back to Britain.

The immediate problem though was to get properly admitted to hospital itself. I was presented with a formidable form to fill in, with questions on four foolscap pages, all of them printed in Russian and Ukrainian and none I could understand. They said it was beyond possibility for me to be admitted to any ward until the questionnaire had been duly and properly completed. So, one by one, nurses and doctors were paraded before me, who spoke to me in a variety of languages, unknown to me though most of them current somewhere in the vast USSR, until at last, as by magic, a nurse arrived who put the questions to me in French. Then I could fill in the answers required and I was asked politely what sort of ward I would like to be in. I said that I would like, if possible, to have a room to myself. This appeared to the authorities a most curious request, but they said they would do their best to cope and so, after not too much more delay, I was taken up to a room with only four beds in it, three of them unoccupied. Much kindness henceforth was shown me.

I was provided with a French-speaking nurse by day and another French-speaking nurse by night – the only two in the place in fact with the language. Nobody spoke any English.

In the hospital, all the rules had to be obeyed. From the start I knew that the period I should have to remain there was six weeks, even though I was not very ill. For the first three of those I had, I was told, to stay in bed. My room was kept scrupulously clean – the paintwork of the door, both sides, and of the wainscot being washed with soap and water every few days. There was a bell-push near my bed which would light a bulb in the corridor outside and a nurse would usually come rapidly. Almost all the doctors in the hospital were women, as indeed, I was told, were three-quarters of all the doctors in the USSR at that time. As the weeks went on and May advanced, the weather outside became warm and a few mosquitoes appeared from time to time in my ward. One night I became a bit worried by their buzzing and used my bell-push. The nurse who appeared had no English or French, but I tried on her the word "mouche", pointing vigorously at the little cloud of flies which were disporting themselves in the air in the centre of the room. To my surprise she rapidly went out shaking with laughter. Soon several other nurses came and I repeated my performance. This made all of them break into merriment and I gave the enterprise up as a bad job. It was a bit mysterious though. The next morning, when my French-speaking nurse appeared, I asked the reason. She told me that the French word "mouche" was the Ukranian word for husband. Hence the laughter!

One of my two French-speaking nurses was a widow aged 22, already with two children. Her name was Nadya, and she was Greek by birth but thoroughly Russianised now. The elder, a kindly soul named Anna, was perhaps 48 or 50 and was looked on with great respect because she was married to a fully fledged member of the Communist Party. Only a small minority of men or women were actually Party members. She and I had many talks together about conditions in Kiev and the parts of the world I knew.

She was an intelligent woman, with a considerable knowledge of France and French culture, though she had never been outside the USSR herself. Her geography however tended to be weak: she thought that England was much nearer America than it was to France – her ideology winning the battle over mere physical fact.

When at last I was permitted to get up and walk about, I was allowed to go into any part of the Hospital I liked and so I wandered into most of the wards, some with patients suffering from complications which followed their illness. But it was exclusively a scarlet fever hospital – as were, I was told, five others in Kiev where the disease at that time was very common. I also was able to visit the doctors' quarters and those of the nurses too.

The great majority of the patients were children and with numbers of them I played games of chess – no intermediary language being needed. It was not unusual for children of 9 or ten to be able to beat me at this game, for it was, and is still, the national game of many Russians. Even in the Red Army clubs, one large room was always reserved for the soldiers to play chess. It was inconceivable that so intellectual a game would be such a popular one in so unintellectual a country as England!

One of the great – perhaps only – worries during my incarceration in hospital in Kiev was the difficulty of keeping in touch with home. An exchange of letters took more than a fortnight and telegrams were both expensive and inadequate. As for reading matter, after the first week or so I was supplied with an abundance of hard-covered books, 17 of them altogether, translated from Russian into English and given me as a present. A few of these were translations of sound Leninist doctrine but some were novels, highly readable, if a little biased in favour of the Soviet regime. I can remember reading *And Quiet Flows the Don* with much pleasure. I also had with me several books of my own which stood up to repeated re-reading without a falter. One of them – *Not Under Forty* – was by Willa Cather. This is a good test of a book's quality.

The time came when, six weeks being up, I was free to leave the hospital. On my first week outside I was accompanied by the lighthearted Nadya and we roamed along the promenade high above the Dnieper. But serious problems at once presented themselves. It was made clear that my visa had now run out and that I certainly could not be allowed to leave the country until it was renewed. This would take quite a time and my meal tickets were on the point of running out too so that, with no money, I shouldn't be able to get anything to eat or drink. The kind hospital however said that it was perfectly willing for me to stay in it until both visa and meal tickets were forthcoming. It was simply a question of filling in time. I can remember filling in a bit of it by taking Nadya to the cinema one day. I did not understand much of what was being said by the characters on the screen, but that did not matter too much in Nadya's company.

When my visa and meal tickets came at long last I was transported to Kiev railway station by the hospital authorities, taking all my belongings with me – for no one would accept any present of clothing from my stock, very much superior though all my shirts and handkerchiefs and gloves and socks, and especially leather overcoat, were to anything any of the Russians had themselves. On the train I was the only Englishman travelling and as we covered mile after mile of the hundreds to the Polish border I became one of fewer and fewer passengers of any nationality on the train. Finally, at the border station it was only I who got out, apart from the few soldiers of the Red Army who were there to guard both the train and me.

It was 2 a.m. but the Polish customs stations were still functioning. I was the only person with baggage to examine, but they didn't seem much interested in the baggage. Instead, they took me to their office and put a long series of questions to me. "How long have you been in Russia?" "How many aircraft did you see in that time?" "How may soldiers?" "Were any preparations for war gong on as far as you know?" ... and so on.

I am afraid that what I could tell them wouldn't have been of much use, but they seemed at least slightly reassured and we parted happily enough as I climbed aboard the train to take me to Warsaw. There, though tired and still a bit weak, I spent part of a day exploring the city before catching another train on to Berlin. After I got back home there was for a time some exchange of letters. They had not charged me anything at all for the care, and food, they had given me. The only request they made was that I should write telling them of the up-to-date ways of treating scarlet fever in England. I discovered that the procedures they had followed were along lines current here in 1905! But I got better – and I think that the cause of international friendship was also served.

Reflections II

I vividly remember, when I visited the USSR in 1936, how keenly some of the young people there were looking forward to the future; how absolutely sure they were that a great age was on the way – of prosperity, unstoppable scientific and technical progress – if only their generation worked hard, behaved properly and held passionately to the vision. It was exhilarating to be with them. But I rather wondered how long any of them could go on being motivated by the hope of realising the future if the promise steadily receded year by year as they moved ahead. What anyway did "ahead" mean?

The hope and the faith were really more significant than any of the hoped-for dividends, but dividends undoubtedly there have been. The achievements of the launchers of satellites, for example, have been immensely impressive. "In the long term," said a glowing commentary in the 1970s, "men and women will move into space permanently." Yes, maybe, but what for? What is any of it for? Something, somewhere, seems to have got left out of the calculation. The crisis of our time, I suggest, centres on what we can really believe in. What meaning, if any, is to be found beyond possessions and productivity?

Wartime Registrar: Durham (1940-44) and
Return to Newcastle (1944-45)

The shadows which the approaching war brought to the summer of 1939 deepened as the months went on. All over the country members of University staffs were leaving for war service of one sort or another. Among those in the University of Durham soon to be given leave of absence was the University Registrar, W.S. Angus, off to join the Civil Service in London. His responsibilities as Registrar covered both Divisions of the University – the one in Newcastle – much the larger – as well as that in Durham itself. Though the Registrar's office was in the picturesque North Bailey, Durham, his overlords – the Heads of the two Divisions of the University – had offices in Newcastle (Lord Eustace Percy) and Durham (James FitzJames Duff) respectively. They alternated as Vice Chancellor of the University itself and meetings which they chaired and to which the Registrar acted as Secretary could be held in either city. Its large Medical School, a very important part of it, was sited in Newcastle (even though graduation ceremonies for medicals were always held in the more aristocratic Durham.)

When it became known that William Angus was about to leave us, the question became urgent who could take over his job – temporarily of course. When I was asked if I would be willing to become Acting Registrar from early 1940, a widely shared assumption was the numbers of students in both Divisions would before long be greatly reduced and that one, more or less imitation, Registrar would be able to cope without too much difficulty – especially if he was given an adequate petrol allowance!

In fact I went on acting as Registrar for more than four years and the student population grew fast instead of diminishing, for Britain came to recognise that trained minds – especially those of scientists, engineers, medicals – were of great importance to the war effort. During those fascinating years I learned a great deal about university management and something too about managing human beings. At first the family went on living at Riding Mill. Sheila's mother died in 1941. Our son Roland was to our delight born in April 1942 – in a Nursing Home at Corbridge about one and a half miles from Riding Mill. Later that year we all moved to Durham – Sheila and I, Rosalind and Roland to a house at North End, overlooking fields whose name we changed from Dormie to Milford [Riding Mill and Oxford]. My parents henceforward lived in a small semi-detached modern house at 4 Sniperley Grove, about half a mile from us. At Milford we had a conservatory with a fruitful vine and a deepish water tank, into which in time Roland duly fell. By then however he had already been christened by the Archdeacon of Durham – in a memorable ceremony at the Cathedral – and Rosalind had started to go to a small nursery school.

My job, which fortunately enabled me to sleep at home every night, entailed frequent journeys by car between Durham and Newcastle – and at first also, of course, journeys between both places and Riding Mill. I grew accustomed to taking the Minutes of Meetings of Senate and Court, and to organising Degree Congregations held in the Castle at Durham or the Great Hall at King's College, Newcastle. But one of the most fascinating aspects of the work was getting to know and deal with Eustace Percy (Rector of King's) and James Duff (Warden of Durham Colleges).

My work as Registrar brought me into close contact with the chieftains in charge of each end of the University. Someone with an acute ear to the ground had chosen them in 1937 to alternate as Vice Chancellor at the University for periods of two years, each becoming Pro-Vice Chancellor when not functioning in the superior capacity. They tended to use the Registrar as a buffer. Both were personalities, remarkably different in shape of mind but of high, almost equal, intellectual ability and of great integrity. Percy arrived at his office before 8.45 in the morning, opened all his own mail – to the perturbation of his secretarial staff – and stayed at the office for much of the day, leaving maybe at 7 p.m. or so, on occasion even cooking his own meals on a stove in his own room. He liked getting some of the more difficult assignments tackled early in the day. Duff, on the other hand, rarely got to his office before 10.40 a.m. in term-time and 12.45 in vacations. But he stayed up late, worked hard and read omnivorously – until perhaps 3 a.m. most nights. He could complete *The Times* crossword in a luminous ten minutes while shaving in the morning.

Percy had a complex character, one which provided a battleground for his aristocratic instincts and his democratic convictions. There were many examples of such conflicts, but I can illustrate them by one example. When he was appointed Rector of King's College, Newcastle, he was very conscious of his political past and his inexperience of academic life. In particular, he was keen to be given a chance of getting in touch with students and discovering what they were really like. So he sent a letter, each copy signed personally, to every member of the College staff telling them to take every possible opportunity to send students to see him so that he might talk with them individually. He was most anxious, he said, to be given a chance of seeing freshmen, and no opportunity must be allowed to slip which would serve as a pretext for sending students to talk with him. He promised that on his part he would help matters as much as he could and he would fasten a welcoming notice to the outside of his door.

The outcome, though prophesiable, was not always what was intended. A young freshman, sent to see the Rector for reasons not entirely clear to him, approached the august door of the Rector's study and saw confronting him the notice, "DO NOT KNOCK. COME IN". The student paused, not being at all sure that this notice could possibly be meant for the likes of him. He then, typically, knocked gently. Nothing happened. Percy disliked having his clear orders disobeyed and took no notice. So the student, after waiting a bit, decided that perhaps the Rector had not heard. He therefore knocked again rather more loudly. Still nothing happened. So the student, thinking that conceivably the Rector was not in, decided to open the door a crack, very gently, and look to see if the Rector was there. By this time Percy was really angry, for had he not been disobeyed three times when the notice clearly said "DO NOT KNOCK. COME IN"? So when the student's head appeared, Percy, swivelling round in his chair, launched a broadside, asking whether the student could not read a simple notice and obey it? The atmosphere was not one that the Rector really wanted at all – but the aristocratic impulses (he was the seventh son of the seventh Duke of Northumberland) had got the better of the democratic intentions.

Yet Percy was, in reality, a very humble man. There were times when, visiting him in the morning, I would find him with his face buried in his hands. (He had a deep sense of guilt that he was a member of the Government, even if a junior member, who had consented to the 1919 Versailles Treaty and he had never forgiven himself for being a party to so un-Christian an act.) Sitting up when he detected my presence, he might say: "Don't think that I am idle." Such a thought would certainly never have entered my head, for I have rarely encountered anyone who worked harder than Percy did. He worked on Sundays as well as weekdays, often giving addresses at services or men's meetings. Though he was himself an Irvingite, he was pretty interdenominational in his church interests.

Perspicacious James Duff was a very different character, who on some occasions would simply yield to Percy when they had a difference of view because he did not believe in spending energy unnecessarily. He would thus accept versions of Minutes he had himself drafted which were much altered and "messed about" by Percy before the latter agreed them. "I have never seen a document so bedevilled," I remember Duff saying on one occasion when his version of some Minutes was returned to him from Newcastle. But there were sometimes fierce battles of principle between the two protagonists, and when he had resolutely made up his mind, Duff could and usually did win these.

There were occasions when Percy would ring the Registrar – me – in Durham before 10 a.m. to propose some course of action which he thought that Duff might not entirely approve. "If you think that worthwhile, Niblett, perhaps you will have a word with Duff about this but I doubt if there is any real need if you think that this proposal is acceptable. I would like to know, though, by half past ten." I knew, as Percy did, that Duff would much resent being rung up at home at that hour in the morning, and since he would not be at his office until 10.30 at the earliest, the easiest thing to do, as Percy was aware, was to concur in Percy's proposal and if necessary make my peace with Duff a little later. Usually there was no problem at all and more often than not, anyway, what Percy did propose was thoroughly sensible and right.

But there were other characters around to tax a Registrar's equanimity, patience and humanity. One of them was Michael Ramsey, the new Canon Professor of Theology who had succeeded the distinguished

Oliver Quick in that chair and was still unmarried. In my first summer as Registrar it was my duty to see that all the examination papers for first degrees reached the printer before the last day by which he could print them (wartime shortages of labour making it impossible for him to cope with anything handed in late). But, by the penultimate day, though everyone else's papers had reached me, Michael Ramsey's had not – and this in spite of urgent appeals in writing and by phone. There was nothing for it but to go to his house in the College (i.e. the Close), knock at the door, talk with him and sit on the steps outside until the papers were put into my hand. This somewhat desperate manoeuvre was successful and I returned to the office with some excellent papers. Before the next summer came, Michael had married Joan, Secretary to the Bishop of Jarrow who also lived nearby in the College, and after that his examination papers were among the first to arrive.

Other unusual characters I encountered included the Chancellor of the University, Lord Londonderry, who lived in the south of the County and normally presided at degree ceremonies if they were held in Durham. But one couldn't be sure until say 20 minutes before the time the ceremony was due to begin that he would actually turn up, so that in the processions and the ordering of procedures one had to be prepared for either eventuality.

Then there was Emeritus Professor Heawood, formerly Professor of Mathematics, who was now over 80, very bent, very deaf, but known to and greeted by innumerable folk as he made his slow way, clad in his black cape, up the hill on his weekly journey to my office. His progress could be followed by the sound of his cheerful responses as he got nearer and nearer. Finally he would with a great effort climb the stairs to my room and, after a pause, produce from his waistcoat pocket a piece of paper on which were two lists. He would then say in a slow and courteous manner, "Mr Registrar, would you very kindly permit me to look at your copy of *Who's Who*; and after that at your copy of Crockford?" Permission having been given he would sit at a table and very contentedly annotate his lists. He did not take at all kindly to my suggestion after many weeks of this that maybe he might like someone to give him a copy of *Who's Who* and even of Crockford when he next had a birthday. "Ah," he said to me once, "there were odd characters about in Durham in my *young* days."

The Dean of Durham Cathedral during my time as Registrar was C.A. Alington, formerly Headmaster of Eton and a great upholder of propriety. He once challenged the minutes of a meeting in which I had incautiously written that a number of candidates would have to re-sit their examination. "There is no such verb as 're-sit'," he declared, "please see that this is amended to 'sit again'." Durham in my time was still in some ways a very traditional place. I can never remember a single occasion during the many lunches I ate between 1940 and 1944 at High Table at University College (i.e. the Castle) on which a Latin phrase was not uttered or quotation made. It was the done thing!

One of the most interesting duties of the Registrar was to act as Secretary to committees interviewing candidates for Chairs, though of course during the war years there were fewer such appointments than would normally be the case. Some curious remarks could be made at such meetings – e.g. at one when a new Professor of Medicine was to be appointed: "There are only two real physicians in the whole of the north of England." Early in my tenure of the post, it was decided to invite Enoch Powell, who had since 1938 been a Professor of Classics at Sydney, to come (without interview) to occupy the Chair of Greek in the University. He accepted the post, but a little later, in the middle of the voyage back to England, cabled me withdrawing. He had decided that the state the war had reached demanded that he should, at any rate for the time being, forsake a university career altogether in order to serve his country. He was never in fact to return to academic life.

Among the most prestigious endowed lectures in the University were the Riddell Memorial Lectures. In 1943 C. S. Lewis gave his famous *Abolition of Man* series and it fell to me to see that they were published by the O.U.P. as soon as possible after they were delivered. I can only say that no one could hope for a more efficient contributor of a neat text and for a more prompt and conscientious reader of

proofs than C.S.L. My relationships with him were of the pleasantest
– though he never remembered that 16 years earlier we had been
fellow students on the Oxford B.Litt. course.

An unusual and somewhat remarkable facility offered by the
University of Durham in those years was an external B.Mus degree.
The Professor of Music, Sir Edward Bairstow, the famous composer
and organist of York Minster, lived in that city and only occasionally
came up to Durham – chiefly for examining purposes and in the
summer. It was indispensable for all candidates to buy and know
pretty thoroughly Bairstow's books on Harmony and Counterpoint.
But however thoroughly they knew them the failure rate both at the
Part I and Part II stages of the degree was very great – on occasion 90
per cent – and at least one re-entry (with fee) a common occurrence.
There was no doubt at all that standards were high! As Registrar I was
more or less responsible for seeing that the team of External Examiners
who came year by year to live in the Castle for a week or two were satisfactorily accommodated. I remember that one year when the bill for
wines and spirits seemed rather high I tried remonstrating with Bairstow
personally. He pointed out very firmly indeed that he was a teetotaller
himself, though this did not seem to me a complete answer to the
University's problem.

I kept my hand in as a lecturer by taking classes on one afternoon
a week in Bede College, to which the students of Whitelands in Putney
had been evacuated. The Chaplain of Bede (a Church of England
college) at this time was Alan Richardson[3] and its Principal, E.R.
Braley ("Give to us our Braley dead," the students were said to pray).
He was in fact a jovial character. "You," he cried to me one morning,
"ought to be the Principal of a Church of England College." "But
I'm not a member of the C of E," I said. "Oh, don't let that worry
you, brother," was his response.

During the war years I gave numerous talks to troops – some of
them stationed on anti-aircraft sites, others in camps for new recruits.
My experiences in Russia were frequently drawn upon (I reckoned
that I gave that lecture 57 times in versions not particularly varied).
Attendance at these lectures was always voluntary, the audiences often

surprisingly big. "Yes they certainly needn't come unless they want; either they do that or they fill sandbags. The choice is theirs."

One of my occupations at night from time to time between 1940 and 1944 was fire watching at Durham Castle (University College). My companions were most of them students who had volunteered for the job and we had conversations together – often on the roof – on a wide variety of subjects. I remember asking each of them one night how old they thought three of the best known personalities in the University were. They looked indeed much more aged than they were – Warden Duff, dignified and slow moving, was then 42; Michael Ramsey, as lumbering of gait as when he became an Archbishop, was 37, and Vaughan Jeffreys, the Professor of Education, was 39. Each of the three, they estimated, must be well over 60!

In London and many other places a lot of thought was being given to the kind of future we wanted for Britain after the war had ended, whenever that would be. A new Education Act was being planned and many consultations were taking place regarding what ought and what ought not to be in it. The McNair Committee on the future of teacher training had been constituted and worked very hard between 1942 and 1944. In Christian circles The Moot was meditating, the *Christian Newsletter* in very lively production and a series of Christian Newsletter books published. One of them, *What is Christian Education?* by John Drewett and Marjorie Reeves, owed a good deal to the discussions we had had on the Auxiliary Movement's Education Committee which I have already referred to. Others on Education, by Fred Clarke and Adolf Loewe, reflected the sociological awareness which was to become so influential an element in the post-war development of Education.

As the war was drawing to its close in 1944 my stint as Registrar came to an end. My father had died early that year, his burial place being the churchyard of St. Cuthbert's church not far from our home. On our return to Newcastle once again my mother came to live in the same house as ourselves. This was at 61 Elmfield Road, Gosforth, and we shared it with Louis Arnaud Reid, Professor of Philosophy at King's College and his wife (who bred dogs!).

I had already got to know Louis pretty well and to find that he operated on a wavelength not too far from mine. Before we left Riding Mill our house had been the meeting place of a lively group which on one seminal evening discussed, under the chairmanship of Fred Clarke, Director of the University of London Institute of Education, some of the underlying challenges likely to face Britain and education in the post-war years. Fred Clarke, who was then External Examiner for the University's postgraduate Diploma in Education, had brought Karl Mannheim with him, who put forward some missionary ideas on the contribution which ideological thinking ought in his view to be making to educational theory and practice. Louis Reid was one of the group, and it was here perhaps that he first encountered Clarke – who a little later captured him to be the first Professor of the Philosophy of Education at the London Institute.

During my time both at Newcastle and at Durham I had become an interested tutor to a W.E.A. Tutorial Class in English Literature – for six years one at Forest Hall, a suburb of Newcastle, and later for four years one in Sunderland. The keen group of students who came to the Forest Hall class ranged in their ages from 17 to 72 and included Edward Short (later to be Minister of Education and a member of the House of Lords) and Alan Johnson, than a lab. boy at a neighbouring soap works, but later Fellow and Bursar of his Cambridge college and Professor of Chemistry successively at Sussex and Nottingham Universities.

It was this interest in extra-mural work which caused me during the later part of the session 1944-45 to apply for the post of Secretary to the Department of Extra-Mural Studies at Oxford – not with any real expectation of getting the job nor indeed the certainty that I wanted it. But at least, looking back afterwards, I could say that the day or so I spent in Oxford for the interview brought with it some fascinating experiences. Before the interview I had to wait for a time in the Senior Common Room at Balliol, and there I listened to an earnest discussion going on about the possibility that the work of the Oxford Extra-Mural Delegacy in the Potteries might be preparing the way for the coming of a new University College to the area. That, they thought, was certainly an enterprise which ought to have Balliol backing. It might well have the support of Sandy Lindsay, the Master, and certainly would have that of Sammy Finer, one of the Balliol dons taking an enthusiastic part in the conversations. And this in 1945 – four whole years before Keele University College came into being with Lindsay as its first Principal (1949) and S.E. Finer as its first Professor of Political Institutions (1950-66).

After the interview I talked with Thomas Hodgkin, another of the candidates, and to my surprise and delight was invited to join Hampden Jackson (a third candidate) and himself at lunch in the Hodgkin home. And so happened my first meeting with Dorothy[4], Thomas's wife, who provided the three of us with a delicious lunch, much enhanced by her presence with us. A good deal of the talk at the meal was an exchange between Thomas and Hampden, who knew each other well, whether either would accept the job, if offered, or give way to the other if he was runner up. In fact it was Thomas who became Secretary of Extra-Mural Studies at Oxford for eight years or so from 1945, before he and Dorothy went off to Africa together.

A Young University College: Hull (1945-47)

Hull is a large city 50 miles down a siding, and in the forties, before there was a Humber Bridge, few people visited it unless they had business there or in the neighbourhood. My first acquaintance with it was on the day I was one of six interviewed for the Chair of Education there for which, backed by Eustace Percy and James Duff, I had applied. The taximan at Hull Paragon Station, when asked to take me to the University College, appeared never to have heard of it, but mention of the road in which it was situated seemed to help him, and I reached it in good time.

The two charming buildings of the College separated by a lawn seemed attractive enough; and before my interview I got into an interesting conversation with another of the six candidates – a man with a Scottish accent named Ben Morris[5]. It was my first meeting with one who was to become a lifelong friend. The chairman of the interviewing panel was the Principal, John Nicholson, under whom 11 years before I had begun my happy time in the Newcastle Department of Education.

The job of finding a house in Hull was made difficult not at all because of a shortage of houses for sale but because so large a proportion – well over 85 per cent – of all the houses in Hull, a city of 350,000 inhabitants, were badly war-damaged. For Hull had suffered physically throughout the war from repeated bombings, and was still smarting and suffering now mentally too – from a sense that the country did not at all realise the extent of her losses or of her courage. Much less damaged cities – Coventry for example – had got far greater publicity and sympathy for the attacks they had endured. But a raid on a town in the north-east (Hull seemed never to be mentioned in the bulletins) might to most people have meant Newcastle or Sunderland – or Middlesbrough perhaps – but few would have thought it referred to Hull. For house seekers in 1945, however, there was the advantage that good houses, once they had been repaired, were available in some quantity at relatively low prices and we were very content with 46 Westbourne Avenue into which we moved that summer. We chose a skilful builder – there was serendipity in the choice – to repair the ceilings and restore the cornices of a well-built house about a mile from the College and on a level with it. (Hull generally is on the level, the highest point being perhaps 30 feet higher than the lowest.)

The College as a whole in the autumn term of 1945 – on its large still mostly vacant site – had perhaps a total of 200 students, those in the postgraduate year reading for the Cambridge Certificate of Education numbering seven. The Department itself, under my predecessor Victor Murray, had been evacuated to Cambridge (I went at an early date to Cheshunt College there to consult him). At first I was the only member of staff of my new Department. One great advantage of having so small a number of students was that one could get to know each really well. I still remember quite a proportion of my first group of Hull students, one a West Indian, one a middle-aged man who came from Grimsby every day, crossing the Humber by early ferry, another a bright maths teacher who later took a post at Denmark Road School, Gloucester, inviting me there to give away the prizes one year in the fifties. The students took the Cambridge Certificate, because at this stage Hull was not a university and did not award degrees or diplomas of its own. By the beginning of the Spring Term of 1946 two good men had been appointed as Lecturers so that now we had three full-time members of staff to teach seven students! An urgent task though was to secure, if I could, that the College should be recognised (for the first time) for Ministry of Education Training Grants, four-year and one-year, and this having been done, to ensure that there would henceforward be a much larger actual entry.

From the start I liked the atmosphere of the College – tiny but with some notable people among its band of Professors, a good Library, and forward-looking in spirit. T.E. Jessop, the philosopher, and Brynmor Jones, the chemist, in particular appeared to me to combine wisdom and vision. And before long, with Roger Wilson appointed to head its Social Studies Department, Richard Hoggart as one of its Staff Tutors in Adult Education, and John Tinsley to be its Lecturer in Theology, the promise in the air seemed to me more and more plucked to earth. I had indeed been allowed to choose John Tinsley more or less myself. In Durham days I had spotted him as an excellent student and had signed his First Class Honours degree parchment when he graduated. John Nicholson was as keen as I that the College should be able to offer Theology as a subject for study and I agreed to "represent" Theology on the Senate until it could be constituted as a Department in its own right. (Curiously, both Roger Wilson and John Tinsley finished their careers in Bristol – John as Bishop of Bristol and Roger as Professor of Education.)

The process of securing numbers of (it was hoped) good students for the postgraduate Education course for the 1946-7 year took me away from Hull a good deal. Since geographically Hull is out of the way, attending an interview there would have been an expensive business for numbers of likely recruits. So I arranged to be myself at convenient centres in various parts of the country at which to interview candidates in that region – often centres not unattractive to myself for one reason or another. Among them were Plymouth, Cambridge, Liverpool and London and such was the success of this manoeuvre that the number of students for the Education Year built up rapidly, as did the number of schools sending students to Hull for under-graduate courses too.

John Nicholson was of course anxious, as were many of his col-leagues, that the College should become better known. He therefore encouraged all sorts of extra-mural enterprises and the establishment of links with the world outside. He was pleased when I became a member of the East Riding Education Authority (whose lively Chief Officer was Victor Clark) and also began to represent the College on the Governing Body of St. John's College, York. Links with local grammar schools could be fostered by going to their Speech Days – occasionally, though by no means always, enlivened by some unusual happening. One afternoon, for example, the report of the Headmaster of the Malet Lambert School in Hull lasted so long (54 minutes; I timed it) that the Guest of Honour (John Buchan) had to go off to catch his train without time to make his own speech at all. On another occasion, at Middlesbrough, the speaker (encouraged by the Head) formally asked the Chairman of the governors, amid the usual cheering, for the school to be granted an extra half holi-day. The Chairman rose with dignity and speed to announce that as the ration for the year had already been used up, this request would certainly not be granted by him. Upon which the Chairman was loudly and fiercely booed. "Just what I wanted to happen," said the Headmaster to me after-wards; "My chairman is a very nasty chap." The plot had succeeded!

The Hull years saw my first ventures – to be succeeded by many others later on – into two new territories: functioning myself as a speaker at school prize-givings (Settle High School was the earliest to invite me) and more important, acting as External Examiner to stu-dents at the end of their Postgraduate Education course (Sheffield University was the first to invite me, to be followed later by most of the others, with Trinity College, Dublin, providing by far the most talkative candidates).

Another experiment started during Hull days was what was soon to become known as the Foundations Conference. The idea was to bring together for a few days a number of outstanding Heads of Schools, University Professors and educational administrators who were sympathetic to a Christian position, though not necessarily orthodox in their beliefs, and wanted to think over at a somewhat deeper level than usual a number of contemporary educational problems. We aimed at a group made up of people from a wide range of the sectors of our educational system who might not normally encounter one another – people from public, grammar and secondary modern schools, from Local Authority administration, from colleges and universities, maybe some officers of the NUT; to hold the three-day Conference annually and house it comfortably in a different place each year; not to have its deliberations reported in the press but to rely upon its members, refreshed and stimulated, going back to their jobs with a new thoughtfulness and awareness that they had allies in other parts of the educational landscape.

In fact the Foundations Conference met year after year for more than a decade (1946-58). It tended to think of Education organically. From a nucleus of some two dozen members, there were eventually well over 200 on the list of those who wished to be invited, though we aimed not to have more than 40 or 45 at any one conferring. Among the most loyal and lively participants were John Dancy[6] and Marjorie Reeves, George Whitfield, Thorold Coade, John Ounsted[7], George Lyward and Roy Rich; those who were keen supporters (and occasional participants) included Walter Moberly, Fred Clarke, Jack Wolfenden, Ronald Gould and Jack Longland. To every Conference my wife Sheila acted as hostess – and often as its Secretary too.

It was the Foundations Conference which sowed in people's minds the idea of a series of shortish books under the general title "Educational Issues of Today". The University of London Press showed much interest in its possibilities and sent representatives to several Foundations Conferences. Those who contributed books to the series were all members of "Foundations" and included Marjorie Reeves, John Wolfenden[8], Fred Clarke and Roy Rich in addition to myself and several others. The bestseller was Marjorie's *Growing Up in a Modern*

Society which went speedily into three reprints.

Should I stay at Hull for a number of years or should I yield to the temptation of applying for the Chair of Education at Leeds becoming vacant in the autumn of 1947? One factor which affected my decision was the importance I had come to attach to the need as I saw it for the universities of the country to establish Scheme A Institutes of Education as outlined in the McNair Report.

The key idea of Scheme A was to involve the universities much more closely with the education and training of teachers, both in the colleges and the universities, so that standards in the teaching profession would gradually but very surely be raised, and through this to encourage the universities to feel a greater responsibility for education in schools – both those from which they drew their own students and the rest. Students in the Colleges of Education within the region served by a university – Leeds had seven – should be awarded qualifications including degrees, underwritten and guaranteed by it, the colleges themselves coming more and more to be looked upon as partners in the higher education enterprise, provided with library facilities of quality, and members of their staff encouraged, with the support of the university, to do further study and research in their own fields.

The strong argument against leaving Hull so soon was my happiness in the developing and fascinating job I had there in a progressive, if small, University College; another was the pain which I knew my departure would cause John Nicholson personally whose kindness to me had been real; yet another was the fact that we had recently moved to a house in Newland Park, very near the College, which had space and light and gardens. Yet a further cause for regret was the unexpected attractiveness we found in parts of the region within easy reach of Hull – with characterful Beverley with its beautiful and delicate Minster, the South Yorkshire Wold country so gentle and unfrequented, and the wide Humber estuary peopled with bird life.

The Leeds chair, however, was a prestigious one and the conversion of Leeds University to Scheme A, if it could be accomplished, was likely to be a highly significant pointer nationally. So I decided to apply – on condition that, if appointed, Leeds would allow me to initiate, as potentially the Director of its Institute as well as Head of its Department of Education, a strong campaign in favour of its Institute's achieving Scheme A status; and that I should be allowed to continue in the Hull chair until the end of the calendar instead of the academic year.

In offering me the appointment the interviewing committee at Leeds agreed to these conditions, though warning me that it would be no easy task to convert a reluctant Vice Chancellor and an even more reluctant Senate to my point of view – particularly as my distinguished predecessor in the Chair, Frank Smith, was not convinced himself that a Scheme A Institute was the right thing for Leeds.

Broadening Horizons (1948-59)

When in the summer of 1947 Leeds University appointed me to its Chair of Education, one of my first tasks, even before the Autumn Term began, was to try to convert the Senate to the acceptance of the Scheme A principle, by which an alliance between the University and the Training Colleges of the area would be strongly fostered. Such oratory as I could muster succeeded in producing a vote of something like 41 to 7 in favour of giving me more or less a free hand with a Scheme A organisation for an Institute of Education. (There were a number of abstentions and the Vice Chancellor himself remained clearly not convinced; but the Local Education Authorities of the area – particularly the powerful West Riding Authority – were solidly in favour and the UGC was pressing Leeds for a speedy answer.) In my tenure of the Hull Chair I had, as I have said, been appointed the representative of the College on the Governing Body of St. John's College, York, so that I had already had an introduction to the outlook of a Training College of quality.

During the Autumn Term of 1947 I continued to hold the Chair at Hull while taking on the duties of the Leeds Chair. I divided the busy week between the two and found it a relief, though also a sorrow, to say goodbye to Hull at the end of the year, as did Sheila too. By that time we had acquired a house in Leeds at 285 Otley

Road in Lawnswood, and had made arrangements for Rosalind and Roland to go to the flourishing Froebel School run by Beryl Davies in two large houses lower down Otley Road, half a mile from our new home.

As I moved from Hull to Leeds there was a sense that this larger stage was nearer the centre too; and consciousness of this grew fast as we lived our first year in our new city. There were several elements helping to nourish the feeling.

First, there was Leeds itself. From the railway line linking the south with Leeds visitors get a decided impression that they are approaching a grimy, dated, place. Actually to live in Leeds quickly demolishes such ideas. It was very much, and still is, a city looking ahead, a blossoming financial centre, with lively theatres and superb concerts, good schools, fine hotels, excellent shops. The Yorkshire Dales are not far away, and over Leeds itself fresh winds from the Pennines blow from the west.

But the University did more than the city to make me feel enlarged. The University Senate, especially after Charles Morris came ito be Vice Chancellor in 1948, had several members full of ideas and able to defend them articulately. They included Fred Dainton (later Vice Chancellor of Nottingham and Chairman of the UGC), Asa Briggs (later Vice Chancellor of the University of Sussex and historian of the BBC), Derman Christopherson (later Vice Chancellor of Durham), Bonamy Dobrée, famous Professor of English, Ronald Tunbridge, a distinguished medical, and many more. Senate met on the first Wednesday of each month at 2 p.m. I found that it was often possible to discover when its meetings would end by finding out which train that evening the Vice Chancellor (who very definitely was in charge of the meetings!) was catching to London.

But there were people other than professors on the staff at Leeds who made the University a particularly humane one. One was Ronald Still, its Chief Medical Officer, always able to give wise advice to students who were ill or worried. He was endlessly unselfish, sometimes going personally with students who were in distress back to their homes. (I once came to know that the previous night he had taken one all the way to Brighton in his car.) Then there was Lady Ogilvie, a perceptive choice by Charles Morris to fill the post he had invented for her of Tutor to Women Students. She was newly widowed and in need of being rescued from sorrowing and given creative work to do. And how blessed to hundreds of women were her years at Leeds before she went on to be Principal of St. Anne's, Oxford. Then there was Peter Ackroyd, liberal Old Testament scholar, and fellow member with me of Headingley Hill Congregational Church. And many more.

My first session at Leeds (1947-8) was a busy one since, in addition to duties at Hull in the first term, I was head both of its large Department of Education (with lectures to give and an interesting but not altogether easy staff to manage) and of its new Institute. Towards the end of that session they gave me a choice of which job I should retain. It was a severe temptation to choose to remain with the long-established and distinguished Department; but since I had gone to Leeds largely because I was so keen myself upon the idea of developing an Institute of Education which mattered, I chose to stay with it. I saw in the Institute idea a pointer ahead to a concept of universities as responsible to society in new and wider ways, in particular to the possibility of their interpenetrating the education given to teachers in every type of school. This called for a university whose concept of the education it could give its own students was one that was multi-dimensional. An Institute, I hoped, might itself be a place which encouraged scholarship, including research, but which also encouraged the growth of whole human beings. And the enlightened George Richards, appointed as the Institute's Secretary, thoroughly agreed, as did the Institute's humane and highly intelligent Deputy Director, Alex Evans.

An Institute of Education, we thought, should have responsibilities both towards the Training Colleges (as they had been called) and towards experienced teachers in many types of school. To fulfil these it would need a lot of help not only from the University's own Department of Education (which would of course be one of its constituent parts) but from many other Departments in the University, especially perhaps those within the Medical School.

The Colleges which came to belong to the Leeds Institute were a varied and enterprising lot. Among them was the large City of Leeds College with an enormous campus and a Principal, Roy Rich, who earlier in life had been the first Professor of Education at Hull; St. John's College, York, one of the foremost of the country's Church of England Colleges; Bretton Hall, near Wakefield, which specialised in the education of teachers of Music, Art, and Drama; Bingley which had had Helen Wodehouse as its first Principal; and a fine Roman Catholic College, Trinity All Saints, just outside Leeds which later developed a strong Modern Languages tradition. We gave the North Riding College at Scarborough a choice of becoming a member of either the Hull or the Leeds Institute. It opted for Leeds and gave us another vital centre for the education of primary school teachers.

From the beginning I was sure the Institute should have a Library, which would be part of the University Library, but be able to offer facilities both to students in the Colleges and to teachers in the region. We were extraordinarily fortunate in the enterprising man chosen as its first librarian and also in finding good accommodation for what before long became its stock of 35,000 books and 100-plus periodicals. The Librarian, E.R.S. Fifoot, later went on to become Librarian of successively the Universities of Edinburgh and of Oxford.

We soon began to put on Diploma courses for experienced teachers, insisting to begin with that there should be at least one term of full-time study in the two-year part-time course which was standard. We provided such courses for teachers in grammar and secondary schools and in primary schools; for teachers of backward children and those tackling religious education. Much depended on the quality of such courses and therefore of their leadership. In addition to members of staff with teaching responsibilities, we were also able to appoint several to be full-time, creatively minded, Research Fellows.

From 1949 we put on an annual Institute Service for students in the Colleges and University itself, attendance being voluntary. It was held every second year in York Minster to which a congregation of over 2,000 came. In the intervening years we used one of the other

Cathedrals in the Leeds area – Ripon, Wakefield or Bradford – or one of the larger Free Churches of the region.

1949 saw not only the start of my membership of the UGC, of which a separate account follows, but of a number of other ploys, which included giving an early morning series of short talks for the BBC on "Belief in God". I also became one of the external examiners for the University of London's Postgraduate Certificate Examination, an annual assignment I retained until I became a member of the London Institute's staff myself in 1960. I found a higher proportion of outstanding students taking this examination over the years than in the corresponding course in any other university for which I was external examiner.

From 1950 I became a member of the National Advisory Council for the Training and Supply of Teachers, a body brilliantly chaired by Sir Philip Morris and intended to bring together representatives of Institutes of Education throughout the country, of Local Authorities and the Ministry of Education itself. It was interesting, and a little ironic, to note that in every official document the Ministry – quite incurably – called Institutes "Area Training Organisations". (We had thought that Institutes aimed to be places of education rather than training.) William Alexander (later Sir William) was a permanent and forceful member of this National Advisory Council and the discipline over him gently and subtly exercised by the Chairman was an interesting phenomenon to watch.

1951 saw my first contact with Westhill College in Selly Oak, Birmingham, which invited me to be its President for one session – the sole duty of the President being to give an address at some suitable point during his year of office. It was not until later years that I became a Governor and Trustee of Westhill and indeed for a time the Chairman of its Governors.

So far in my account of my days in Leeds I have said nothing of the family, but for all of us Leeds in fact was proving a happy city in which to be. Sheila developed links with the old-established Yorkshire Ladies Council of Education and took the initiative in developing a very special sort of residence for the elderly under its auspices. She continued to examine in English for the University of Durham School Examinations Board and for some of her Leeds years was its Chief Examiner in English. After a few years at Miss Davies's Froebel School, Rosalind went on to Leeds Girls High School and Roland to the Junior and then the Senior Departments of Leeds Grammar School before going off to Bryanston in his early teens. My mother died in 1953, well looked after at the end by some kind Leeds friends as well I hope as ourselves. From the start in Leeds I became a member of Headingley Hill Congregational Church whose excellent Minister, Harold Leatherland, became a family friend (indeed it was he who conducted my mother's funeral service, coming with us to Durham for the interment of her body in the grave at St. Cuthbert's in which my father had been buried nine years before). Sheila found in St. Chad's Church, Headingley, a place of worship to suit her. In the early fifties, being interested in the history of the Moravians, a sect which was decidedly non-conformist and yet had bishops, she became a Governor of Fulneck Moravian Girls School near Pudsey.

I am not quite sure how I found time to write anything, but in fact my short *Education and the Modern Mind* was submitted to Faber in 1953 and published in 1954. Its American edition, with an introduction by Margaret Mead, followed a year or two later under a better title: *Education – The Lost Dimension*.

It was in 1954 that the University of Leeds granted me a sabbatical term. I was anxious to spend it, if I could, in the States which I had not yet visited. A Kellogg International Fellowship came my way and this covered most of the costs for a three- or four-month stay excluding travel to and fro across the Atlantic. One condition of the Kellogg Fellowship was that the planning of the trip should be done acceptably and that I should visit in person the little town of Battle Creek, where the headquarters as well as the chief factory of the firm were sited. I was also given a Fullbright Travel Grant which paid the costs of crossing the Atlantic both ways.

The voyage over was made in the Queen Elizabeth. I can remember vividly sitting in the cinema during one of several great storms with

the big ship rolling from side to side and the enormous curtains swinging across the edges of the screen as she rolled. The film itself was
accompanied by the music of the Swedish Rhapsody, which now I
always associate with that memorable afternoon. We finally made
New York five hours late at dusk one evening, its multitude of sky-
scrapers looming gigantically through the mists, with some of their
floors still lighted. It was an unforgettable sight as the liner moved
slowly and smoothly to the quayside with nearly all her passengers on
deck as this fairy-like city itself seemed to be approaching.

My first month was spent chiefly in New York – at Teachers College,
Columbia – where I met several scholars with whom I was to have closer
contact later on, notably Freeman Butts, with whom I was to edit *The
World Education Year Book* for 1972/3. I saw a good deal, too, of my old
Teddy Hall friend, Allen Walker Read, now a Professor of English at
Columbia, and I was a frequent guest at his house at 39 Claremont
Avenue, near the campus. From New York I visited Washington and also
the University of Maryland nearby.

My second month in the States was spent chiefly at Harvard where
I was accommodated in a large ground floor room in one of the residences in the famous Yard and soon began to feel part of the place. At
first, however, I found sleep difficult because of a student who practised perseveringly on a clarinet for an hour between 12 and 1 every
night, and then because of a mysterious noise which seemed to emerge
from the room exactly over mine, diagonally across which someone
seemed to be treading heavily. There would be a pause and then the
heavy tread would be resumed diagonally in the other direction, and
so on indefinitely. When the journeys were finished at last there would
be the clump of what seemed to be a heavy boot with leggings, taken
off and thrown down, first from one foot and then – after a pause –
from the other. This went on every night for about a week, when I
felt that I could stand it no longer. So I composed a polite but firm
little note and took it up to put through the letter box, if there was
one, of the room above mine. I had not ascended the stairs before
and was surprised to find that on the door concerned there was a
notice "The Rev. Father ... "! All the same I dropped the note into

the letter box and after that all was quietness. What could have been the explanation for the treading? Perhaps the Father was saying his prayers, meditating between each.

After my month at Harvard where I made good use of the superb Widener Library and attended various seminars in the School of Education (I had to take some myself), I went on to Chicago, from which I was able to visit both Ann Arbor and Battle Creek, as required. I had expected that my two days there would include a visit to the factory and show me how the famous cornflakes were made. But it was made clear that this was certainly not part of the programme. I was told however a good deal about the support which the Kellogg Foundation was making to Extra-Mural Departments in Universities, not only in the States but in other countries; and I was told also something of the history of the Kellogg firm, including the famous quarrel between Mr Kellogg and Mr Post in the early days, which caused Mr Post to set up a rival establishment and to market Post Toasties, Grapenuts, etc.

From Chicago, with the warm approval of the Kellogg Foundation and at their expense, I was able to make quite a number of journeys and visits to other universities and cities. I went, for example, to Denver, the mile-high city, and had my first sight of the Rockies. And from there I went on to St. Louis, much further south, before returning to Chicago. The impressions of academic America given by this first visit made me keen to follow it up with others when chance offered. And an opportunity did occur a good deal sooner than I expected.

Back in England I found plenty to occupy me that summer and autumn – partly no doubt making up for lost time, but partly because there was much fascinating work to be done. The meetings of the governing body of St John's College, on which I served, were at first a bit handicapped by the obvious lack of interest which the Chairman – the Dean of York – took in them. Occasionally, indeed, he had to be fetched to the meeting. But since he was *ex officio* Chairman, it wasn't easy to know how someone else might be inveigled into taking his place. When, however, Michael Ramsey came to York as Archbishop, we wondered whether we might be bold enough to ask him, knowing that he was keenly interested in the Church Colleges, whether (a) he might be willing to become Chairman, and (b) he could negotiate in some happy way the disappearance from the Chairmanship of the Dean. All went splendidly and during the whole of the time that he was Archbishop he never, as far as I can recollect, missed a meeting of the Governors and always knew the content of the agenda beforehand. After the meetings, though, he was not at all good at socialising and it was easily possible to go up to him standing by himself and have a talk with him about this, that and the other – a talk which could sometimes blossom in surprising ways.

Another fascinating "outside" body on which I served was the West Riding Education Committee. This was made fascinating chiefly by the presence of, and sometimes conflict between, its enterprising Chief Education Officer, Alec Clegg, and one of the most formidable and knowledgeable members of any Education Committee in the country, Alderman Hyman. Clegg had keen aesthetic interests and great devotion to the education of children and was proud of his pioneering efforts in the West Riding to provide for both these enthusiasms. Hyman's strength lay in his mastery of every agenda – his intelligent and careful study of all the items before a meeting and his forthrightness in airing his views on matters which concerned him. No manipulation of the agenda would prevent his being awake when some matter of vital interest to himself was being discussed.

In 1955 Keith Murray, who had become Chairman of the UGC, asked me whether I would be prepared to chair a meeting of a new Sub-Committee of some eight people to report on Halls of Residence in Universities and their future. I should be able to have a considerable say in who should be members of it. Clearly this was not an offer to be rejected!

It occurred to me soon after it started its work that it might well be of interest and use to draw upon the experience in countries other than Great Britain of providing residences for students – particularly the USA. Keith Murray, approving this idea, wrote to the Rockefeller

Foundation to ask if some money might be made available to finance a trip for me in the USA lasting something under two months. They agreed and so September and October 1956 saw me in the States again, this time visiting, to start with, several universities in the far west. I crossed the Atlantic from Liverpool to Montreal on the Saxonia making my first acquaintance with Canada. From Montreal I flew to New York and thence to Los Angeles and San Francisco where I made my first acquaintance with the University of California. I visited the University of Oregon at Eugene and the University of Washington at Seattle, going on by ship to Vancouver where I saw something of the residence halls provided by UBC. After crossing the Rockies by the spectacular Canadian Pacific Railway route I went on to Minneapolis, and thence in turn to Universities and Colleges in Wisconsin, Indiana, Illinois, Ohio and upper New York state. I was intrigued to see how imaginative was the planning of some of the buildings for student residences in the States; how enormous some of the residences were; and the care taken to segregate men from women according to floor – theoretically quite a safeguard, but in practice not one as strong as the authorities had intended.

There is no doubt that the second half of the 1950s marked the beginning of a period of lessened optimism in educational circles. As far as Institutes of Education were involved, the starting-point for their concerns about their financing and future came as early as 1952. For in that year the University Grants Committee had to consider whether the earmarking of funds which had been provided for the starting up of Institutes of Education could be continued for a second quinquennium. All of them were very young in 1952 and in my view one more quinquennium was an imperative. But the whole principle of ear-marking was unpopular both to members of the UGC and to universities themselves; for a grant that was earmarked represented, from a university's viewpoint, a curb to its freedom to allocate its funds according to its own judgement.

Not surprisingly, therefore, a battle took place inside the UGC before a decision was reached whether or not earmarking for Institutes of Education should continue in the quinquennium 1952-57. The

Committee was narrowly divided on the matter. Eric James led the opposition to a continuation of any special grant to Institutes and I led on the other side, strongly supported by Henry Magnay, the Chief Education Officer for Liverpool. But my side lost – by one vote! – and so there was no earmarking of funds for Institutes from 1952 onwards. Before long most of them were feeling the pinch – their universities were not supporting their expansion in the way the Grants Committee itself had done. Roughly speaking those Institutes which had succeeded by imagination and skilled footwork to secure a generous grant for the first quinquennium were better off when times became harder than those Institutes – such as London – which had asked for only meagre support at the start.

In spite of commitments elsewhere I spent most of my time during the later fifties in attending to work within the University of Leeds and its Institute. But increasingly I was concerned that there and throughout the country the desire of both University Departments of Education and Institutes of Education for the autonomy of each should not become a source of weakness to both. The foundation of a separate Conference of Directors of Institutes and of a Conference of Heads of University Departments of Education seemed to me a danger signal, and to bring about a union of the two became one of my major concerns. That involved much delicate persuasion and negotiation, with a little discreet pushing here and pulling there, enlisting support from this Vice Chancellor or that if it seemed helpful. The final success of this quiet campaign did not occur for some years but it certainly was helped by the foundation of the National Advisory Council on the Training and Supply of Teachers which drew its representatives both from the Departments and the Institutes.

Among the more curious happenings in the University of Leeds one session was this inexplicable episode. Each term, by tradition, a University Sermon was preached by a distinguished visitor. One Sunday, I think it was in 1958, an excellent 35-minute sermon was given us by a famous Scottish Presbyterian. Two terms later exactly the same address was delivered by a well-known Anglican professor from England. How come? The very words were the same! On the Monday morning following this second sermon I asked the Vice Chancellor, who had sat by himself, chin in hand, on the front row of pews on each occasion, how such a repetition could possibly be explained. "Oh, were they the same?" he inquired.

Never in my life having visited Rome, I found myself there in the spring of 1958 twice within three weeks. For under the auspices of the British Council I gave a lecture in the University of Rome one March morning. The Professor of Education in whose Department it was given was ill in hospital at the time and the following day I went to see him there – to find him lying in bed by himself in a large and luxurious room, with crowds of visitors circling round, all of whom seemed to be talking animatedly to one another, while he was left quietly reading – though very ready to talk with me and in excellent English. From Rome I went on to Florence, where I spent a very cold, cloudy day.

The second trip, three weeks later, entailed merely a touchdown at Rome airport for Sheila and me *en route* for Iran. I had been invited to make a report to the Iranian Ministry of Education on transforming its system of teacher training. In Teheran (we had had a day in Baghdad on the way and found that no direct travel by air between the two cities was possible even then) we were given a warm welcome by people on the University's staff, an attractive programme of lecturing and visits being arranged for us. As for the main assignment I was to my surprise presented straightaway with a lengthy report on how the teacher training system of the country might be improved. This had just been handed in by a team of US educationists who had been in the country for a month or two immediately preceding my visit. I was asked as my first job to let the authorities have an analysis and critique of this report (which they had not yet read) – a task I found easier than I expected. For the recommendations from the Americans were in three parts. Part I described the present system of teacher education in Iran; Part II described the present system in the USA; and Part III recommended that the system contained in II should be substituted for that in I.

Sheila and I much enjoyed our first experience of the Middle East, including two or three days spent in Istanbul on our return journey, at a hotel overlooking the Bosphorus, and arrived back just in time for the start of the summer term.

During the latter part of 1959 one of the most difficult decisions of my life had to be made: whether to stay on at Leeds probably for the rest of my career or move to the London Institute to share its leadership with the newly appointed Director, Lionel Elvin, but taking *inter alia* special responsibility for its work with the Colleges of its widespreading area. I had been at Leeds for more than 12 years and another period of about the same length lay ahead before I reached retiring age. I had been happy – often intensely so – in Leeds but the pioneering days of its Institute were over and the money supply was becoming tighter. Rosalind had already been at Cambridge for two years and Roland was in his first term there. But could the interlocking of posts at London possibly be a success? Granted that the bringing together of Institute and Postgraduate concerns in the education of teachers on which I was keen seemed to be perfectly exemplified in the structure of the London Institute and that it was without doubt the most prestigious institution for teacher education in the Commonwealth, would I find the somewhat impersonal character of the University of London uncongenial and any adequate equivalent there to the friendliness on which I had really depended rather a lot both in Newcastle and Leeds?

We finally decided that I should take the risk and so my job at Leeds came to an end with the end of 1959. My ten years with the UGC had finished a few months before that. We were about to open a new chapter in our lives.

The UGC as It Was in 1949-59

I joined the UGC in 1949, the invitation having arrived out of the blue. For I had had no reason beforehand to think that I was at all the sort of person who would receive such an invitation – which came from the Chancellor of the Exchequer in a personal letter, since the Treasury was the department of state under which the UGC functioned. The Committee met in a characterful room on the ground floor of 38 Belgrave Square, premises which in those days accommodated all the staff working for it – to the best of my recollection a single-figure number.

The Chairman for my first year was Sir Walter Moberly – the first full-time chairman the Committee had had – and there was no Vice-Chairman. The Secretary, whose name was de Montmorency, was also full-time and a career civil servant – responsible, able and well liked by all of us. He was especially knowledgeable about universities, having in the course of the job learned a great deal about them and he was a skilful and penetrating writer of minutes and reports. The Committee met for a day during most months, the meeting lasting from 10.30 a.m. to around 4.30 p.m. The Chairman, of liberal and scholarly mind, presided with an urbanity and informality rather typical of the Oxbridge tradition. But there was a certain missionary sense mixed in with his overview of universities. He was interested in educational purposes as well as policies; but not, I came to think, all that interested in finance. It was possible indeed for any financial matters that we had to consider not to come up until well after lunch and there were occasions on which they were condensed into the last hour or hour and a half of a meeting.

When I became one of the new "younger" members of the Committee, R.H. Tawney and Margery Fry had only just ceased to belong to it, both of them people with a strong individuality and sense of vocation. Several of those who continued to serve, as well as three or four of the newcomers, were undoubtedly people of character: among the continuers I think of Sir Charles Darwin, a descendant of the original Charles and himself aristocratically Cambridge with a very acute mind; and of David Hughes Parry, Head of the School of Advanced Legal Studies in London who later on became Vice-Chairman of the Committee. He brought a feeling for Wales, and especially for Aberystwyth, into our counsels. Among the newcomers there were Eric James (later knighted and afterwards a lord). He was then High Master of Manchester Grammar School and a robust defender of grammar schools in general. George Pickering, Professor of Medicine at St. Mary's Hospital Medical School and later Regius Professor of Medicine at Oxford, concealed under his modesty the shrewdest of judgements about higher education and its need to be enterprising. Henry Magnay came with much experience of ways of Local Government and was always conscious of the need to keep a watchful eye on what Central Government might be up to.

The company was human and friendly. We normally lunched "around the counter" at a pub in the neighbourhood of the office; but each year there was an annual dinner to which all past members of the UGC as well as present ones were invited. A good many of us belonged to the Athenaeum and since a number of Vice-Chancellors (whom we referred to as "customers") also belonged to it, there was a chance of natural and informal contacts on occasional evenings. At that time there were fewer than 30 universities in the whole country.

Among those who attended meetings of the Committee was the Permanent Secretary of the Ministry of Education. At the beginning of the fifties this was Sir Griffith Williams who was succeeded after his retirement by Sir Gilbert Flemming. Neither of course was a member of the Committee and on the very rare occasions when something was decided by vote they would not have voted. But they were encouraged to contribute points to our meetings and their massive knowledge of the thinking of the Ministry of Education (and of other government departments too) was a great asset. If their advice was asked for specifically, they knew how to give it in the right way. From Scotland came Sir William Murrie of the Scottish Office – a shrewd top civil servant from Edinburgh.

What has to be remembered in talking of that period in the Committee's life was the importance of the common traditions fostered by Public School, Oxford and Cambridge and Civil Service life, all of which flowed into the atmosphere. So much could be taken for granted by all of us that it hardly needed to be mentioned. One particularly good illustration, as it seems to me, of the behind-the-scenes working of the best sort of civilised and human spirit is this: Gilbert Flemming, powerfully intelligent, with a great capacity for objectivity but very English, was a pretty close friend of Charles Morris, who after being a don at Balliol for a number of years became Vice Chancellor of Leeds University. I discovered – much later on in fact – that Flemming and Morris when they went up together at the age of 19 or so as scholars to Trinity College, Oxford, were put on the same staircase and had begun to know each other well from freshman days. In due course Gilbert became best man at Charles's wedding and when visiting London

Charles sometimes stayed overnight at Gilbert's home. It is unthink-
able that two men so devoted to the development of what they thought
of as the right sort of higher education should not have discussed a
number of its problems together and found one another's up-to-date
viewpoint. Since Charles Morris at the time he was Vice Chancellor
at Leeds had Philip Morris, his brother, as Vice Chancellor at Bristol
and since John Fulton – a fellow don at Balliol with Charles – was
Principal of University College, Swansea, and later the first Vice
Chancellor of Sussex University, there was scope for much inter-rela-
tionship and much complexity of influence.

One of the ways in which members of the Committee itself came
to appreciate each other's viewpoints and to respect one another's judgements was through the visits we paid once every five years to all the
institutions in receipt of grant. These visits lasted a strenuous day, sometimes a day and a half or even two days, each. Some members might
travel to the place of the visit in a railway carriage together and there
were a few occasions upon which a journey from one university to
another, being visited the next day, was by private coach. At the start of
the decade beginning in 1949 there were no permanent sub-committees of the main UGC so that all the official visits which took place
were by the Committee itself. Obviously this was a very time-taking
business and not all members could go on every visit, since most had
heavy responsibilities in their own universities, firms or schools, as well
as serving on the UGC and maybe several other national bodies. But
my recollection is that the attendance at the visits averaged 50-60 per
cent of all the members, who then totalled 16 or 17. Very full notes
were kept of all visits and of the impressions we formed.

As the fifties went on the Committee changed somewhat in
character, though not in essential spirit. Pressure of business made
it inevitable that the attention given to financial matters grew greater
and closer. Under the chairmanship successively of Sir Arthur
Trueman and Sir Keith Murray this was achieved in a natural way.
A Vice-Chairman had started to function in 1950; the office staff
increased almost year by year. Specialist sub-committees began to
be appointed from the early fifties to help the main committee and

started to visit institutions on their own. The chairman of each specialist committee was however a member of the main committee and could report back to it whenever necessary and at any time. The Medical and Education sub-committees made a particularly important contribution during the 1950-60 decade. A Halls of Residence Committee with a limited life was appointed in 1955 with the duty of producing a Report on its remit. Soon an architect was appointed to "vet" the plans for new buildings which were coming into the office from the universities we sought to serve.

The Report of the Committee on Halls of Residence was published in 1957 and had some influence, even if a limited one. It encouraged universities to develop more Halls and regard them as integral to the education they provided. Among the universities which took its recommendations really seriously was Nottingham under Fred Dainton's Vice-Chancellorship.

The London Experience (1960-73)

It was clear enough from the start that my experience at the London Institute was going to be part of a wider one – of living for the first time in London itself and, what is more, living near its centre. For, through the good offices of one of my former students from Newcastle days, Hamish Stewart, now Clerk of the Court of the University of London, we were apportioned part of a delightful house belonging to the University: 41 Gordon Square. Quentin Bell had once lived there and it had had close associations with the Bloomsbury Group. It overlooked the central, at that time private, garden of the Square itself, where Arthur Waley, famous for his translations from the Chinese, who lived a few doors away, could be seen quietly walking on many a day. We ourselves as residents were given a key to the garden so that we could wander in it freely at any time we liked.

More than thirty Colleges "belonged" to the London Institute, some being in or near London itself, others far flung in Sussex, Kent, Surrey and Middlesex, including several as far off as Eastbourne, Canterbury and Dover. The feeling of spiritual closeness to the University which it had been possible to encourage in Leeds was clearly going to be hard to foster here. The London Institute's Library, wonderfully extensive in its stock of books and periodicals, if not its accommodation, was not available to students from the Colleges; nor was an Annual Institute Service a possibility, for the overall atmosphere in what came to be called the "Central Institute" was decidedly cool towards religious belief, and of course distances were a handicap as was the sheer number of students – over 21,000 – to be accommodated. All the same I started to explore what possibilities for development there were, making initial visits to most of the Colleges and lecturing in some of them during my first two terms and making contacts with many of the 170 or so men and women who were my new academic colleagues on the Central Institute's staff.

A feature of the London Institute was and is, of course, the immense strength of its work with students from other countries, and the depth of its interest in comparative and overseas education. So that maybe it was not so surprising that after two terms or so of "shaking down", I found myself setting off for a period of some five months overseas. For the first two of these I lectured in the 1960 Summer Semester at the University of California, Los Angeles.

With me on that flight to the States were my family – Sheila, Rosalind and Roland – for all of whom it was their first visit to that stupendous country. We had exchanged houses and cars with one of my opposite numbers at UCLA for two months – with no exchange of money between us but an agreement to pay compensation if the number of miles covered by one of us in our borrowed vehicles greatly exceeded that of the other. In the event the mileages were much the same – some 3,200 – with both parties convinced that they had had the better bargain. At Los Angeles Rosalind and Roland each took some courses of their own choosing in the semester programme and we were able at weekends to travel around, our most notable visit being to the spectacular Yosemite National Park with its inquisitive bears, mighty mountains, lovely streams and all.

After Los Angeles we had a few days in San Francisco, Sheila and the children departing then by train for New York and the journey back to England while I sailed smoothly across the Pacific to Australia in the luxurious *Mariposa* of the Matson Lines, where every cabin was first class, all were occupied, yet there were still more crew than passengers. We stopped off at colourful Tahiti on the way, where I spent much of a day driving round the island in a hired car and savouring memories of Gauguin. There was no airport in Tahiti in those days and it was not overrun by tourists. Then, calling at Auckland *en route*, we made for Sydney where I spent a few days at its university before going on to Melbourne.

Both at Sydney and Melbourne I was invited to receptions put on by former students of the Institute now in influential positions in Australian education. My base was Scottish-flavoured Melbourne, where I lectured and led seminar groups, but I was able to fly to Adelaide, Perth and Hobart before leaving the country. I shan't easily forget the return journey by train from Perth to Adelaide across the Nularbor Desert, 300 miles along a completely straight track with only telegraph posts breaking an entirely empty expanse on both sides of the line. Strangely, on the cross-members of the telegraph posts birds were to be seen perched. What could they find to eat? Where could they find a place for their nests?

The journey back to England was not direct. I flew from Sydney to Singapore, and thence, after a short stay, to Bangkok with its amazing Buddhist temples, before arriving at Hong Kong where for a week I conducted a course for the British Council. Sitting invisibly on the back row when I gave my first lecture was an old fellow student from Teddy Hall days, trustworthy and affectionate Li Sheng-Wu, whom I had not seen for 30 years. After the lecture he came shyly up to identify himself and we had ten minutes together. Later that week he arranged an authentic Chinese dinner party for me, where some 15 members of his family and closest relatives sat round an immense, round, very low table, with me as an honoured guest, for a splendid meal which seemed to have as many courses as there were people present – varied and delicious soups coming along as intermediate but integral parts of it.

From Hong Kong I flew to Delhi for four days. On one of them I visited the Taj Mahal at Agra – a building unforgettable, unforgotten,

which fulfilled all the expectations I had had of its loveliness and
peace. The journey home brought further experiences – a sight of
Mount Ararat, glimpses of Istanbul, views of the blue seas of the
Greek archipelago.

Back in the Institute in London, the early sixties saw much re-
shaping of the curriculum in the Colleges, with both pattern and
content altered for the new, post-Robbins type of teacher education
courses they gave. Committees and committee meetings galore were
needed, many of which I chaired, a number involving staff from parts
of the University of London other than the Institute. All the same,
the hopes both of the McNair and of the Robbins Reports for a teaching profession of high status were becoming dimmed once more in
spite of valiant efforts all over the country, including London, to
establish a B.Ed. degree which would have nearly the prestige of a
B.A. or B.Sc.. But neither the Universities nor the Government seemed
convinced at any deep level that this was all that important! More
and more it appeared to be accepted that the first concentration for
Universities – the one that would give them prestige (and money
too) – was research.

In these circumstances what did seem possible for a Dean of the
ULIE, with few teaching duties possible within the Central Institute
and its somewhat lessened hope of a new era arising from its relationships with its Colleges, was to begin to develop work within a fresh
field of educational study, one already beginning to blossom remarkably in the USA, that of higher education itself. Nor did it seem
improbable that finance might be obtained from appropriate Foundations and Trusts for researches in this area.

By 1963 the Niblett family had already been turned out of 41
Gordon Square to make room for a giant new and expensive University Computer which hummed night and day and filled all the space
in three adjacent civilised Gordon Square houses. (It was replaced by
a more efficient, much smaller, though equally expensive, computer
housed elsewhere a few years later.) After a period spent in a house in
Bedford Way – one now demolished to make room for the spreading
National Hotel – we moved to another owned by the University, 33

Tavistock Square. Sir Fred Clarke, whose thought and enterprise had done so much to create the Institute itself, had once lived in it and during our tenancy, in the basement a busy, much-visited, lawyer resided who was soon to become famous as one of the founders of Pakistan. From that rather secret basement of his, appetising smells of hot curried dishes arose evening after evening.

The first half of the sixties saw me active in other ways than those I have mentioned so far. From 1960 to 1963 I was Chairman of World University Service (UK), with a very articulate Council largely made up of students keen on WUS concerns, drawn from universities throughout the country. They were ruthlessly determined that the percentage of costs devoted to administrative purposes should not exceed four per cent of the annual budget. (This is a principle many charitable organisations have still to consider!) I was of course continuing to widen my experience as an external examiner and I had become first a member and then a deacon at the King's Weigh House, a congregational church which had the very able Daniel Jenkins as its Minister – Simon then being one of his teenage family and still a long way from the Editorship of *The Times* and his later achievements.. I had also widened my range by being chosen as a member of the Army Education Advisory Council and of the Council of Royal Holloway College at Englefield Green, on which Lady Lucan served before the period of her suffering began.

After an intensive period of chairing Committees, visiting (and lecturing in) the Institute's Colleges of Higher Education during the winter and spring of 1962, I went with Sheila to New Zealand for several months as William Evans Visiting Professor at Otago University. Based in Dunedin in a delightful flat provided for us by the University we were allowed to intersperse my numerous lecturing and official commitments with journeys in the Austin A40 they had put at our disposal. So we were able to see much of the magnificent scenery in the west of the South Island – approached along roads wonderfully free from traffic – and use the car too for getting to Christchurch and other places at which I had been invited to lecture. Indeed they allowed us, when we departed, to drive to the North

Island, see something of its scenery as well (including the bubbling hot springs) and finally leave the car at Auckland from which we sailed on the *Gothic* as two of its twelve passengers across the Pacific (calling at the lonely Pitcairn island) through the Panama Canal (spending a day in a hot Trinidad) and then across the Atlantic to Tilbury. Our cabin was the one said to have been occupied by the Duke of Edinburgh on some previous voyage. Magnificent!

Back in England, there were absorbing and at times challenging duties to fulfil. The Council of the Institute with the friendly Sir Ronald Adam as its chairman met regularly with future plans for its expansion under consideration. The Advisory Council on the Training and Supply of Teachers of which I was now a member was, under the chairmanship of Philip Morris, a livelier body than its name might suggest, with every meeting full of interest.

During a vacation in 1963 I took part in a conference sponsored by the World Council of Churches at Salisbury, Southern Rhodesia, now Harare in Zimbabwe. From it I went on to South Africa to lecture, under the aegis of the British Council, in a number of cities with universities – including Johannesburg, Pretoria, Cape Town, Stellenbosch, Pietermaritzburg and Durban – with opportunities to see from time to time something of the sun-drenched landscapes and varied scenery of the country and visit impoverished, sad Soweto. At Durban I was given the chance of visiting an operating theatre in the huge hospital for black people. I witnessed most of a Caesarean section operation, though in the chloroformed atmosphere of the very hot theatre I was overcome with faintness and after a time had to go out. But the messy baby, complete with some of its umbilical cord, was produced and washed in my presence in another room, as testimony that it was a proper – and complete – human being!

Early in 1964 I visited another operating theatre in London, this time with myself as the patient. I left my gall bladder behind at the hospital but recovered after a period to resume my busy job at the Institute and in July to go to the States again: first to make personal contacts with people in a number of the Foundations, including Ford, Rockefeller, Carnegie and Hazen; and then to lecture at Chicago

University. Hearing that I was in the States, the British Foreign Office offered me a chance, during the August about to begin, of lecturing on their behalf for a period of three weeks in whatever towns I liked to choose. They would pay all my expenses although not a fee for the lectures – which had to be given chiefly during lunch hours to Chambers of Commerce, Rotary Clubs, etc. and were meant to introduce American businessmen to British ideas on schools and school systems. Since I could choose which cities I was to speak in, I selected places I had not visited before – e.g. Cleveland, Cincinnati, Nashville, New Orleans, Houston, Austin and Seattle. During the tour I met many people from circles I did not normally move in. (One night, for instance, I stayed at the house of a millionaire oil man.) I also had opportunities to explore something of the cities I was in, New Orleans being a special delight. Between Austin in Texas, with its magnificently endowed University Library, and Los Angeles, I was able to spend a weekend visiting the Grand Canyon – endlessly spectacular, incredibly vast.

The success we had in 1964 in renting a cottage for a few weeks at the aptly named hamlet of Paradise near Painswick in Gloucestershire was quite a factor in determining our choice late in 1965 of Pinfarthings Cottage, Amberley, as a characterful house to buy. We intended to use it during vacations while I was still working and to retire to it when the time came. Our children, Rosalind and Roland, and later all three grandsons came to approve the choice and it was to prove one of the most successful ventures – and investments – we ever made. The front lawn offered just the right scope for childhood cricket and the views from the back were of peaceful Cotswold landscapes.

1965 saw me as occupied as ever – if not more so! – with Institute committees and some outside it. It was in that year that a national Society for Research in Higher Education was formed, with such early encouragement as I could give it, of whose Council a few years later I was to become Chairman for a period. Within the Institute itself we applied successfully to the Joseph Rowntree Trust for a grant enabling us to appoint two full-time Research Fellows to investigate the changing functions of Halls of Residence in British Universities.

A significant development with the beginning of the session 1965-1966 was the setting up of a Centre for the Study of Educational Policies. Its concern was to study the purposes and assumptions which lie, often unrecognised, behind different policies as well as studying the policies themselves. We particularly needed, I thought, to find out much more about the self-image held by differing types of places providing higher education. What was their understanding of the range of their responsibilities? How far did it include the education of social attitudes, of manners and morals? What criteria did they use in estimating their own success? And so on. We had a distinguished consultative committee to support the enterprise. Its members included, in addition to people from the Institute itself, Lord Robbins, Charles Morris, Richard Hoggart and John Fulton, and in due course we found we were discussing such matters as academic failure (on which some research papers were produced), student discipline, the qualities required in members of staff and problems met in their recruitment, etc..

My interest in and knowledge of higher education in America was fostered by further visits to the USA and Canada between 1965 and 1969, but perhaps the most exciting visit overseas during those years came from my appointment for two months in 1967 as Japanese Government Visiting Professor to the Universities of Japan. It would not have happened but for the good offices of Joseph Lauwerys[9] and it was on the condition that I should pay special attention to some aspects of moral education. The Japanese Government offered a return air passage first class but were willing to agree that if I took Sheila with me this could be transformed into two economy class fares, the only proviso being that when we arrived in Japan we should be seen descending from the first class exit of the plane and that when we departed we should use the first class entrance. It was also required that both our arrival and departure should involve aeroplanes marked JAL. They did not mind if we used other airlines for a number of sectors of the journeys. In fact I wanted to show Sheila something of Bangkok and Hong Kong so we took in both those places on the outward journey, the homeward trip being broken at Hawaii, with its deep blue skies and seas, and Los Angeles.

Our two months in Japan were full of new experiences. At Tokyo airport we found a cortège of large cars waiting for us and a company of moralogists to welcome us. These were for the most part businessmen concerned about the moral education of the young in Japan and with a fervent hope that moral standards in their country would be raised. Throughout our extensive travels in the two main islands of Japan, the moralogists looked carefully after us, appointing some able young men to travel with us on various trips. Among numerous other places I lectured in were Tokyo, Sapporo and Hiroshima. Everywhere we went there were Japanese meals to eat and Sheila was always regarded as an honorary man – often being the only woman present at a dinner apart from those who stood behind the tables and served the various courses. On one occasion as a particular treat, we and the whole company were provided with a plate each of Japanese blowfish – one of the greatest of delicacies – prepared by an expert chef. We were told that unless this dish had been meticulously prepared, the poison it contained was so powerful that within a minute of eating it death would ensue. As honoured guests we had to start sampling it and to show our pleasure, before the rest of the party – a large one – would be able to begin to eat. In fact we did not die and rather apprehensively enjoyed the dish.

More and more of my most interesting work was, well before the end of 1967, being done in the field of higher education studies. For it was becoming clear to me that the post of Dean of the Institute as originally envisaged was no longer viable. Part of my dissatisfaction with it was due to the impossibility of making the scattered Colleges of the Institute into a family or filling them with a hope for the future that would be creative. All over the country Area Traing Organisations were in serious decline, with lack of money and of governmental enthusiasm among the causes. But part was due to my own deficiencies. I was better at being a leader, able to pioneer and take the initiative fairly freely. As well, I found the permeating humanist

climate of the administration in the Institute too cool for comfort
and the lack of any sympathy for religion among so many of the brightest and best of the members of its staff – highly intelligent and excellent at their jobs though so many of them were – more inhibiting than
I ought to have done. I was out of sympathy too with the plans likely to
be adopted for the new building we had so much looked forward to,
for I thought that a new library should be one of the very first priorities
within it and I was not successful in carrying the Planning Committee
with me in this matter. It seemed that to use my capacity as an entre-
preneur might be more possible as a Head of Department than as Dean.
So when Lionel Elvin offered me a choice between remaining Dean
and becoming the first occupant of a Chair of Higher Education –
which would not be merely a personal one – I had little hesitation in
opting for the latter.

It had of course become clear long before 1968 that there ought to
be a place in the London Institute for Higher Education as a study. (To
the objection that such a subject was not a discipline – such as were the
Psychology, History, Sociology or Philosophy of Education – one could
retort that neither was Comparative Education nor Education in Overseas Countries, in both of which fields there were already Chairs.) Before
the Department of Higher Education came formally into existence
enterprises relevant to its concern had been sprouting, among them
the research work in Student Residence already mentioned, the group
discussing policies and purposes in higher education and the organisation of a forward-looking Anglo-American seminar which had met in
North Carolina in the spring of 1968.

The members of this Quail Roost Seminar were a small but distinguished lot drawn from both sides of the Atlantic. The great transformation in American higher education had begun. Henceforward
it would cater for masses of students; and the energy and hope going
into that movement were widespread in the country. But a sense of
the history and the traditions of thought and scholarship from which
Universities in the past had gained so much of their strength seemed
very much less so. Papers were contributed to the Seminar by Northrop
Frye[10], Marjorie Reeves and Asa Briggs[11], which showed their under-

standing of the humane traditions upon which both Continental and UK Universities had so richly drawn; Martin Trow dealt penetratingly with the growing difference between the élite and the popular functions in American higher education, the significance of which was much in the mind of every participant and especially those from Canada and the USA. A book arising from the Seminar – *Higher Education: Demand and Response* (Tavistock 1969) – was well received on both sides of the Atlantic.

It was in the Autumn term of 1968 that the Department of Higher Education finally came into being. It took under its wing – but at first very lightly – the fine work, financed by a grant from the UGC, being done under the leadership of Ruth Beard on the improvement of teaching in universities. It was of just the kind the UGC's Hale Report (1964) had sought to encourage. Ruth's skill and energy were shown in the variety of activities her Unit initiated – including conferences, courses, and research projects. She interested the Medical and Dental Schools of the University in searching for ways of improving clinical teaching. Like me, she was particularly concerned that more thought should be given to the objectives of higher education. We began to consider what the content might be of a postgraduate diploma course in Higher Education.

More importantly perhaps, it was decided to bring together a high-level national group to consider some policy issues in Higher Education and the direction in which it ought to develop. Clearly better linkage was needed between people in universities thinking about the future of higher education and the actual makers of policy. But how bring this about? If such a group was constituted, it seemed wise to include several Vice-Chancellors, if possible a couple of top civil servants, at least one economist, some leading scientists and scholars, maybe a Director of Education from an LEA. In fact the group we were able to bring together included all these elements, though the two Civil Servants who belonged to it, both from the Treasury, insisted that their names should not appear on any published list of its members. It met between 1969 and 1971, its members including Alan Bullock,[12] Asa Briggs, Brian Pippard, Richard Layard[13] and Michael Brock.[14]

Its 1971 Report argued strongly that access to universities ought to be given to potential undergraduates whose entry qualifications were unorthodox but who had had, since leaving school, good experience in industry or other employment. And we wanted those who had gone into employment without having a higher education, to be assured of their right to transfer to it after a few years. We thought that the choice of a particular course within a university should only be confirmed when a student had already joined the institution; and that transfer to another course within it ought to be readily possible, credit being given for work actually done. We were strongly in favour of two-year higher education courses being available, with students entitled to return later for a third full-time year with resumption of grant. We viewed as essential much more flexible and varied arrangements within our higher education system, whatever the organisational differences between its sectors. Closer relationships between the two parts of what was then the binary system would, we held, be likely to bring financial as well as other benefits with them.

The Group with some changes of membership continued its work for two more years, its thinking being fed by two working parties, one on the contribution of the humanities to higher education, and the other on the liberal education of the technological expert. Its Report in 1974 attracted a good deal of attention and maybe what we said in both our Reports helped in producing a number of the changes made in the following decade.

My increasing interest in the actual curriculum of studies offered by universities was much stimulated by a visit to Canada in 1970 (after I had become the recipient of a CBE) at the invitation of Professor Ted Sheffield of the University of Toronto. He brought together about 60 lively representatives from faculties of Arts and Science in some two dozen universities all over Canada, a mixture of older and younger, to take part in a Workshop on Curriculum Innovation. Each university reported first upon experiments in new curricula and plans for curriculum change within it, my job being to listen and then analyse and comment upon what I had heard. I was a little surprised to find how easy it was in such a stimulating environment to speak more fluently than usual.

I have found, as many others have done, how much less inhibiting North America is than Britain!

In London very early in the 1970s we began, with the aid of a grant from the Social Science Research Council, to research into the antecedents, concept and development of Institutes of Education. Two devoted scholars – Darlow Humphreys of the University of Bristol and John Fairhurst – worked with a will to investigate the history of nine of the leading Institutes, so that when the book was finally published under the title *The University Connection* (NFER 1975), it was a pretty authoritative volume. Unfortunately from the first couple of hundred or so copies distributed, including all those sent out for review, the title page was omitted, so that the book was not to begin with much notice at all.

The Institute of Education movement in a number of ways foreshadowed developments in higher education later in the century. The challenge which Institutes presented to a conventional understanding of what a university was for lay in the conviction of their sponsors that a university had more responsibility for the education of the nation's teachers generally than so far had been accepted or even perceived. A university certainly was responsible for extending the knowledge of its own students and for equipping them to judge objectively a wide range of evidence. But the Colleges around it, where far more of the country's teachers were being educated than in the university itself, would profit greatly from a closer relationship with it. Those Colleges would find their status improved, hopefully too the standard of their scholarship and surely their own recognition nationally. So that the profession of teaching would itself in time come nearer both in reputation and attractiveness to medicine or law.

The pioneers of the Institute movement – McNair, Fred Clarke, Charles Morris, Philip Morris, later supported by Robbins and Lionel Elvin – were men of humanity and vision who believed in widening the territory universities should occupy. This happened with the creation of the binary system in the 1970s. Henceforward a period of higher education would become the normal thing for many more of our skilled experts – electricians, bridge builders, constructors of cars,

office managers, those dealing with communications and computers. The arrival of the so-called binary system no doubt owed much
to Toby Weaver (who had himself come early under the influence of
Philip Morris) but it occurred at a time when society was becoming
far more aware of how dependent it now was on its capacity for technological advance.

And if the orthodox universities still seemed to hold their skirts a
bit too closely about them to welcome speedily so considerable a
widening of their function, then polytechnics must be created – with
as nearly as possible the standing of universities if not as yet the name
or the wide range of disciplines those could offer.

The first half of the seventies for universities in this country (and
some others) was a time of deflated hopes and much frustration. For,
as in the States a dozen years earlier, the transformation of our system
of higher education from élitist to mass was now under way. But
shortage of money, a sharply increasing competition for jobs and the
need for more expertise to improve one's chances, were beginning to
transform the landscape. Underlying all the problems was the fact
that in a late twentieth century world we had become unsure of many
traditional beliefs and values. I wrote a small book which made little
impact and had the rather meaningless title *Universities between Two
Worlds* (1974) – a reference to Arnold's diagnosis that we were "wan-
dering between two worlds, one dead, the other powerless to be born".

The subject of the 1972/73 *World Year Book of Education* was
Universities Facing the Future. Freeman Butts of Teachers' College,
Columbia University, NY, and I as its editors were able to get a
number of thought-provoking contributors from many countries
to write its 30 chapters. They included Eric Ashby, Ladislav Cerych
and Harold Perkin from Europe; Prem Kirpal from India; Michiya
Shimbori from Japan; Leland Medsker and Warren Martin from
the USA. But where the readers for such a volume would come
from, who could tell? The *Year Books of Education* are not the reference books the series title may appear to indicate. One is simply
casting bread upon the waters in the hope that some of it will be
rescued and cater for an invisible hunger.

In 1973 I gave an address to the Inaugural Congress, in Rotterdam, of the European Association for Research and Development in Higher Education whose President I had for its first year become. In it I asked for different researches to be carried out upon the *educational* consequences of size of institution or size of department and upon a number of other topical if intractable problems. I considered some of the assumptions hidden within our use of such familiar terms as "decision-making", a common one being that this is largely an executive affair.[15]

By the time I gave this talk I had already reached retiring age. But my last five years at the Institute had continued to bring with them a variety of fascinating activities outside it, some within the University of London, including service on a variety of commissions inquiring into the future relationship of Goldsmiths College to the University as a whole. Its Wardens, first Ross Chesterman and then Richard Hoggart, had much to cope with!

Being appointed by the University as a Governor of Cheltenham Ladies' College involved going several times a year to meetings of a responsible but somewhat conservative body (the Principal herself was not a member but invited to come into each meeting). On it however some of the keener people, including Peter Spicer and John Dancy, were, like me, concerned to look into some of the possible outcomes for that very fine school of the changing social composition of the parents who sent their daughters to it (few clergy now, few university teachers, many fewer servants from a far-flung empire). So we produced some statistics and prophecies which might at least challenge thought.

During these years too I paid several visits to Strasbourg to take part in the deliberations of the Education Committee set up by the Council of Europe. I also chaired a commission appointed by the International Association of Universities which met in Constance to discuss the provocative subject of the "comprehensive" type of university now being experimented with in Germany.

In 1972 a further visit (when I was accompanied by Sheila) to lecture at the University of California in Los Angeles had been extended by a trip to Santa Barbara where I spoke at the Center for the Study of Democratic Institutions, that much loved brain child of Robert Hutchins. Thence, after visits to some other campuses of UC, including the delightful, wooded Santa Cruz, Sheila and I went on to a hot Mexico City, with its wonderful Museum of Modern Art, returning through St. Louis, visiting the main campus of the University of Illinois at Urbana and finally catching a plane back to Britain from Chicago.

In England, with the aid of funds lovingly collected by Amy Buller, a project was beginning to blossom of transforming St. George's House, Windsor, into a seminar and conference centre on a Christian basis. The plan was to use it for residential refresher courses for clergy in the mid-week and at the weekends for residential conferences attended by "high up" participants who would meet to thrash out answers to questions – especially moral ones – whose subjects included industry, education, crime, the functions of the civil service, etc., etc. There were to be some 28 bedrooms. One of the problems considered by the initial small planning committee of which I was a member was how much should we charge for the accommodation and meals. The businessmen present were in favour of rates similar to those charged by a luxury hotel for accommodation in so prestigious a place, many times as much as clergy – or teachers – would be able to pay. Compromise solutions were of course arrived at eventually!

The end of my time at the Institute had come fairly unnoticeably. Certainly London itself, in which we had lived for nearly 13 years, and its challenges had greatly appealed to both our children. (One of Roland's early driving lessons involved taking a car round Trafalgar Square!) And the invitations which came to Sheila to become in succession Deputy Chairman and then Chairman of the Domestic Coal Consumers Council brought her a place on the national map and eventually an O.B.E. To reconcile the interests of coal consumers and coal merchants so that each feels that justice has been done may be fascinating but it is no easy task! She was also active in the University of

London Women's Luncheon Club. During her year as its President, in 1971, she had the duties of inviting and in due course of welcoming Mrs Thatcher (then Minister of Education) as speaker and was rather impressed to find that her diligence, or that of her advisers, had enabled her to discover beforehand an astonishing number of things both about Sheila herself and her husband.

Retirement: Leisure Occupied (1973-)

At the end of 1973 we went to live in our Cotswold cottage at Pinfarthings in Gloucestershire and became country dwellers, though for the next few years I often visited London for one ploy or another. They included chairing a Committee of the United Reformed Church on the Future of its Ministry; becoming a part-time backroom boy in Church House, Westminster; and encouraging the nascent Higher Education Foundation to think about values in higher education. For some seven years (1975-1982) I acted as Chairman of the Editorial Board of the journal *Studies in Higher Education*, admirably edited for much of that time by Sinclair Goodlad of Imperial College.

Not long after we left London I ceased being a member of the Athenaeum Club to which I had belonged from the days (now no more) when many bishops belonged to it too. I carried away happy memories of its great drawing-room on the first floor, reached by the wide staircase on whose steps Thackeray had paused to shout defiance. In that enormous room it was possible to have quite intimate conversations. I remember, one evening, seeing in the distance Toby Weaver[16] having a very long talk indeed with Eric James. What were they discussing all that time? Was it connected in any way with the announcement which came a few weeks later that Sir Eric was to chair an important committee on Teacher Education?

The United Reformed Church Commission on the future of its ministry had among other things to consider how many of its Theological Colleges it would really need in future and which, if any, should be closed. A vexatious matter indeed and one which came in due course to involve me in one of the most difficult and painful conversations of my life. For we decided that our College in Hampstead must cease to

exist – a College with a long history and a famous Library. John
Huxtable had been its Principal and my close and very old friend
from Oxford days Geoffrey Nuttall, for a quarter of a century its
distinguished Lecturer in Church History. He defended the College's
continued existence with well-informed arguments and great passion.
And it was left to me to break the news to him of our recommendation
that now it should close, its Library to which he was devoted be
disbanded, and he himself retire.

The pleasurable task of producing a report on the Church of
England's Colleges of Education was made the more so by the ex-
traordinary privileges afforded me by the Secretary of the C of E
Board of Education, Canon Robert Holtby – among them freedom
of access to all his correspondence regarding this (and other) matters.
A man of great intelligence and robustly held opinions, he was no
respecter of persons who might favour policies he considered (not
without reason) to be regressive. Had I received some of the letters he
could send to Bishops, Deans and Archdeacons rebutting their views,
I might have taken time to recover.

My labours at Church House led on to the setting up in 1976 of
a Working Party on Christian Involvement in Higher Education which
I chaired. Its job was to consider in particular the situation arising
from the closure of ten of the 26 C of E Colleges. Soon however it
extended its concern to cover higher education more generally – and
the values it stood for, secular as well as religious. This Working Party
came in due course to recognise the similarity of its concerns with
those of an older body, the Higher Education Group. Originally set up
in 1949 as the Dons Advisory Group, it had changed its name in 1960
to the University Teachers Group and in 1977 to the HEG. Throughout its history, the Group had acted as a forum for Christians and
others to discuss issues, philosophical and practical, of deep concern to
higher education. Its established organs were an annual conference and a
newsletter, both of which have been continued by what was now called
the HEF.

For the merger of those two bodies in the later 1970s led to the creation in 1980 of a Higher Education Foundation which had charitable

status and could seek funds from a variety of sources. Like the Higher
Education Group before it, the HEF was not concerned with propaganda
for any preconceived theory or belief. Though many of its supporters were
Christians, many were not, and its religious position should more properly be
described as Christian-compatible than as Christian in any exclusive sense. In an
article in the *Times Higher Education Supplement* in 1981, I summarised its main
stance in three points:

(1) We share with all forms of liberal humanism a deep con
cern for scholarship, for the advancement of learning by research
and teaching.

(2) Nevertheless of ultimate concern are persons. And we see
them not just as thinking but as feeling and choosing people;
so we aim at a balance between objectivity and commitment.
Persons are not just individuals but inescapably social beings.

(3) So higher education has a responsibility to society at large
exercised not just by meeting its expressed and conscious needs,
but also from time to time by challenge and criticism.

In 1981 and 1982 the Foundation sponsored five major Consultations which aimed to explore the underlying philosophical issues,
to identify areas for research, and to suggest action. Its twice-yearly
Newsletter became the *Higher Education Newsletter*. Among the most
remarkable of the articles it was later to publish was Stephen Prickett's
profound *Failure as Education*.

Sheila and I paid two visits to the States in the seventies. In 1976
the University of Chicago had asked me to give a lecture on "The
University as a Critic of Society" and I went on to speak at Emory
University in Atlanta, Florida State University in sunny Tallahassee
and, on the other side of the continent, at the flourishing University
of Utah. We noticed that its famous President David Gardner (soon
to be President of the University of California itself) in entertaining
us to coffee did not, as a good Mormon, drink any himself and that
at the lunch which followed he was correctly abstemious.

Our visit in 1979 was to New Mexico, Santa Fé being our base.
We were loaned a luxurious, marvellously equipped house, 7,000 feet
up, with spectacular views from its wide windows. I was able to spend

some time at St. John's College to explore how its "Hundred Best Books" programme worked. Under good and enthusiastic teachers, I thought, some students were finding it a highly rewarding – and civilising – course. (They were of course mostly middle class students to start with.) With the help of the Subaru car put at our disposal we "did" many things on our own – visiting Indian settlements, Los Alamos, the D.H. Lawrence shrine near Taos, and the stupendous valley of the Rio Grande still 600 miles from its mouth. We spent a day too at the University of New Mexico at Albuquerque thrilled by its splendidly designed library and other buildings.

Other commitments for periods of a few years in the decade following my retirement included being Chairman of the Governors of Westhill College, Birmingham, and a Trustee of Lucy Cavendish College, Cambridge. Westhill, the largest of the Selly Oak Colleges and now an integral part of the University of Birmingham, is in a number of ways unique. It is Free Church in origin and orientation, and always has an interesting admixture of Christian overseas students in it, some on the Church Education courses the College puts on for training laymen to serve their churches better as teachers, administrators, and workers in the environment.

Though the College of St. Mark and St. John had moved from Chelsea to a windswept site on the outskirts of Plymouth, I went on for some years being one of its Governors. But the meetings of the Trustees of the former St. Luke's C of E College at Exeter tended to be more exciting. For when Exeter University bought the College, the capital which accrued was put into the hands of 12 trustees, four appointed by the Cathedral, four by the University and four (of whom I was one) as independents. These it was thought could act, under the wise chairmanship of Michael Brock, in a non-partisan manner when circumstances required; and with the formidable and generously hatted Margaret Hewitt – always 100 per cent certain of the rightness of her views – as one of the University's representatives, a balanced judgement did sometimes call to be exercised.

For some years too I served both as a member of the Gloucestershire Education Committee and as its representative on the Governing Board of the Bristol Polytechnic. But I found the extent of that Board's subservience to the Bristol Education Committee rather alarming; for only minor recommendations from it ever seemed to be accepted. Any more significant ones which involved policy changes were either rejected or more often simply "lost": we heard no more about them. So after three years I quietly resigned. No better argument for the withdrawal of the Polys from Local Authority control could have been found than the disregard the Bristol LEA paid to the views of the Governing Body of its own Polytechnic – happily now the University of the West of England.

The invitation which reached me to become a Trustee of Lucy Cavendish came as a surprise. It is a College for women students only, most of them mature, who have missed having a university education earlier. Itself young and expanding but greatly in need of more money, its Trustees had some fascinating characters among their number, including Dorothy Emmet (once upon a time a fellow lecturer with me in Newcastle and later a Professor of the Philosophy of Religion at Manchester) and Margaret Braithwaite, original of mind, affectionate, dauntless in defending her views on College policy and no respecter of persons. I was taken by her on one occasion to an hour of Buddhist meditation and one night I stayed at the home in Cambridge shared by Margaret, her husband Richard – retired Professor of Philosophy – and Dorothy Emmet. That brought experiences. There were conversational exchanges starting at 7.45 a.m. which called for thought, breakfast being prepared at the same time – albeit a little chaotically – by some of the participants, very much including Margaret of course. But at least she wasn't now driving her Mini along the Trumpington Road and turning round to talk to me on the back seat while intelligently and robustly conversing.

From 1975 to 1977 I was Chairman of the Council of the Society for Research in Higher Education – a period in which it had to decide how broadly it should interpret the word "research". Should it pretty emphatically include in the term "development" as well? Happily, in my view, it opted for the more comprehensive interpretation.

The mid-seventies period had been one which had brought me some health problems: two operations for cancer in 1975 (it has fortunately not recurred) and a chest condition kept under control by inhalers and drugs which can, however, be self-administered. Rosalind, following her undergraduate years at Girton, a postgraduate one in Bristol and a Diploma course at LSE, was now an experienced social worker in London. Roland, after five years in the Birmingham City Transport Department – during which he added a Birmingham M.Sc. in Transport Planning to his qualifications – had gone in succession to posts in Manchester and Strathclyde. But all the family, including Jill and our three young grandsons, came to visit us at Pinfarthings from time to time – all three relishing "cricket" on the front lawn.

During the years 1983-7 I served as a member of the Editorial Board appointed by the Conference of Vice-Chancellors of the European Universities to produce a *History of the European Universities in Society*. The Board met several times a year, usually in Berne or Geneva. The four authoritative volumes to which our discussions led, two of them largely by members of the Editorial Board itself, ought when published during the 1990s to have perhaps exerted more influence than their scholarly nature ensured.

With leisure increasing – as from the early eighties, commitments in London and elsewhere became fewer – I had, or at least should have had, more time to think. My long-standing concerns – for the future of higher education, religious belief and with the civilisation of the West – did not grow less. The potential for fresh inter-relationships between the three both intrigued and challenged me.

The days were now past when vice-chancellors were expected to have time to remain academics and even, in some cases, maybe develop into prophets. More and more they were finding themselves compelled to be managers, keenly aware of trends in the great world outside and of the imperative need to capture more money for their institutions. The selected technical colleges which had become new universities in the middle sixties and the now fast-developing polytechnics powerfully strengthened the part which technology and its applications henceforward would play in our higher education system. This was the direction in which our nation, like so many others in the world, wanted its higher education contribution to go.

During the seventies the proportion of the people attending the conferences run by the HEF who were on the staff of polytechnics rose sharply. The universities themselves in this situation were becoming more and more aware of the prestige – and funds – which research could bring; and more and more departmentalised too, with inter-disciplinary studies in many of them somewhat timidly confined to a linkage of subjects already felt to be akin. The Foundation Year at Keele had been abandoned, its four-year undergraduate course reduced to three under financial pressure. The ambitious Sussex redrawing of the map of learning had been curbed. Bold experiments in cross-disciplinary studies were sometimes to be found in the more enterprising of the polytechnics. But in these the apparent diversity of the subjects linked together in the modular courses they offered was in fact quite often determined fortuitously rather than on any principle, the cross-fertilisation between them being minimal, and its significance left to the students themselves to discover, if it was discovered at all. How indeed secure a strong unity in a degree course, however desirable its components and however well taught, if for most students it was made up of a pretty miscellaneous assortment of pieces? And who should guide or compel students to study units which seemed to them – and often to the man in the street too – irrelevant "abstract philosophisings" and "up in the air"?

I remember being struck during the years in the 1970s when I had served on the British Fulbright Committee (which selected people for Travel Grants for study in the US) how many of the brightest of the many outstanding ones in fierce competition for them had chosen a course in an American university designed to equip them with an expertise in advertising or media management. Short-term rather than long-term considerations were in the seventies increasingly influencing the choices of objectives made not only by students but by institutions of higher education themselves. At a time when the nation as a whole was becoming more and more market orientated, with unemployment beginning to be a threat even to graduates, and with an increase in student numbers in many countries partly because there were fewer and fewer jobs for the unskilled, it was not surprising that in Britain as elsewhere the knowledge and discipline a higher education was expected to provide seemed to be growing more limited in range and depth than idealists had once hoped would be the case. The values to be incorporated in it were those most obviously useful in an industrialised society in which technical efficiency was imperative, for it was no longer a society in which the beliefs and assumptions of a clerisy were expected to filter down and be accepted uncritically, even gratefully, by the rest.

How secure in such a mental environment the values implicit, for example in Christianity, should be examined, maybe adopted, when the large majority were growing up in a society in which humility, fidelity and forgiveness were not widespread virtues and religious worship an unknown category? A large question and one beginning to be asked in many countries.

The period ahead for the West seems likely to be one bringing profound challenges with it. These will be not merely to peace and contentment but to civilisation as we have known it. For what is at risk is not only at the level of behaviour – widespread though drug-taking, sex, promiscuity, ministering to self-interest and escapisms of many other kinds continue to be – but at those deeper levels of pre-supposition and belief, threats to which involve the stability of both the individual and society.

Post-modernism may or may not be a fashion which within two or three decades will be outmoded. But if so it will have left a legacy, for it has sought to face the facts that all the conscious processes of human reasoning are subject to concealed biases and motivations from which there is nowhere to run; that much of our knowledge comes to us through the medium of a language, whichever it may be, that imposes severe constraints and limits upon understanding; and that we are inescapably condemned to being a contemporary people.

Can people however retain depth for more than a limited time without any fundamental beliefs? These were brought to us in the past by narratives handed down from generation to generation by ancestors we could trust and validated by experiences of our own and loves we knew to be real. Can we get on, even survive, as fully human beings without recognising any authority that is more than evanescent and more than superficial? I doubt it. We must and shall continue to rely intimately upon beliefs which resonate with our experiences and loves.

As far as religion is concerned, it appears by no means improbable that in this country within the next 50 years churches are going to change almost out of recognition, a full-time paid ministry having gradually disappeared. Much then may depend for the transmission of an attitude of receptiveness to religion upon an educated, trained and dedicated laity. The content of that religion may well give greater place to the promptings of what Christians know as the Holy Spirit but whose influence is not confined to Christianity. The possibility that such a faith will be both informed and disciplined will depend not only on tradition but on the life and activity of the communities who share it. The influence of these could be seminal, small though some of them may be.

The schools and the places of higher education to which the young go, while still efficient at training the mind to reason and be critical, will need to recognise again, far more than now, the power of a loved community both to educate and discipline its members. The young need help and human examples if they are to absorb the heritage freely offered by literature, music and the arts. Schools themselves need to see that insights of great importance to human development are given by failure as well as success and that hope – which has many dimensions – matters enormously.

Introduction to Part II

The chapters which follow, largely on education and religion, give some indication of my thoughts about both and of how they developed over half a century.

In these days it is not easy to write about the content of either education or religion in a way which seems relevant to the concerns uppermost in people's minds. For in both cases short-term considerations dominate those concerns. In schools and colleges today the emphasis is strongly on the vocational, on what will help their country to secure and retain as a high place as possible in a competitive world.

Attainments in management skills, media skills, computer skills are highly valued – they can certainly be exacting if taken to a high standard but when acquired produce a relatively quick pay-off; as also, though less immediately, can such studies as medicine, surgery, engineering, economics. There is a feeling however that such subjects as philosophy, theology, history, literature, are more peripheral. Studying them won't yield either quickly or slowly the dividends that matter!

Though this tendency to narrow the remit both of education in schools and of higher education should not be *exaggerated* it is a very real one. Consideration why it has happened and how conceivably it might be reversed will take us well outside the province of education itself. Among several of the factors involved, one of the more far-reaching and subtle is the decline of religious belief – and of concern with the spiritual.

And I have to agree that a proportion of those who very genuinely believe in Christianity tend today to limit their focus: concentrating upon personal salvation, the text of the Bible, and doing good deeds. They are reluctant to reckon fully with the existence of other religions having a spiritual content, nor are they greatly concerned about the movement, strongly backed by the Christian West, especially in the US, towards the globalisation of a materialism guided in the direction of its progress by a limited technological frame of mind.

It is large problems such as these, both educational and religious, which now chiefly interest me.

In Part II, one of the early chapters illustrates my concern that teachers should be humanely educated and well trained. (The address I gave to the Headmasters' Conference in 1951, here reprinted in part, was in fact the first on the subject of Teacher Education which that influential body had ever asked for.) There follow chapters which deal with the development of education in Britain, and in particular of higher education, during the last half-century. And then several on society as it now is in the West and the future this implies. Finally consideration is given to the place of religion in a world becoming smaller but more and more in need of compelling humanity to face some fundamental challenges.

The Needs of the Child

In the later forties and during the fifties I lectured and wrote a good deal on problems facing homes and schools as children grew up in a society increasingly complex, mechanised and secular. The Macmillan Lecture I gave in the House of Commons Dining Room in 1955 was on "The Young Child and the Life of Today". The extract that follows, which continues the argument, is taken from an article on "The Needs of the Child" published during that period in the *Durham University Journal.*

The need for a home

One fundamental need of the child is for a home – and home in this sense involves of course not merely dwelling-place but family as is now generally recognised. We are becoming much more aware than we used to be of the subtle and far-reaching effects on the child which an institutionalised upbringing may have. Obedience to rules simply as cold rules is apt to be destructive of personality. Home influence is an inward influence, organic, intimate. But the need for a home, of course, is not a characteristic of the child only. The grown-up who consciously or unconsciously is homeless will be unhappy, hungry and emotionally unstable. Much delinquency is to be explained on the principle "He who steals, steals love". It is with the growth of people into completeness that the educator is concerned.

The need for sense-experience

The need of people to experience is so obvious that we often do not notice it, just as we do not consciously notice the light of day but take it for granted. The interest in all things interesting comes because of an appetite for experience. Capacity for learning is closely related to capacity for experiencing. And if this capacity becomes silted up there is little chance of much education happening. It must therefore be one of the main tasks of the educator to conserve and enlarge in the pupil his openness to experience.

One of the most absolute of barriers to the teacher is sheer inability to experience, whether in a child or himself. Even our capacity to see things or listen to things vividly is limited. Life for most people can easily become a daily set of facts or mere objects. They can sometimes, as it were, learn no more until they get a fresh supply of vision with which to learn it.

During childhood an imaginative way of looking at things is almost universal. "A child in the full health of his mind," says C.E. Montague, "will put his hand flat on the summer turf, feel it and give a little shiver of private glee at the elastic firmness of the globe. He is not thinking how well it will do for some game or to feed sheep upon. The child's is sheer affection, the true ecstatic sense of the thing's inherent characteristics." But this imaginative power to take delight in the world just because it is so full of an interest native to it is apt to become more and more unusual, unless we are artists or poets, the older we grow. The capacity is often sacrificed on the altar of correct behaviour and the pursuit of things useful: often it seems merely to diminish and finally disappear. This, perhaps, is natural and it may be retorted that we can get on just as well without such heightened awareness as with it. After all, if this elemental sort of ability to sense the world is lost, there are many compensations – the ability to reason, for example, and to think logically. But these are not really substitutes. And fundamentally we are dependent all our lives upon our ability to perceive the world vitally enough. If the elementary power to experience vividly through the senses be lost, then, though we may not know it, life is a poorer and more shrivelled thing. At bottom each of us creates his world for himself: no one in the last resort can see for us or hear for us, though they may tell us of fruitful ways of looking.

The need for feeling

One of the needs of the child and the adult too, if he is to live a full life, is the need to feel and to express feeling. In most western countries, at any rate, educators tend to take little official account of this and to regard it somewhat ashamedly. As our civilisation has advanced, there has been a breakdown in many of the communal activities – for example, the ritual dance or the choric chant – which nourished this need and freed the spirits of those taking part in them. There is psychological truth in Coleridge's description of the dryness of the Ancient Mariner's soul at the time when he could not feel and of the release which feeling brought:

> A spring of love gushed from my heart,
> And I blessed them unaware: ...
> The self-same moment I could pray;
> And from my neck so free
> The Albatross fell off, and sank
> Like lead into the sea.

One of the several reasons for the popularity of the cinema, the dance hall, the football match and the greyhound racetrack today is that at these places people can release feelings. It is for the educator to reckon with the existence of such a need in his own nature and that of others, and to provide the means by which feelings can be loosened and freed in ways not damaging to other people or likely to fixate emotional development at a primitive level. In Germany and Italy during the Fascist era the emotions of the crowd were systematically exploited by mass rituals and displays. The problem is to find how to give free expression to fundamental human emotions and not misuse them when they are liberated. We must provide in varying ways moments when "the dykes of personality are broken down". Perhaps this loosening operation is best effected through the arts – good literature and music, films and pictures – which, springing themselves from "more than usual emotion with more than usual order", are the best teachers of a sense of ordered freedom.

The need for coming to terms with things

Very early in life a child begins to learn the sheer objectiveness of objects. There is no arguing with a wall which hurts you when you bump into it. But things small enough and light enough can be moved about; they will obey desire if you are physically skilful enough to make them. And some very important early lessons are experiments with things. The desire of the baby to push and pull, to manipulate and arrange objects, is the essence of most early play, even if the objects at first be merely his own legs and toes. The play-material it is so important for him to have is material from which he learns with his muscles, though not necessarily with his conscious mind, the laws of gravity and friction. He learns slowly which movements he can cause to be subject to his own will, and which he cannot. Some of the stubborn obstinacy of fact is borne in upon him. That lesson is one never completely to be mastered all life through. But there is joy in control and joy too in being able to dominate. No one who has watched a baby delightedly scattering a pile of bricks to the four winds will hesitate to believe that the impulse which moves him is a deep-seated one. So is the impulse for building, for arranging, for planning, which develops later. Practical work often gives these impulses scope – for young children brick-building and similar play; for older children and adolescents gardening, tree-felling, team games played with a ball. But most impulses can of course find outlet in less practical occupations. Some of the essential attraction of the hero is the sign of him hacking his way through circumstances to victory. A good deal more use might be made of the biography of great men in the teaching of a number of school subjects. Not enough scope is always given to children to criticise sensibly and initiate changes. Change itself can have stimulation power, especially for the young, provided that it be not too violent or overwhelming.

In children, to construct and to plan are apt to be more closely and directly related with things objective than in older people. The building of a castle on the sands of the sea-shore is an educative business. There is no good reason that I can see why Meccano should not be on the school time-table, and later on Chess – a game which demands so much of the same type of foresight and imaginative calculation as is demanded by what is later called "administrative ability". Much of the educative value of craft-work lies in the ability that is involved to work to a plan – and so also with making a composition, a play, a story, or designing a chemical laboratory of one's own.

The need for communicating with other people

Long before he is able to understand and to use language, a child can communicate quite a wide range of desires, dislikes and feelings to other people – for human beings are instinctively social. Even crying itself is a form of social intercourse. As the child grows, his power to communicate becomes more and more subtle and inclusive. Compare, for example, the ability of a child one year old to convey interest or disappointment simply through facial expression, with the ability of the same child to do so at the age of four. The body is throughout life one great medium for communication. But with the gradual acquisition and mastery of man-made techniques for communication the range is enormously extended. Part of the importance of a capacity to use words is just that, as Croce has pointed out, impression and expression are reverse sides of the same coin. The abilities to form ideas, to pursue a logical train of reasoning, to receive delicate sensings into the mind for its own nourishment, are themselves dependent for most of us upon the ability to use words with effortless certainty, both in speech and writing. But verbal symbols are not by any means the only ones needed by the child as means of communication. He will need to know how to use figures, and will be the poorer if he can express nothing through musical notes, drawings, paintings and craft-work of several sorts.

A person unable to communicate an emotion or idea because of lack of mastery over some medium of expression is apt to suffer from frustration. Such frustration is often visible in a baby but in older people it is noticeable more rarely even though it may be powerfully present. Frustration due to lack of power to find words or symbols for expression is a more frequent cause of the world's ills than we sometimes imagine – a most potent source of unreality and misunderstanding both between individuals and between nations.

The difference between the truly cultured person and the less cultured is largely to be found in the range, delicacy and precision of personal communication which the one has attained compared with the other. It is sometimes the quiet and reserved who really have most ability both to understand and to convey their understanding – interconnected needs of the individual human being and of human society.

The need for judging and reasoning

Growth of the ability to think is largely dependent, as has already been said, upon growth in power to use words. But not all judgement needs to use verbal symbols. To distinguish between shades of colour or to judge the relative heights at which this or that aeroplane is flying does not demand any notable mastery over words. Many a carpenter and many an engineer has brought great ingenuity to his work without an extensive word-store. But it takes words to enable any person to learn how to reason. And to understand the reasons for things is not merely a luxury – it is a need of humanity. The young child's question, "Why?" may often be a mere indication of wish for social intercourse. But the same question in the older child is the question above all others which marks him out as a human child and not an animal. And it is in the fleetingness of the satisfaction which the child so often finds in his attempts to answer his own questions that one of the chief opportunities of the educator lies. The child must grow in power to deduce and draw conclusions if he is to become a responsible citizen later on. But more than that: if he is to find a coherent purpose in life and any principles on which to rest his conduct or his faith, he must be able to recognise the authority of reason and of reasoning. Man remains a slave in proportion as he is unable to follow reason whither it leads. But there is of course much of the slave left in all men at the stage of their development they have yet reached.

We have now glanced one by one at a number of the needs of the child. The fulfilment of each of them involves social relationships, some intimate and personal, others with people as functionaries, and yet others with men as vehicles or voices of Reason or Truth. The field of education is as wide and complex and subtle as life itself; and always it is a human business – a matter of growing into traditions and acquiring standards and gradually learning to take steps as an increasingly responsible person in the same general direction as other civilised men, but along a path of one's own.

Of all writers on education in past years, Wordsworth perhaps is among those who have most to say that is valuable as a corrective to those modern tendencies in educational theory and practice which fail to recognise this need sufficiently. He believed that knowledge, real and worthy of the name, is organic, a living part of the mind which receives it, growing and developing within it and gradually modifying the person of whom it becomes a part. Such knowledge as this is sharply to be differentiated from information which has been received merely into the rote memory and stored in a compartment of the self separated from the rest. The mind of the child is in essence creative. It works upon the external world brought in by the senses and creates an interior living and personal world from it. Just as it is possible to make a ball roll by applying a hand to it, so it is possible to make a child's mind revolve and work by artificially exercising it. But the sort of knowledge which matters is not to be gained in this way. Knowledge which is significant comes to the child as experience; it is three- or four-dimensional, not merely factual, though facts are a part of it. Knowledge so come by that it is a living part of the mind does not impede power; but dead knowledge coats the mind over and dulls it.

Though the normal child is constantly active, there are moments when he is quite spontaneously passive. Often they come in the tiny period of relaxation following some special effort or fearfulness; and these are the moments in which insight and understanding come to birth.

At the time of receiving an experience which means much, the child may be able to answer no questions about it. It is only at a later stage, and very likely not even then, unless he is very self-conscious, that he will be able to point to a certain day and hour and know that then and there an act of creation was going on within him. Nevertheless it is such moments which help to make a person into an individual, an identity, giving him standards which are not merely man-made, binding his days each to each, so that even a butterfly may be an "historian of one's infancy", because it brings back to memory experiences and moments of feeling of long ago.

The child is the father of the real man not merely chronologically but at every instant. The man separated from any return to the child in him is separated from the springs of his own being. He may have developed that precise technical control of the mind which we know as the power to think, but his instinctive life will have dried up and all his thoughts will be out of touch with what really matters. In a word, he will be disunified, his thoughts lacking in creative power.

Book IV of *The Excursion*, the finest in the poem, called *Despondency Corrected*, gives an account of how the Solitary, who is in some ways a product of a typically modern diseased society, can regain unity of personality and health of outlook. He has lost his religious faith, has lost confidence in man, and has become apathetic. He must go again to his native mountains and take part once more in worship, in company with men who still have simple faith. He must give himself, as a child gives himself, to an interest in animals and people. He must deliberately set himself to remember from the inside his high moments of the past. Recovery of self-unity and happiness lies not in more and more scientific research or reasoning but in keeping open, as a child keeps open, the passages between the senses and the heart.

One of the fundamental needs of the child as he grows up is for keeping alive a central simplicity, faith, humanity – call it what you will – what Wordsworth thought of as the creative spirit of nature awake within. A childhood which is to nourish later life as it needs nourishing must be an experiencing childhood. Abstract knowledge is not a substitute for life neat: holidays and freedom are not just recreative but of elemental, spiritual importance. The child has need for experiences of the vast, for moments of such sheer awe or happiness that he loses all sense of time and egotism in them.

A child whose need for these things has not been filled will later on hardly be capable of living a first-hand life. There will be something hungry in his conduct, a desire to escape from belief and from all that acceptance of life which is involved in real and full maturity.

The Training of Teachers
[Address Given to the Headmasters' Conference in 1951]

Of course everybody here knows that teachers ought to be trained, that they must be trained and that training must go on for a long time. Where we may differ is that while some of us think training should begin in an Education Department of a University, others will contend that the only place in which training can possibly go on is a school itself.

Perhaps the width of our basic agreement is greater than might at first appear. Whether we believe in a period of postgraduate training in an Education Department or not, we surely all know that the actual business of teaching children can be learned only with children themselves in a school. For teaching is a very practical art, having a lot in common no doubt with other practical arts such as the art of the orator, the entertainer, the actor, the journalist, the statesman. For example, managing a class in a classroom is rather like managing a country or managing a set of people anywhere; it is a political business, as it were, calling for a capacity for quickly estimating a situation, for rapid and accurate judgements of human nature, for a sense of the possible. And learning how to be a statesman can obviously be done only by practising trying to be a statesman; it is no use merely relying on psychology, educational or otherwise. It is no good simply reading up the subject and having a bit of theoretical knowledge. Certainly psychology and theoretical knowledge will help. On all that we are perhaps already agreed.

Further still, we may all be together in holding that there is much to be said for a man having a postgraduate period in which he can try himself out as a teacher and learn how to co-operate better with himself as a teacher in several schools. He may make only a partial success of one period in a school and yet be able to start anew in a permanent, paid job with that failure or partial failure behind him, having learned from his lack of success as he could not possibly do in any other way.

We may be agreed on all these things, but "What is the use," some people will say, "of a man spending a whole year in an education department having his time largely taken up with academic and abstract lectures and discussions on educational psychology, the history of education, child health, teaching method, the philosophy of education and goodness knows what?"

Now, as you would expect, I believe in a period of teacher training – a year at the postgraduate level – for almost all people who are going to be schoolmasters or schoolmistresses later on. I believe, too, that the only time at which it is practicable for most people to spend a year in this way is immediately after graduation. I wish, personally, that it was possible for at least part of the period to be spent after one had taught for three or four or more years, but that simply is not possible at present. If we take that for granted – that it is not possible for the large majority – I would also have us take for granted that however much we wish this postgraduate training period to be longer, in fact it will not consist of more than 30 weeks, of which at least 12 will be spent in schools and probably a couple in swotting up for the final examination. As a result, there will be only 16 weeks' theoretical training at most.

Nor in defending a policy of teacher training for all graduates would I for a moment want to defend all that in the past, by tradition, has gone on in Education Departments. Of course, you may very rightly think you would like to hear me do that – "We know there is a lot to be said in its favour, but the other would be more interesting." But I should be less justified in trying to defend all that has gone on in the name of training in Education Departments through past years than you would be in trying to defend all that has gone on in public schools in the name of education of boys. No doubt there was a time when not to have spent a year in an education department was in some sense to have been preserved as a gentleman and an amateur. I should deplore any year of training which made a man less of a gentleman than he was to start with; but I contend that it is even more important to his career now than it was 20 years ago that he should have this period of training, and that within 20 more years practically nobody will dispute the fact.

In the time I have at my disposal, my plan will be first to try to answer the question, "What justifies a young graduate of 22 or 23 spending a year, no doubt at the Government's – that is the taxpayer's – expense, in a University Education Department before he starts earning his bread and butter?" After that I hope to suggest some ways in which present practice in our education departments is tending to change.

First, then, why is the training year more necessary than it used to be? For a long time now degree courses in Universities have been tending to become more and more specialised. Even under the best conditions of college life in Oxford or Cambridge there is a good deal of separation between the science people and the arts people, and that separation is growing – not merely in language and vocabulary but also in the things they take for granted. The Fred Hoylish part of Fred Hoyle must find it very difficult to understand what T.S. Eliot is trying to say, even in his prose.

The separation between specialists in individual subjects is increasing. The young philosopher can hardly be understood by the young economist, if by anybody else, and the young physicist by the young historian. It is certainly possible to get a good honours degree in any University, if you have a mind that is good enough, by application and without having thought about life as a whole for very long at any time during your degree course. As somebody recently said, "Specialism we must have; it is fragmentation we are getting, because the technical insides of well-fenced subjects are studied by technical bits of persons." There is truth in that. Only some graduates during their degree years are going to find out as much as one would expect of them about either life or themselves. As with so many boys and girls in sixth forms today, they can get up things excellently, their intelligence quotients are high; but their power to experience is much narrower than one might suppose and at the age of 22 they are often far from realising how unawakened they still are in their imaginations, in their sense of the possibilities in education and the career they are about to enter and in their minds as a whole. One of the jobs of the training year, as I see it, is to get men and women, fresh from the study of their academic subjects and their different specialisms, to think about some pretty big questions. You may call this a humanising function, if you like: I think it is quite fundamental.

I want people to do some of this meditating alone and some of it together in small mixed groups. One of the functions of this education year, in fact, is restorative – bringing them back from being specialists to being humans. It is extremely significant and important that at this time they should be brought into touch with children, because children, and especially young children – and I want all my students to meet some very young children, below the age of eight – are in some senses more typically humans than grown-ups; by which I mean that they express human desire and human will, human faith and human greed and ambition and love, without as much concealment as we get in the grown-up. They express it far more directly. That is not to say that children are simple beings to understand; only that they have a smaller and less subtle array of armaments under which to conceal themselves as they deal with the world outside.

In the first place, then, the training year should, I suggest, be a thoughtful year about life in general, as well as concerned with education in particular; for nobody can come to have any philosophy of education who has not at least a bit of a philosophy of life itself; and that is a very immediate and first-hand thing to get. In these days of a planned society it is quite easy to get a great many of one's sins committed for one; if we are to do any thinking, it is not possible to get one's thoughts committed for one, too. The year has got to encourage people to some first-hand meditating.

But remember that we are working with a very wide scatter of people. We have the man who has a first class honours degree – not many of these going in for teaching these days, I fear; we have, in considerable numbers, the man with a good second; and we have the man who has managed to scrape an ordinary degree or the lowest class of an honours degree, whose studies may well have been such that at the beginning of the education year, while his neighbour may possibly have read a good deal of Plato in the original, he himself has very little idea whether Plato was a Greek or an Egyptian and in any case cannot see that Plato can have anything to say relevant to 1951.

First of all, then, it should give general encouragement to thought. The second justification of the training year is, I suggest, that it can do very much to open students' minds to sound and possible methods of teaching which otherwise they might never encounter. The tendency for the untrained schoolmaster, even more than for the trained, is to teach his own subject by much the same methods as those by which he was taught that subject. Unless he learns all other methods of teaching in that field, it will not be surprising if, before he has been teaching for many years, he becomes a little unenterprising in his approach. If he is lucky, in the first school in which he teaches he will learn a great many of the possibilities. He will see imaginative experiments going on all around him. But he may not be lucky.

The same is true not merely of methods of teaching a subject but about advice on incentives and punishments that can be used – the use of competition and a marking system, and a great many other things. So often, conventional methods are defended on the dog's leg principle. A salesman was trying sell a dog to a lady, and she complained that its legs were too short. "Too short, madam?" replied the salesman. "They are long enough to reach the ground, aren't they?"

What is needed is much more than throwing out suggestions about possible methods, about ways in which good teachers have successfully practised the teaching of that subject. We have to get down deeper than the question "How?". Sometimes, at any rate, we have to get to the question "Why?". Fifty different methods can all be good methods. It takes a greater discipline of humility in a young teacher than perhaps in an older one to realise that. But the method will only be a good one for any individual if the teacher can teach by it without frustrating himself and without becoming simply a "schoolmaster". The sort of instruction in teaching method which is a giving of hints and tips is not of much use to anybody. What we want is to get a man's mind exercised as an educator's mind instead of as an academic mind. That takes a bit of doing. To teach in one particular way because you do not know any other way of teaching that subject is the worst possible reason for teaching like that, even though you may teach well by it.

In the long run, the teacher, like anybody else, is saved from chaos only by principles – principles which he has learned both with the mind and with the heart. In a time like our own, with so many different, so many opposed, ideas about teaching methods, it is more important, I think, than it used to be that the young teacher should have thought ahead a little about them. I am not referring only to the possibilities opened by films, gramophones, radiograms, broadcasting and television – which is surely coming into schools. (I think the importance of these things can quite easily be over-estimated, as it can quite easily be under-estimated too.) I am not talking only about dramatic work or a new understanding of the arts in education, or so-called activity methods.

There has never been a period of 30 years in which greater progress has been made in the shaping, the printing and illustration of text books than the last 30 years. In the text books which we have now a vast amount of thoughtful and creative work in educational methodology has been incorporated. Clearly, a good deal of so-called teaching method is simple common sense – a mixture of sound common-sense and a real understanding of boy or girl nature. "Start where they are" is a useful enough maxim which no doubt we have all given in one form or another to young teachers. But not all the principles of teaching method are so obviously common-sensical. Take, for example, the modern approach to the teaching of reading. It would appear to be common-sense to teach people to read at first letter by letter, or word by word, or syllable by syllable, and not to start, almost from the beginning, sentence by sentence.

Or take the modern approach to the teaching of art, the Marion Richardson approach, which has meant so much in schools of all sorts, including your schools – even though you may not know anything about art. It makes art an entirely different subject from what it was before, whose aim is to develop courage of imagination and a sense of freedom in expressing it, such as you could never produce with older methods of teaching art. To teach English language or literature by too analytical a method, with too frequent an emphasis on memorisation, or grammatical examination, or the purely intellectual comprehension of prose passages, may get in the way of doing something else with the subject, of making real personal expression possible – and expression creates, as well as releases.

Any proper consideration of teaching method must raise, too, the subject of the content of the curriculum as a whole. It is important that students, in their education year, should grow somewhat worried about the content of the curriculum, should come to wonder how many subjects really ought to be introduced into the school timetable. Just as young men ought to be worried about big problems – the problem of time, arguments against the immortality of the soul – so, if they are going to be teachers, they should be worried about really fundamental problems like the problem of what we are to teach in the school.

A third factor which makes the year in an Education Department more necessary perhaps than it used to be is the increasingly democratic nature of the society in which we all live, and, in consequence, the increasing unity of our educational system, in spite of the increasing diversity and complication of the kinds of school in it. If a man is educated at a primary school, and then a grammar school, and then a University, he will have a very limited acquaintance with the educational provision in this nation as a whole, and that may be even more true if he goes first to a preparatory school, then to a public school, then to one of the older Universities and then, again, to teach in a preparatory or a public school. Unless he has been a year in an Education Department he may never have had an opportunity of finding out or seeing anything of how 95 per cent of the children of this country are being educated.

How are we to make the educational system of this country come alive in the minds of students at this stage? I am no great believer in very much history of education for very many students. Never more than to people of that kind is the adage true that history repeats itself and historians repeat one another. It is a dull subject. I do not very much mind if a student emerges with huge gaps in his knowledge about the educational development of our country, but I shall mind if he has not begun to see that changing educational provision, even in the public schools, comes out of changing social need – some of that social need consciously realised, but a great deal more of it probably unconscious.

I want him to see that particular changes have been the offspring of personal vision and some personal determination. I mean, that it is dependent on actual men – theorists like Locke and Rousseau, practitioners like Arnold and Montessori and Caldwell Cook, administrators like Kay Shuttleworth, Morant and G. N. Fleming. I want to endow him with ancestors among the keen.

But most students will learn most vividly about the nation's schools not by any theoretical treatment or dosage of history, but by having a very simple map of the system put before them and then being given a chance of some preliminary descents into schools of various kinds in which they are not practising during the year. I think it is very important that they should see for themselves, even for the inside of a day, what is going on in a good infants' school, or a good nursery school. If there is an unorthodox primary or boarding school in the region, I should very much like them to go and see it, not because I expect them to agree with all that is going on there. Schools like Summerhill, Frensham Heights, Dartington or Wennington are very useful schools for teacher training purposes.

I want them to see schools for children grossly handicapped in some way – blind, or deaf, or mentally defective or having two of these conditions at once; seeing what can be done by modern educational practice for children so hopelessly unfortunate; and coming away experienced and wondering as a result. I want them to see something of schools other than the grammar school and to have had at any rate a couple of weeks as a semi-member, if not a full member, of the staff of a school teaching children under 11 and of a secondary modern school.

The future is bound to bring many more contacts between schools of the various sorts in our country than the past has done, and I would suggest that a University Training Department is one of the few places which is really in a strategic position to mix its students and, by visits and discussions, as well as lectures on the English educational system, to broaden their consciousness of and their acquaintance with many types of school where they will never teach and never even practise.

How is present practice in Education Departments tending to change? There is a far greater awareness among psychologists than there was a few years ago that we do not know much about a human being when we simply know his intelligence quotient and do not know anything about the shape of his mind or, more important, about the kind of society in which he has been brought up.

We are very much more conscious, psychologists in particular, of the importance of attitudes to children and their effect upon the outlook of a child from a very young age. I should say that one of the directions of change is towards less teaching of individual and abstract psychology.

Sociology is rising in importance as a subject of significance to Education Departments partly because of the vast amount of work done in these fields by anthropologists during the last 30 years. The emphasis in psychological study itself is on group and social psychology; and, in particular, Karl Mannheim, the first occupant of the Chair of Educational Sociology in the University of London, has brought a very considerable influence, for good or ill according to one's point of view, upon teacher training and sociological study in general. But this emphasis on a sociological approach has meant a great many changes in the department of one kind or another. Take, for example, the kind of books we should recommend in a number of departments for preliminary reading. These might include, Margaret Mead's *Growing up in New Guinea* and *Coming of Age in Samoa*, Whitehead's *Leadership in a Free Society*, George Orwell's novel *1984*, with its profound and terrible perception of the effects of social organisation on the individual, and Charlotte Fleming's *The Social Psychology of Education* and Marjorie Reeves's *Growing up in a Modern Society*. The human interest of that sort of reading is great. It tends to introduce education to students as a live subject.

Secondly, the effect of the sociological emphasis has been to change the whole conception of the scope of education as a subject. It still deals, of course, with what goes on in schools and what should go on in the classroom, with the preparation of lessons, with the right planning of what one is going specifically to place before children in a given period. But much more the emphasis of sociology is upon the training of the unconscious mind of the child while he is at school and before he went to school; and upon the importance of the school in giving him roles to play and some responsibilities to take – the role of being properly an Etonian or a member of Manchester Grammar School, the responsibility, personally accepted, for being a prefect or for getting through an examination.

The educational sociologist is concerned with teaching the importance of right attitudes and the transformation of attitudes from one into another. I wish I could say more about that, because it seems to me, personally, quite important that education should be the study of human change under control and not only of what goes on in a school or a classroom. A baby born of intelligent parents, even the child of a headmaster of one of our leading schools, perhaps represented here, brought up from early days in a South Sea island among savages, would, without doubt, himself develop into a savage, nasty and brutish, even if tall, and come to take for granted, without a moment's hesitation, what everybody around took for granted.

A third effect of the emphasis on the importance of the sociological approach has been a new recognition of the importance of environment. Even as recently as ten years ago, in the battle between heredity and environment, heredity seemed to be winning hands down. One of the effects of the new trend has been to emphasise that we still have very much control over environment, but our use of the term has become more subtle so that it is now not merely thought of as classroom and school walls, of pictures and physical surroundings, but of the environment within the mind. A child may be brought up in a place materially slum-like and yet educationally have a quite promising environment because somebody has made what he learns fascinating to him or because somebody has confidence in him and knows how to use praise.

A third development in the education year is much more difficult to define. Perhaps I might call it an enlivening of the year – a greater attention to the experiential value of the year. We realise the need for sharpening blunt-ended B.A.s, of whom there are quite a lot, and this is to some extent being done by lessening the number of formal lectures, more of the work being done in tutorial groups. The individual is catered for more and one hopes is stretched more by the work set. The practice is growing rapidly of having some residential weekends or periods for at any rate groups of people in the year. It is very important to have the education people living together for a time.

The range of places visited has tended to widen and, with the stretching of experience in mind, may in these days include factories and art centres, and youth clubs, as well as the types of schools I have already mentioned. The number of visitors invited in to talk is greater. The whole thing is more lively and more personal. But even with these changes in its character, no doubt for some years yet there will be people who still ask, "Is the year of training really worthwhile after all?" They will ask, "Will all this knowledge and these jaunts of various kinds do much to make a man a better teacher?" I would not claim that the year will help a student directly to more than a certain extent, but I do claim that it will give him a point of vantage from which he can look at things in general. It will tend to make him philosophical in the proper sense of the word. It is justified on much the same ground that higher education generally is justified; the air higher up is fresher. It is true that one can learn what is immediately practicable only by practice. A man is worth what he wills, but one learns to be much more fully human by seeing visions and the possibilities and seeing them with the right kind of thoughtfulness.

The Job of the Humanities

One of the astonishing things about life is that we have to submit to happenings of the greatest importance to us without being consulted at all. Our birth – in which country or what century – was not of our choosing. We weren't asked what sex we wanted to be. And all sorts of developments have their way with us without our being able to do much to stop them, or even make their onset faster or slower: the coming of adolescence, for example, or middle age, or old age. In spite of what all the advertisements proclaim, we can control only a little how pretty or ugly we are. Birth and death, looks, illness, disablement, come unsought; neither wholly prophesiable nor fair. But some things we can do – and must do: keep up to date with what is going on around us and keep pace with ourselves. These are inescapable conditions for experiencing that matters. And without that we can never become "experienced" or stay so. To sense, to love, really to enter into life are conditions of understanding and conditions of being fully human; and there are no short cuts.

It might be thought that the teaching of the humanities would have exactly this purpose – the purpose of nourishing humanity in people. But has it? How often, especially in these days of the national curriculum and frequent examinations, the life in the subjects we teach gets lost in "objectivity". The same basic conditions, which are essential for keeping people human outside the classroom, are essential for keeping teachers human inside it.

The humanities I have in mind are literature, whether written in English or another language, music and the arts, history and religion. The humanities are distinguished from the sciences by having as their main interest not groups or classes of things but aspects of life in their uniqueness. They are concerned first with what happens or has happened, not with deducing laws or theories. They face life with all its rocks and all its surprises; only after they have done that is it their concern to speculate about the human condition or attempt to improve it. The implacable offensive of technology is not for them. Their first aim is to convey immediate experience through the senses to the heart and mind. When experiences have been achieved they can be evaluated; and the study of the humanities can indeed help us to educate our values and make judgements. But though evaluation is important, poetry, music, or sculpture are successful first and foremost if they add to our experiences and help us to find meaning in them.

It is difficult in a world enthralled as ours is by the sciences and scientific method to find more than a tiny bit of room for the humanities. Physics and chemistry deal with the processes and structures of matter viewed from without, psychology and sociology view people and society from the outside. And this procedure has led to enormous and welcome results: how much we owe to the very limitation of the scientific frame! The sciences with their clean, passionate exactitude, their dedicated common sense, have done so much, so obviously, for mankind; already they have doubled or trebled our life-span. It is difficult to believe now that as recently as 1852 the average age of death in Dudley, a typical industrial town, was 16 years and ten months, and that three-quarters of its population never reached the age of 21. Our hopes today of progress and happiness, like our hopes for prosperity, are closely bound up with more inventions, with tapping the universe to see what it sounds like, and, with the help of computers, finding out more about how scientific discoveries can be applied. Scientists are concerned with the truth, but the impersonal truth. Their concentration is on the observable and the measurable; that which cannot be checked is suspect.

Such is the reputation of science that its detached, neutral, objective way of looking at the world is taken by many to be the only way that will yield knowledge that is really true. Many clever men and women think of all real knowledge as capable of finite statement in words. What can't be known like that simply isn't knowledge.

It is tempting to think that in the long run everything will come to be understood by a purely external approach. But if all our actions can be explained in terms of chemical reactions which generate electrical impulses within the nerves; if what we think is nearly all due to sociological causes; if what we feel is largely self-deception, what have we left? Values may be on the way out, their significance reduced until they are abolished altogether – together perhaps with most of what makes life worth living.

Now this obviously is not the destination we really want to get to. All the same we do often find ourselves in life at places we didn't want to be. The danger is illustrated, I think, if we make a check of terms and words in common use that are very much O.K. and approved by the intellectual contemporary ear though subtly tendentious in the emphasis they carry. Take, for instance, the word *problem* which is definitely up in the world as compared with *mystery.* The late twentieth century presupposition is that we *ought* as far as possible to reduce mysteries to problems. *Mental health*, again, as a term is all right, but *wholeness,* even *goodness* are to be queried. One can test mental health (for we think we know what is normal), but goodness knows what goodness is. The modern disposition, in fact, is to concentrate upon dimensions of truth which we can master. We are happier with a "group consensus" than with the idea of individual commitment; one never knows how to cope with that.

But the humanities are very apt to be concerned with suffering, goodness and evil, joy, commitment, the mysterious; *King Lear* and *Electra*, the Gospel of St. John, Mozart's *Piano Concerto in F Major*, Van Eyck's *The Arnolfinis*, Dostoevsky's *Crime and Punishment*, Henry Moore's *Ecce Homo*. There is feeling, civilised and tightly controlled, but impassioned, in all of them, and insight too. Take away the feeling and you take away the capacity they give us for interiorising them and finding a meaning in them. To make use of them only for some extraneous end, such as passing an examination, is not enough.

A really human approach to the humanities in these days is subject to a multitude of threats and pressures, some of them subtle, several more obvious, but all tending to reduce the noise of their implication. In Richard Hoggart's phrase, pressure is on us to "thin out the sense of life". And the need for getting through examinations does not help those we teach. Since one can only examine the examinable, we have to teach things, more than we would otherwise do, in an examinable way, life being as instrumental and competitive as it is.

Education as a Humane Study

Education in a university or college course ought from the start to be taught in such a way that a student can really inhabit it. It should be a discipline, but of a kind that will lead its students by stages to an informed and increasingly personal concept of what schooling and learning involve. Feeling and imagination should be disciplined by it as well as reasoning power.

Just as the prime subject-matter of literary study for a B.A. is not literary criticism or even literary history but literature and man revealed in it, so the fundamental subject-matter of Education is people learning things, people learning to live in their time. This is in part an intellectual study, in part an exercise involving sympathy and intuition. At the relevant stages in the study of literature it is imperative to study the history of literature, to read the critics and see the point of their criticisms; at the relevant stages in the study of Education it is of importance that one should learn to think in psychological, sociological and philosophical ways. But these are no substitutes for contact with children and an entering more and more personally into an understanding of their growth, the way they learn, the way they are influenced by society, by the family, by the school, by the class, by friendship. And the same goes for personal understanding of the school and its quality and qualities, its deficiencies and possibilities. Cognitive knowledge, important though it is, is no substitute for that interior knowledge on which in due course cognitive knowledge will draw and by which it will be enriched or remain a knowledge of externals only.

It will be a mistake to seek to develop in our students an extensive technical knowledge about the theory of education in ways that are too out of touch with their buried knowledge of their own childhood and their own society, so that we replace the more generous discipline we might have produced – with its delicate sensitivity to developing human beings and its critical observation of the effects of educative material upon them and upon society – by one that is more barren. It is true of course that without submission at the right time to the "inside knowledge" which can be communicated by the philosopher, the psychologist, the sociologist, the historian, the student's capacity to understand what education and the educative process are about will remain limited. The insights and methods of the sociologist, for example, can wake in his mind truths which otherwise would never have lived. But everything still depends upon the capital of experience and understanding which he himself is contributing and can contribute.

Humility remains a very appropriate desideratum for anybody teaching or learning about education. For however much more we go on discovering about the development of the child and the influences of society upon him and about what the school can do with him, our sheer ignorance of the subject remains immense. Perhaps, indeed, this must always be so. We know well enough, for instance, that the normal child will learn his own language quite easily and become fairly fluent in using it; he will learn, as time goes on, to find more and more meaning in the words and sentences he hears and to put meanings of many kinds into what he says himself. But we know little about how fact and meaning realise themselves to sense and throat and the other instruments by which we speak so as to convey what we intend. A child listens to words and their meaning comes to him. But why and how? Why should children who are not very clever reach the limit of their understanding of meaning at a certain point? What limits the range of comprehension which is possible even to the cleverest? We can annotate our ignorance on these subjects by references to Intelligent Quotients or Learning Quotients or inherent differences of verbalising ability. But these are useful shorthand terms, not fundamental explanations. The process of understanding remains inexplicable. It is natural, we say, that people should learn to dance and speak and draw and, later on, to reason. And we leave it at that. We know far less than we shall do by the year 3100 about the best stages in a child's life for teaching it particular things. Doctors realise that it is especially important that the development of the embryo in its uterine life should proceed unhindered by handicaps which certain diseases in the mother at certain periods may entail.

May it not be that in later life there are times when certain mental stimuli are peculiarly harmful? We do not yet know enough about such subtle causes and consequences. Humility is called for.

Again, we know that a child growing up in a particular society will learn to take many of the habits of that society for granted. But we often underestimate the extent and depth of the permeation. How indeed can we calculate it and in what terms? What would a child uninfluenced by social habits or presuppositions be like? We are quickly brought up against the boundaries of human understanding. However much we can explain, there are irreducibles in many directions which we can only accept. If by the study of education we mean only the external study of processes of learning, and of socialisation, or the history of how the formal provision of education has been made in the past, we shall not make it a particularly humane study – nor one worth more than a little attention by those going to be teachers.

What then ought to be the beginning of educational study for those, fresh from school many of them, who come to our Colleges and Universities? First, I suggest, to learn to understand children more knowledgeably, without sentimentality, but with an increasingly disciplined and relevant intuition and sympathy. They need to put themselves back into the position of children so that they will be able to imagine controlledly yet from the inside what it is like to be a child and a child at various stages. The first help to this may be the recollection of their own childhood; and a stimulus to this, and to self-awareness in general, will be an attentive reading of the childhood chapters of good novels, biographies and autobiographies. A meditative study of Wordsworth's *Prelude* has much to give some students. But they must be helped to read it slowly and not simply be told to read it. To learn how to read savouringly goes against custom today. The second means to our goal is encouraging our students to undertake a relaxed but increasingly close observation of children, both individually and in groups, and in both informal situations and more formal ones.

What we want is that they should begin to reflect on their own experiences, recognising in the motives and impulses which actuate them some of the drives and compulsions in children too. But little progress will be made unless they have to realise that there is nothing which they see other people doing to which they cannot find the key inside. They have to come to feel acutely that they and the children are akin as human beings – not merely as behaving, but as living, people. "To produce habits out of rats" is a common ploy among experimental psychologists these days. The psychologist concerned with human education has no such magic. His main concern is the more difficult one of producing in human beings more understanding of how human nature works. Education is concerned with the laws of growth, and with theories of learning, and methods of teaching only as a means to an end. This is a subject which, properly taught, should compel people to ask questions that jolt – and about themselves as well as about children.

At the early stages, an impetus to thought about education for quite a number of students is the reading and discussion of such books as Orwell's *1984*, Hoggart's *Uses of Literacy* (a book that contains much dynamite done up in bonbon wrappers) and Michael Young's *Rise of the Meritocracy* – books that toss into the arena problems that disturb. For education is concerned with far more than schooling, important though schools and efficient teaching are.

The earliest stage is not the one in which to separate educational studies into the divisions that will come later. This period corresponds to that during which ideas are collected and recollected before one starts to write an essay. Many students early in the course will also need to find out for themselves how they get on with children in the classroom, and the college or department will need to discover whether any student is so unpromising as a teacher as to merit being dropped altogether, before too much money has been spent on preparing him for a career in which he will be unhappy. To find that after all he *is* some good with children and that he can teach a bit is a wonderful remedy for unconscious fear. Supervisors at this stage are never in danger of being people throwing straws at those who have already landed. Schools in special association with the department or college, whose members of staff come to know it and the people in it well, can be of great value where such association is a practicable thing.

Before long the student's powers of observation should be more directed, and his concept of human nature and its varieties expanded and informed. He should be asking himself from time to time what portrayals of human nature are really adequate and what leave out, in fact, a good deal of what supposedly is being studied. In what respects are human beings really like Skinner's pigeons? In what respects unlike?

The tendency should grow more marked to separate out the strands within the subject. It should already be becoming clear that one thread is that of child development; another will be sociological – the trends and influences in society around the child which haunt him as he grows; a third will be philosophic – one which asks questions about goals and purposes in life. Then there should be thinking about how schools, society itself, came to be as they are now; in other words, historical thinking. It will, in my view, already be helpful for students to glance at ways of dealing with the education of children other than those employed in their own country. In addition there will be concern about curriculum content – what to teach to particular groups and how to teach it.

But all the time the chief standby and remedy for too fragmented a treatment of Education as a subject must lie in continued recollection of children, schools and the actual conditions of life. There is an imperative need for professors, lecturers and students to be in touch quite often with children – both in person and in fiction – and to go into schools frequently. There is a sense, of course, in which it is primary school children who are most essentially and intensely children. Only exceptionally imaginative teachers of Education can afford to be separated from real children and real schools over long periods. If most of us are, our approach to the subject will be insensibly modified. Fresh observation of life, an unjaded sensitiveness to what the young do and how they feel are necessary if lectures are to be relevant professionally as well as really treatments of their discipline from within, and not simply straight History, or Philosophy or Sociology. It is in a continuing reference to actual situations that we may find the link not only between the different aspects of the study of Education but between those and the study of other subjects. Such a deliberate effort to betake oneself back to daily life, to observe anew children and situations at first hand, is itself a peculiarly hard discipline for the academic mind and one from which we may often escape. For the effort may seem an impediment to thought; we may take refuge in strenuousness from daring to experience, which demands moments of openness and relaxation. It is sometimes hard to escape far enough from one's own presuppositions to retain either an eye that is innocent or a compassion that is correct.

But do not mistake. I am not saying that the study of Education can be pursued far without reference to the disciplines at least of educational philosophy, psychology and sociology. The further we go on with serious thought about education and educating, the more indispensable are these to clear understanding. In the later parts of an Education course this will have become true for almost all students. There is no way to an adequate comprehension of the teacher's task, and therefore their own, in an actual and professional world save one which demands thought about children's development irrespective of the kind of culture they inhabit (that is psychology); knowledge of how a culture is communicated through the family group, one's contemporaries, the school, through workmates and the nation (that is sociology); and equipment with which to think coherently about objectives and values (that is philosophy).

Each of the disciplines can bring with it a capacity for new insight about one's profession and what one is engaged upon in pursuing it; and with each there has to be a moment of cognitive comprehension if its meaning is to be secured. But how can we go further and help our students to incorporate some of their insights in professional actions, in teaching in the classroom? It takes exceptional tutors – at once sympathetic, knowledgeable and humane – to get far with this. I am not saying that all teachers of Education are the right people to supervise much school practice; but they should see something of at any rate some of their students in the classroom. A study of the Foundations of

Education will not at all necessarily at once affect practice. But theory of Education should not be separated from practice more than can be helped, or examiners in Theory arbitrarily put into a separate category from examiners in Practice.

One debit of the separation of educational studies into disciplines, necessary though that is, is that it becomes difficult to find adequate or even possible niches for quite worthwhile writers about education who are not themselves single-mindedly philosophers or psychologists or sociologists. We know where to put Locke, of course; by a slight straining, or patting, of the conscience even Rousseau and Dewey may be classed as philosophers, though Goethe's writings about education are usually forgotten altogether. But what of Comenius, Froebel, Wordsworth, Pestalozzi, to say nothing of Maria Montessori and A. S. Neill? By some sleight of hand they are sometimes miscellaneously classed as writers about educational method, which seems a bit blasé; or as coming into the history of education, which would apply of course to Locke, Dewey and the others if we had not already got them safely under cover.

If we divide educational studies into separated disciplines it is also important to see that attention to a number of matters of professional concern does not fall through the gaps between the intersecting circles of those disciplines. For example: the shape and balance of the school curriculum; relations between parents and teachers; the startlingly parallel movements in education between one twentieth-century country and others; and so on. We want our students to be dissatisfied with the *status quo* in a disciplined way and to be able to retain that dissatisfaction creatively all their lives. This calls for an approach to the disciplines themselves which does not rule out an expression by the lecturer of views and convictions that are personal as well as an objective presentation of his subject. It is also important, especially in the later stages of the course, to introduce students to some of the major issues of current educational policy – identifying them and treating them as neutrally yet frankly as possible, and seeking to show the practical consequences of different policies. Professional concern must spread more widely than the classroom if it is to be adequate.

The suspicion of so many people and students is that for Education as a subject to be an academic discipline, it must be removed from life, not concerned about really real things. And, they think that if it is like this, it cannot be very important. I have maintained that a study of Education must be one in which the student is personally involved. The subject our student will be inhabiting is not education in isolation from life. The questions raised by a philosopher of education are questions about the significance of things which have to be answered by the learner not the textbook. The aim is not to give students a philosophy of education on a plate but materials for realising where they stand, so that they will not be so much at the mercy of the *zeitgeist*, the sport of every random gust of their time that is strong enough to blow them off course. A sufficiently skilled teacher could perhaps teach an intelligent child anything within reason. But mere skill is an external accomplishment. A technical knowledge of navigation is no doubt immensely interesting in itself. But the course an aircraft is to take is chosen for other than technical reasons; they include amongst other things the destination it is to go to.

The study of education indeed is rarely about matters that are safely settled and dead; nearly always about matters that are of ongoing human concern. To acquire such knowledge takes insight and sympathy as well as thought. It is not flat and two-dimensional; but to be tested by its relevance to John, Mary and the teacher. The questions raised are never more than partly to be answered by three-hour papers or even essays that can be continuously (how continuously!) assessed; rather by how one feels and thinks on the job; by what one does there; in one's decisions about what to say, how to act and when to stop.

On Existentialism and Education

I

Those who are profoundly deaf do not listen, for there are no sounds for them to hear. But people who can listen perfectly are nevertheless likely to hear with effectiveness only words and sentences which seem to them to have relevance and meaning. A message may be lost for at least two reasons: because it is expressed in a code too hard to decipher, or because it appears to have no significance that is worthwhile. Soren Kierkegaard lived from 1813 to 1855 and all that he wrote might have remained buried till now in its obscurity but for the sufferings and experiences which the 20th century has brought to men, making audible some of the things he poured forth in his books and journals as he searched and strove for truth amid the incomprehensible nothingness by which he felt himself enveloped.

By "existentialist" thinking I mean thinking like his, which does not consider a situation from the outside, as something to be analysed, but rather as one in which the thinker is himself all the time involved and for which he must take responsibility. It was Kierkegaard himself who first applied the term existential to thought which was thus deeply "authentic" and which led to a personal "commitment". And diverse though the writers are to whom the term existentialist has been applied, the theists among them have at least this in common: their writings are full of a sense of the sheer importance of life and of the need for a deep personal involvement in it; they believe in the freedom of man as against the inhumanity of the machine; they are sure that reason is not the sole way of coming to an understanding of existence; they suspect the tendency towards the mere planning and categorising of human beings inherent in Marxism and in some of the teachings of sociologists and psychologists.

In spite of all the suffering and courage of Englishmen during the war and the challenge to new thought which the war brought – a challenge answered on the more practical level by the White Paper on Educational Reconstruction, the Education Act of 1944, the McNair Report and the Fleming Report – there was in England no national disaster comparable with the ideological falling apart which so profoundly affected France, Germany and Italy. Since the early 1930s the thought of Heidegger, Berdyaev, Sartre, Karl Jaspers, Martin Buber, Emmanuel Mounier and Gabriel Marcel has been deeply influenced by the struggle within the mind of their compatriots, a conflict which within Englishmen and Americans has been kept for the most part unconscious and unresolved. The threat, as they see it, is of life left everywhere meaningless though "happy", of states peopled by men whose feelings and ideas have been subtly and skilfully given them by propaganda, of human beings superficially civilised but lacking depth. It is this threat which constitutes the basic problem for education the world over; that is why the existentialists – and especially the more profound existentialists – may have something to say at this juncture which is significant.

The names of Jaspers, Buber and Marcel have become widely known in England since the mid-war years – a fact that has something to do with our slowly increasing realisation that "freedom from" is no philosophy; that little hope is left in rationalism, now a creed for the old; that a cult of the practical for its own sake can take us everywhere and anywhere – and up many garden paths; that mass-satisfaction and mass-culture can lead men into a complete futility in which only their self-deception protects them from despair.

If we draw back and look at it as a whole, the existentialist movement can be seen as a protest against the broad current of thought from Descartes onward which has regarded the reasoning power as the most distinctive of all human attributes and as offering the greatest hope of human progress. *Cogito ergo sum*, said Descartes; *sentio ergo sum, respondeo ergo sum* the existentialists tend to say, according as they are less sympathetic or more sympathetic to a theistic position. Not that existentialism despises intelligence – rather it holds that for man to neglect to use his mind is to betray himself and become robbed of the very possibility of self-unity; nor that it runs away from fact – rather it points to facts about the human mind and the human predicament from which rationality runs away. "We must come to ourselves where we are" – that is the message of Kierkegaard,

Heidegger and Jaspers alike. And so, though existentialism from one viewpoint may be seen as a protest, from another it is a call to more authentic living and experiencing, to a truer communication with others; in Buber's well-known phrase, "All real life is meeting"[17]. The call is for a more complete taking of individual responsibility – with reason and feeling awake together.

It is by no accident that Sartre and Marcel have found the play and the novel more natural and powerful vehicles for some of their teaching and philosophy than the treatise and the lecture. For in the novel and the play ideas can be embodied in living characters, who clash and react, the appeal being to the feelings and the reason at the same time. Indeed, had the word existentialism been coined, we might long ago have thought of writers and poets from other centuries as in some respects existentialist in their attitude. In essentials, for instance, Pascal, Blake, Coleridge, Keats and Dostoevsky are existentialists. There are strong existential elements in the thinking of Nietzsche, Unamuno, Bergson, Santayana and Ortega. When Pascal wrote *Le silence éternel de ces espaces infinis m'effraie* he was expressing an idea related in spirit to Kierkegaard's dread at *le néant*. Much of Wordsworth's greater poetry is a record of his authentic experiences and his sense of commitment and involvement. There is a sense in which all existentialist philosophy is similarly autobiographical.

In this essay I shall first attempt to define the existentialist position of Jaspers and Marcel[18] somewhat more in detail, bearing in mind especially those aspects of their thought which have particular relevance for education in our own time. I shall then note how remarkably Wordsworth's writings apply a number of existentialist ideas to education, and in the final section consider briefly the relevance of these teachings to contemporary educational values and practice in home and school.

II

Jaspers and Marcel both start from a conviction that real experience can never be wholly comprehended by the reason. We must accept the mystery which is part of life, never pretending to ourselves that we can define or capture truth whole. No truth can be completely expressed in words; it is multi-dimensional; and is not to be set out on one plane.

Though Jaspers is emphatic about the quite indispensable contribution made by scientific knowledge – as witness for example his address to the Medical School at Heidelberg after his election as Rector of Heidelberg University on 15 August 1945 – he has much to say of the proper place of the scientific truth within our knowledge of truth proper. The scientific spirit means knowing what one does know and what one does not know. It is knowledge accompanied by a consciousness of the limits of knowledge; all knowledge which assumes that one can have knowledge of the whole is unscientific.

When science is neglected, fantasy and deception become a substitute for faith; and the absence of the scientific spirit provides a soil in which inhumanity grows. The scientist, however, must not forget that each individual man is an infinity; no scientific conception can embrace him as a whole. The scientist must never lose the sense of the inexhaustible mystery of every individual.

"In a world like our own," says Marcel, "which is becoming more and more completely subjected to the dominion of objective knowledge and scientific technique, everything tends to fall out as if this observation of our situation from the outside were a real possibility. ... Both biologists and Marxists are seeking to arrive at an interpretation of life at the purely objective level, only, unfortunately, the kind of objectiveness they are aiming at entails a preliminary, and complete, elimination of the subject as such. ... With the scientist the self has, in so far as it possibly can, vanished away. His task is to bring order into a world which is as little as possible *his own* particular world"[19]. The whole truth about an object cannot be the scientific truth, for the whole truth cannot be known without experience of what it is like to be that object. The use of symbols, diagrams or figures to define a living being leaves out its essence, though it is necessary to employ them for particular purposes. We reach an understanding and a perception of the human situation not after outward examination only but through a deeper involvement and commitment.

The existentialism of both Jaspers and Marcel is in this way a protest against undue extroversion, against the tendency of our time (and of education in our time) to use "intelligent" as a term of praise chiefly for analytic, external, objective comprehension. Full comprehension, they maintain, involves the being; and being is what "withstands an exhaustive analysis bearing on the data of experience and aiming to reduce them step by step to elements increasingly devoid of intrinsic or significant value".[20] Marcel accuses Freud of attempting an analysis of this kind in his theoretical works.

Both Jaspers and Marcel attack the psychologist not for making observations about mental phenomena but for interpreting them with the aid of a philosophy which they regard as superficial. "Psychoanalysis," says Marcel scornfully, "seeks to explain away the child's myth of the 'real place' in terms of subconscious sexual symbolism; but in the last analysis we must recognise that this discipline, seeking to destroy all the old myths, offers us a new one in their place, that of the pre-natal Eden of the embryo in the womb"[21]. Jaspers accuses psychoanalysts of talking as if a life without tensions were more or less attainable, as if there were some possible social order in which all men would enter into their rights, and as if the conscious and unconscious parts of the mind would be friendly together as soon as our complexes had been purged. Psychoanalysis is apt to regard man as nothing but the puppet of his own unconscious. "The true but logical outcome of psychoanalysis is that man is to return to that nature in which he no longer needs to be man."[22] Too often the psychologist assumes that the possession of high intelligence is almost synonymous with a guarantee of really authentic living, true existence. Far from it. The intellectual can be the most ingenious of escapists, refusing to be committed, refusing to take responsibility, content to look at everything from the outside in dilettante fashion.

One of the objects of a humane education must be to increase the capacity for communication. Incapacity for communication is inability to hear anyone else – or to admit honest questioning of oneself. "There was," says Jaspers, "almost until the present time a cohesion among men which rarely permitted communication to become a special problem. People could content themselves with the saying: we can pray together, but not talk together. Today, when we cannot even pray together, we are at length becoming fully aware that humanity implies unreserved communication among men."[23] There is danger and temptation in believing that one possesses the whole truth whether moral, religious or scientific in any situation; for that may easily prevent further experiencing and cause a breaking off of real communication with other human beings. And experiencing and being in touch are the essence of living. To be self-centred is one form of being cut off. It is to be unavailable, not having one's resources at hand – in Marcel's word *indisponible*, incapable of responding to calls made upon one by people or events.

The appeal of Jaspers and Marcel is for greater depth in living. We deceive ourselves if we think of life merely as a succession, a series, of occurrences which can be adequately expressed in terms of story or film[24]. The important part of man is his deep central inwardness and much of the proper concern of education must be with the nourishment of inward being and the growth of power to see into, to understand.

In a world wholly given over to technologies and technical achievement no man could really live. And the revelation to us of fundamental ideas about our own humanity, of ideas that we are never merely units, is one of the most important of all the functions of the home. The home is "a symbol of the world which is the child's necessary historical environment",[25] more organic and deep-reaching in the education it can give than in many countries the school can ever be. An upbringing in a good home may safeguard the child from loss of himself in the impersonal superficiality of much modern city life. And the spirit of fraternity which it inculcates must be carried over into relationships outside the home – in school, in factory, in public life.

But both Jaspers and Marcel, and particularly Marcel, are concerned to distinguish between fraternity and equality. The two indeed are incompatibles. They are spiritually far apart: while fraternity says "You are my brother", the anxiety of equality is to claim what is one's due. In these days there is great need for strengthening the bonds between man and man and not founding society upon an hierarchical system based upon money values or educational qualifications whose human significance is practically nil. But this must not blind us to the fact that children are far from equally educable. Education must distinguish between what is comprehensible to all and what is attainable by an *élite* through a nourishment of mind and heart together.

In an important section of the preface to his *Men against Humanity*, Marcel, after calling intelligence and love "the most concrete things in the world', goes on to point out that most people today exist and develop only at a level far below that at which intelligence and love are possible. "Do not let us seek to persuade ourselves that an education of the masses is possible; that is a contradiction in terms. What is educable is only an individual, or more exactly a person. Everywhere else, there is no scope for anything but a training. Let us say rather that what we have to do is to introduce a social and political order which will withdraw the greatest number of beings possible from this mass state of abasement or alienation.'[26]

The society which looks to education and the school as if they could create faith out of nothingness is looking for the impossible. If education is to help in "the development of human beings possessed of full selfhood, that can only ensue through a faith which amid all necessary strictness in learning and practice indirectly conveys a spiritual value".[27] Jaspers criticises an indulgence in "interminable pedagogic experiment" – for that is almost certainly a symptom of the absence of real values and purpose. In much schooling today "immense demands are made upon the young as regards the acquisition of facts, so that immature minds are strained whilst no imprint is effected upon their real being".[28] Facts matter and so does the teaching of facts, but their "reverberatory power" matters still more.

Among the final aims of education are the attainment of freedom (in the only sense in which freedom exists) and in consequence the ability to make personal decisions that are really personal. Freedom is not to be defined or described, though it may be experienced. "The free act is essentially a significant act." Freedom lies on a different plane from determinism. Ultimately, to say "I am free" is to say "I am I".[29] But important though it is to act significantly and come to take decisions that are really personal, deeply involving the whole man, it is nevertheless a fatal fallacy to transform the absoluteness of existential decision into a knowledge of truth that can be stated in the form of moral propositions or laws valid for everybody at all times.

The main contention of both Marcel and Jaspers is that education must be of the inner being, not merely of the memory or of the intellectual capacities. True remembrance is assimilation, not collecting in the mind an infinite number of antiquarian details. Too much of modern life, and of contemporary education also, is a "positive gratification of the mind without personal participation". What matters most of all is the inward attitude a man acquires during his formative years, the way in which he contemplates his world and grows aware of it. For this is the origin of what later on he *does*: he must learn how to hold himself towards the world; he must learn, too, that he must be involved in it. The challenge to education in our age is that it shall bring people up, in a technical society, so that they shall be still capable of living real lives; of entering into profound communication with other people whose otherness they respect; of making decisions that are significant and personal, and not only a following of the crowd; of transcending the temporary and transcending the "triviality of enjoyment".

III

No one coming fresh after a study of Jaspers and Marcel to a reading or re-reading of any two dozen pages of Coleridge's notebooks[30] or of Wordsworth's greater poetry can fail to see that their approach to life, too, is existential in character. In *The Prelude*, at the age of 30 or so, Wordsworth looks back over his development, attempts to remember and set down the significant periods of his upbringing, to recall and recount the events of his childhood and youth which brought him real experiences. Many of his shorter poems are annotations upon the same developmental theme. And certainly a number of his ideas, as he saw himself, have a direct application to education: the living nature of true knowledge, for instance; the educative value of awe and fear; the importance of "communication" at a deep level; the need for a preservation of inward unity if superficiality is to be prevented.

Wordsworth sees the natural child as a creature delighting in his senses, unconsciously receptive of a thousand sensations. The young child often is haunted by his own sensings, and the process of haunting is the process of being created. During youth consciousness begins its work – that of co-ordinating, criticising and disciplining; youth is a period of self-examination, of introspection. And there is no way to manhood save by this route. A person whose childhood has contained but few sensings is permanently impoverished of life; as is someone whose youth has had little richness of feeling. Even during maturity it is important that the grown man should keep open the ways back to childhood and youth, for childhood and youth are moments, and permanent moments, of his life. "The child is father of the man" not merely chronologically but at every instant. There is an intimate connection between receptivity and creativeness; the man separated from any return to the child in him is separated from the springs of his own being. He may have developed that precise technical control of the mind which we know as the power to think, but his inward life will have dried up and all his thoughts will be out of touch with what really matters. In a word he will be disunified, his thoughts lacking in inspiration.

For Wordsworth, the meaning of this experience or that cannot be found save from an intense participation in it. He tries to express in his poetry moments of profound *being*, in the existentialist sense. It is such high moments which eventually make an individual into a person, an identity, with his days "bound each to each" by a "piety" which can be the offspring only of feeling. If men are to understand the world they must bring to its comprehension a heart and mind which are awake together. But any such understanding will contain a recognition and acknowledgement of mystery; there is in any deep experience an over-plus, a comprehensiveness, not expressible in words. Here again, there is a link with contemporary existentialism.

The product of right growth is a mind which is not merely an instrument but a power; an originating, active, yet comprehending

centre. From the retained possession of such a mind come
> ...sovereignty within and peace at will,
> Emotion which best foresight need not fear,
> Most worthy then of trust when most intense,
> Hence cheerfulness in every act of life,
> Hence truth in moral judgements and delight
> That fails not in the external universe.[31]

Much of what passed for education in his day (and still passes) Wordsworth regarded as superficial: it was education of the eye, or the reasoning powers, or the memory rather than of the living man. All real education, he insists, is education of the individual child, however much it may have to go on in classes or teams. And much of it will be the outcome of deeply human "meetings" between the one who gives and the one who absorbs.

He defends the dame school because of the human, personal contact between the dame herself and the children. "I will back Shenstone's Schoolmistress by her winter fire and in her summer garden seat," he says, "against all Dr. Bell's sour-looking teachers in petticoats that I have ever seen." Wordsworth condemned the infant schools of his day because they separated children from their parents; and because they robbed the child of many chances of affection, of feeling and experiencing. "The bent of the public mind," he says in a letter written to the Revd H.J. Rose, "is to sacrifice the greater for the less – all that life and nature teach, to the little that can be learnt from books and a master. ... Our course is to supplant domestic attachments without the possibility of substituting others more capacious. What can grow out of it but selfishness? ..."

The central question of Wordsworth's reconsideration of his own childhood is this: how have I developed from the child which once I was into someone still capable of creation, someone still possessed of self-unity and "the deep power of joy" when so many other men seem to have lost these things? And in brief the answer to his question is: in bringing up a child we must first of all be loyal to his own nature. He needs the nourishment of inward life which comes through being surrounded by an environment of human love, of natural beauty, of scenes and circumstances which can give opportunities for quietude and relaxation, and yet the fiercest activity, which bring challenge, and yet discipline the spirit by the fear they hold.

IV

It seems likely that existentialism, whether represented by Jaspers, Marcel or Wordsworth, has a good deal to say that is relevant to education in our own country and our own time.

(i)   Because of the large and indispensable part played by schools and colleges in education there is a special temptation to speak as if the whole of education took place within them. Parents more and more look to schools to educate their children for them; but it is difficult if not impossible for schools to give as intimate an education as the good home. Perhaps the fundamental vehicle of education is one of relationship, not even of words. Quite inevitably a great deal of the effort of schools and universities today must be given to training people to function usefully and efficiently in a technological society. Economic necessity alone would bring this about, but in addition it is easier to give them this training (and to test their attainments in it) than education of a deeper sort. One question posed by existentialism is whether our conception of the scope of education, even within the school, is adequate in a contemporary society where the home has progressively less power.

A strong case can be made out for regarding the grammar school, at least, as first and foremost a place in which intelligence, in the sense of power to reason and think, is exercised and developed. The curriculum will be one in which music, the arts, religious knowledge, even the literature of one's own country, are given comparatively little formal place, the assumption of course being that the boy or girl will get much very important education from home, from church, from the reverberatory effect upon heart and mind of passionate good teaching by enlightened and cultured teachers. There will be, it is taken for granted, personal contacts with people within the school environment itself – no matter what the subject they teach – which will light up wide-ranging interests, philosophic, artistic, literary, musical, more authentically and personally than if more space were given to these things on the timetable. Where conditions are favourable this will happen. But in these days when nearly ten per cent of the inland postal traffic of the country concerns pools[32]; when the quality of family life, of reading, listening and looking, is under threat from so many directions, when the influence of an active religion is powerful only within relatively few homes, when so much of a man's working life in office or factory will probably be spent under conditions which take little account and make little use of his humanity, is this an assumption which ought to be made save in a small number of highly selective schools? Perhaps there is need for greater attention to be paid than is usual in most secondary schools, even grammar schools, to subjects in which reason and feeling are disciplined together. It is still true that on the whole we tend to exercise the young mind in school hours for most of the time in fields from which emotion can be excluded at will. Jaspers's warning is worth reflection: "We cannot, with the logicians, escape into a set of clearly defined symbols to avoid the difficulties of an existence experienced as metaphorical. Instead, to be truly logical, we must capture the logic and language of that existence itself."[33] It is not cerebration alone which matters most.

(ii)   Marcel's contention is that we are much more ready today to face problems than to acknowledge mystery; the inclination indeed is to pretend that a mystery is merely another problem. It is, of course, more difficult than it was once for children to come into frequent touch with the greater than man. Separated from silence, from loneliness and vastness, from mountains and sea, even from sky, by civilised and mechanised town life, children are also protected as far as we can manage it from contact with great suffering and the fact of death[34]. The danger is that they will be isolated from the infinite. In a materialist atmosphere of competitive, functional rivalry it will be easy enough to get them concentrating actively upon problems, much more difficult to secure that willing acceptance of their forked humanity which is necessary to an acknowledgement of mystery or to make worship possible.

It is the atmosphere of our homes and schools which will make this deeper education natural or prevent it from happening. One can hardly have dealings with religion, or beauty, or some of the other kinds of knowledge, in an examinational climate or one in which there is no tincture of leisure. One of the key duties of homes and schools and universities is to keep selves open to experience: open to insight, open to faith and belief, open to love, open to hope, open to knowledge.

(iii) The repeated emphasis of the existentialists is upon the need not simply for action, but for commitment. The word has an old-fashioned ring and it may be that individual responsibility is the only goal on this ground at which we can deliberately aim. But the will is never to be trained *in vacuo*. A sense of responsibility is to be developed only by the exercise of responsibility under conditions which open the eyes to a realisation of the consequences of one's own actions and decisions. Perhaps we underestimate the extent, and the depth, of the responsibility which the boy or girl of 14 or 16 can take, rich in its educative power to himself and, by a subtle alchemy, to the community too.

One of the tasks is to show young people how wide is the gulf between conformity and a taking of moral responsibility. There is no freedom in mere conformity; that is only to be attained through deeper living and a willing acceptance of perceptions of duty. A sensitive recognition of duty is never unindividual: each must find what his duty is as no one else can do. And he must act upon insight when he has had his moment of perception: freedom, commitment and a sense of responsibility go together.

(iv) We certainly lack today a conviction that the education we give children has an overriding purpose. Rather we think of it as having many diverse, separable purposes. The existentialists have no simple remedy for this state of affairs, but their stress is upon the need for educating the person, not only the functionary. Their central concern is for "men as they are men within themselves", their message that it is important in education to be

… studious more to see
Great Truths, than touch and handle little ones.[35]

For always, even in matters of knowledge, "in order to *have* effectively it is necessary to *be* in some degree."[36]

Education: The Status Quo Is Not an Option

I

The world contracts year by year and almost everywhere the Western technology which enables it to do so is desired, sought – and feared. Western wealth, too – and the way to wealth is through specialisation, competition, control, management, the directed mind.

This is the world our young are growing up in, and it isn't surprising that throughout the West schools and places of higher education, too, are being urged to strain towards these golden goals. The proportion needed of skilled to unskilled workers is rising everywhere. The emphasis is on acquisitiveness and individualism, for these are the "getting ahead" virtues. And education is seen as providing the instruments necessary not only if we are to be prosperous, but if men and women are to be able even to fit themselves into a future bound to be more complex, more dominated by the useful (and interesting) mechanisms that have to be mastered. And so almost every country is making the teaching given in its schools more directed, transforming its system of higher education into something more functional than it used to be.

The concentration then is on the useful, the examinable, the attainable, on "getting ahead". But what then? One hot day a man was lying on a beach in Italy in the sun. A rather interfering passer-by (probably British) went up to him and asked officiously: "Why, my man, what is your trade?" "A fisherman, sir." "You ought to be catching fish and earning enough money to buy your own boat." "What for?" "Well, with it you could make a good profit and by and by you could own a whole fleet of boats." "But why?" "There you could earn a simply tremendous lot." "What for?" "Well then you could retire and come and lie on the beach."

The national curriculum for our schools fits into the broad picture of educational intention I've been indicating. Its emphasis is on the basics – literacy and numeracy – and on applying the basics to real situations. But does it reckon with more than some levels of human purpose? Among the terms approved are such words and phrases as "performance", "attainment", "equipping every pupil with skills", "an assessment of performance unit", and so on. Officialdom likes what is measurable. But it all seems a bit external.

What in fact have we to motivate us when we've got ahead, when we've secured the sort of future we were working for? A lot of life seems to have been left out including quite a bit of the sense of belonging, of being part of a community of other people with whom we are in close relationship.

Living well takes more than knowledge and skills. It involves, too, feeling, insight, understanding other people, sympathy, a sense of beauty; all these things in addition to the mastery of technical tools. Such capacities have an internal reference: and they are not competitive. It takes humility and receptiveness and imagination to nourish them – and not too directed an effort.

We need, I think, both the main types of education – that concerned with the external world, and that involving a deeper, more feeling entry into things – if we are to secure either that our country is a community with some sense of a family about it, or that the individual is to live a life that is more than superficial. There is a story about Prince Metternich which illustrates what ultimately can happen if the only motives which drive people are competitive and thus that their understanding of others is self-interest. When a military aide whispered into Metternich's ear at a royal ball that the Czar of Russia was dead, the Prince paused and whispered back, "I wonder what his motive could have been."

I know of course that it can be argued that it simply isn't the job of the school to give any religious education or education which involves belief. That is something for the churches (even if only ten per cent of children any longer have any contact with them), for the family, perhaps for television or whatever, but not for the school. If it does anything at all in this area, it is said, let it confine itself objectively to the facts, not seeking to inculcate the beliefs, or even the set of values, particularly associated with any one religion. Indeed, better steer clear of consciously attempting to educate values at all except those of neutrality and objectivity which are, of course, "OK".

And yet is not such a trading out of the human situation in the long run a kind of betrayal? Beliefs, including religious beliefs, are necessary to health – both social health and individual health – and the more they involve both insight and reason in harmony the better. Without beliefs we have no standards of *importance* to draw upon.

To belong to society, even to be a member of a family at other than a superficial level, means sharing in experiences of many sorts with other people, suffering with them, and recognising one's kinship with them. "Till it know loss, no heart can learn to give," wrote a young New Zealand poet with fine penetration. Experiences brought by literature, music, pictures, videos, and shared with the teacher in the classroom, can matter. Joining in an act of worship in school or in church as one of a family of fellow human beings can sometimes be a help. Of course school worship will rarely be intimate or deep; and in a multi-faith school or where (as is now commonly the case) the majority of the children have no religious faith at all, religious observance involving prayers or hymns or readings will hardly look for more than a reasonably polite degree of attention. But sometimes, at least, periods of school worship – which should, I agree, be occasional rather than daily, at least in maintained schools – can enable some children to reach places in themselves they will not otherwise often encounter. Only sometimes. About a hundred years ago, when I was at school myself, I recollect (can still recollect) how the antiseptic way in which the second master read the lesson proclaimed his non-belief in the whole thing. And that was certainly destructive of faith in others. (I think that he might well have been excused from taking part.)

If schools today are to educate their boys and girls in more than the useful and the examinable, they are more likely to do so if they are communities which really matter a bit to their pupils, or at any rate contain communities, which may sometimes consist only of a teacher and a group of those he or she is teaching. But teachers certainly need the backing of society far more than is now the case – and to be given a respect, a trust and therefore a freedom which is no longer common.

When, in 1936, I spent ten weeks in Russia, I remember the

exhilarating sense of expectancy which then prevailed there, affecting what the schools could do both in and out of the classroom, with the daily newspapers keenly following their doings and a community interest in them which could be relied upon.

I suspect that the status quo in education in Britain will not, and cannot, change very much unless our society wants it to, and unless that society becomes more really a living community of people. If it doesn't, we shall be in danger of producing a population which, though maybe more alert, sophisticated and knowledgeable than now, and with money in its pocket, finds it difficult to cope with – or use – more than a little of its humanity and its real potential. Such a continuation of the present state of things is unacceptable; for in the long run it must lead to what C.S. Lewis years ago frighteningly called the abolition of man – leaving only unreal men and women, those who looked like people and believed at bottom in nothing.

II

Higher education today is developing along largely specialist lines with a rapidly increasing use of technical devices in teaching, research and administration. The idea that universities should be places of liberal education is at best recessive. The early history of Keele University with a whole Foundation Year devoted to General Studies, nearly 100 per cent of its students offered residence, and a large proportion of the degrees awarded not in single honours schools, seems to belong to a faraway era. The changes which have happened and the rate of change at which they are continuing to occur make higher education a fascinating field of study. There is little doubt that the general direction of change is one favouring subjects which have an objective content, concentration upon which will lead to jobs and careers. Subjects which are "applied" have greater power to attract today. From Electronics to Business Management, from Medicine to Media Studies, the emphasis tends to be of this kind. And if one's first degree is in a field which has little "applied" content – for example, Classics or History, Pure Science, even Psychology, the tendency now is for a student to return for a postgraduate degree or a professional diploma more immediately related to a profession.

Recommendation 31 of the Dearing Report (1997)[37] said: "Institutions of higher education should, over the next two years, review their postgraduate research training to ensure that they include, in addition to understanding a range of research methods and training in appropriate technical skills, the development of professional skills, such as communication, self-management and planning." Specialisation and professionalism are indeed more and more necessities for university teachers themselves if they wish to get on – from those who are Assistant Lecturers to those who hold prestigious Chairs. Much concentration is now placed for almost all members of staff upon research and success in research-based enterprises. "Absorbed in our scholarship," says the thoughtful William Bouwsma, distinguished American professor of History, "we have given minimal attention to the needs of students, to the inherence of their educational experience, to problems of meaning and value." Nor does it look as if higher education here or in the US is likely to give much more attention to these matters in the period which lies ahead.

As Dr. Kenneth Wilson has perspicaciously pointed out, in the Dearing Report much is said about quality. "But the quality discussed concerns the delivery of courses (we must have standards for university lecturing), the content of educational programmes (we must be sure that the "system" supports the nation, in particular the national economy), and the Government investment (we must be sure the taxpayer is getting value for money). Nobody would disagree. But as a complete statement of what Higher Education is about, it is lamentable."

The university must certainly be involved in the production and transmission of knowledge. Essential to its functioning therefore are research and scholarship without paying much regard in the first place to whether or not they have applications which promise to be "useful". It has a duty to teach those it tries to educate the importance of pure knowledge, of looking for the evidence, of developing the ability to think logically and without bias, of discovering at a cost what the facts are and what are some of the things of basic importance within whatever area or areas one has chosen as one's special province.

But this most essential among its functions must not rule out of court a number of others. It is entirely right that it should also equip at least some of its students to be ready to enter upon a career (or perhaps a variety of careers), able to apply the standards and disciplined principles they have learned within occupations that will enable them to earn a living in the contemporary world. And if it be retorted that the best means in many cases of doing this may be that they should from early in their undergraduate years have been studying an "applied" subject or subjects, I would not deny the contention – provided that there is incorporated in the approach to the subject or subjects that respect for principle and for objectivity, that regard for seeking out the real truth, that exercise of power to think, which are central to a university's approach to subjects that are "pure", its approach to research and scholarship themselves.

But a university should also be a place in which its students can absorb the principles and knowledge which are its *raison d'être* without losing its humanity; can enrich their lives and gain maturity in more dimensions than an equal number of years spent entirely in the world outside might have enabled them to do. Included in such maturing could be the acquisition of a certain openness to life and experience. There are approaches to experience, even to truth itself, which are not within the territory ruled by argument or logic. The unexpectedness – and the holiness – of the heart's affections have much to teach us.

For objective knowledge, the kind which research and scholarship yield, is not the only kind which is of worth. Knowing, for example, every possible fact about a poem – the date of its composition, when in the life of its author it was composed, its choice of language and metre, the skill with which it makes use of reminiscences of other works, etc., etc. – may be interesting enough, but no substitute whatever for feeling its beauty. Knowledge *about* a painting, a piece of music, a play by Shakespeare is not the same as a real knowledge *of* them. There is indeed a sense in which knowledge *about* them is to a real extent irrelevant. Reading about love can have little meaning unless we have some understanding ourselves of being loved or of loving or – almost certainly – both. And the same is true of other experiences, good or bad, which life brings us – experiences of failure, of hatred, of jealousy, of delight, hope and joy. Surprisingly perhaps if we think of the matter at all, we find that we can speak in sentences, can sing tunes, can walk, can climb mountains. And not merely do things by imitating what other people do but do so on our own originally and, it may be, creatively.

There are in the history of mankind whole developments which can now be studied because they happened – but which only happened because some individual or some group gave a lead which was pioneer. There is more to life than its past, yet no serious study of the future can ever exist because of the unprophesiables.

The university is centrally concerned with encouraging its students to look for the evidence and to think logically. But what we see as logical tends to be confined to what has already happened or to the probable outcome of traditions or occurrences already in being. If viewed at the time when they happened or were about to happen, new events could not necessarily have been seen as the *logical* consequences of their predecessors. For creativity is not in its essence a logical process: the thrill which a highly original painting or piece of sculpture or play can bring us is in part due to its very unprophesiability, its non-obedience to what could logically have been expected. For there is mystery in all creativity, including the imagination, enterprise and risk-taking so intimately a manifestation of the human spirit. It was the venturesomeness in that making of the earliest music to which Rilke refers that eventually led on to Mozart. And who could have foreseen that eventuality? George Steiner has pointed out that theorems and experiments aim at proof and that proof is, in essence, terminal. But there is nothing here to appease our desire to find a meaning in things, a desire voiced and fleetingly answered in the greatest music, literature and art. Within that desire and that answer there is, inexplicably, a closeness to the transcendent. If a sense of the transcendent is lost so too will be much of what gives life its importance. "What I affirm is the intuition that where God's presence is no longer a tenable supposition and where His absence is no longer a felt, indeed overwhelming weight, certain dimensions of thought and creativity are no longer attainable."[38]

Being, Having and Believing

I

The crisis of our time centres on what we can really believe in. A belief in progress is of course still widespread – even if progress is equated with being simply carried along as pleasantly as possible by a succession of events that seize the interest. Many perhaps do not want to live in the present so much as in a future which is always just about to arrive.

Some two and a half centuries ago western man lived in an age of much greater stability and confidence. Handel's music with its sureness and central range was one of its typical products To appeal to objective facts came to seem more and more an extension of common sensen. Enlightenment was both goal and promise. The age called the Age of Enlightenment, as Langdon Gilkey has pointed out[39], saw itself as introducing a new era for human history on three grounds. (a) Correct, cumulative and fruitful methods of knowing had now been discovered and developed and through our expanding knowledge we could count on an increasing control over the natural forces threatening human welfare. (b) The practical application of this new and expanding knowledge of causes in an expanding technology and in an expanding industrialism would provide a plenitude of goods for general consumption; and, with the banishing of ignorance, poverty could also be banished. (c) The curse of traditional superstition and of unexamined authority (especially in religion) could now be eradicated, making rational structures possible in the political, legal, social and moral domains. By the beginning of the 21st century we have seen all of these grounds for optimism radically questioned, if not shattered.

Even a hundred years ago many certainly saw in history plain evidence that God backed the West. The continuation of such optimism was encouraged by the imperial possessions of the western countries and by technological victories which affected wider and wider areas of life. Such recent, late 20th century, achievements as Concorde, the moon-shot, the computer, video, the microprocessor, subtly continue this apparent age of confidence. And certainly many of the changes of horizon they are bringing with them are not likely to be reversible.

All the same the climate of opinion is slowly altering. More and more people wonder where progress is leading us. They are beginning to question whether progress itself is necessarily so good a thing. Many western societies are no longer in a state of robust health, though affluence may increase and consumer goods multiply in variety enough to satisfy ever more ingeniously invented needs. This has come to be known as a high standard of living; but the proliferation brings small dividends of satisfaction. If productivity is all – with developing nations treading the same path half-centuries, decades or merely years behind, where has meaning gone? "A technocratic society is not ennobling," says Daniel Bell.

Material goods provide only transient satisfaction or an invidious superiority over those with less. Yet one of the deepest human impulses is to sanctify their institutions and beliefs in order to find a meaningful purpose in their lives and to deny the meaningfulness of death. A post-industrial society cannot provide a transcendent ethic ... The lack of a rooted belief system is the cultural contradiction of society, the deepest challenge to its survival[40].

Have we reached the end of the age of enlightenment to substitute for it a world described by Nietzsche? He foretold an era to come which would be dominated by two groups: "the last men" and "the nihilists". The last men are those who believe in leisure and happiness for all. They would concentrate on making use of the achievements of technology as ends in themselves and for their own comfort. " "We have discovered happiness," say the last men and blink." "A little poison now and then: that produces pleasant dreams. And a lot of poison at last for a pleasant death." Nobility and greatness would become categories without meaning.

The other group, the nihilists, would rather will nothing than have nothing to will. For them violence is the way to mastery: it is an end in itself, it stirs the blood. The individual takes it into his own hands to hold his countrymen, and the world, to ransom. There is, Nietzsche implies, at least more truth in nihilism than capitulating to an anodyned life of ease. Our present post-enlightenment age certainly seems to have large numbers who, without knowing it, are like last men or nihilists. How shall people escape from such a condition?

It has yet to be seen if a communism dedicated to a great future of material production will eventually be in a different case or develop in a different direction. The aim of Marx was "to overthrow all the structures by which man is humiliated, enslaved, abandoned and despised". But when you think you have done that, what do you put in their place? The past century has brought relative prosperity and many more possessions to vast numbers of people in Europe and America. But is the outcome at all the kind of freedom Marx was seeking? To turn the television on for 20 hours every week (the present average for British adult viewing) may represent a different kind of enslavement.

Many have now come to query whether education really justifies the confidence we have had in it, and whether it either does or can yield the dividends people used to expect from it. Even the so-called evidence of history is under question, as inevitably biased, however hard we may try to protect ourselves against all prejudices. The temper of the time encourages confrontations rather than social unity; criticism not approval; having political parties "out" rather than "in"; cut-throat competition in production and more and more violent competition in sport. Even the research projects which attract funds are those which seem likely to pay early dividends of a material kind; faith in fundamental research is at a low ebb. There is an emphasis on money-making, getting ahead, sexual prowess. In all these there is an element of escapism. There is significance – and fear – in the prevalent habit of taking only the short view ahead and finding the long view unrealistic, a waste of time.

The West is of course no longer unchallenged as a bringer of civilisation. It may bring "achievement"; but peace, happiness, fraternity, do not seem to be its products and hardly equality either. Both Europe and the USA are more and more aware of the rest of the world than they were and sense that the growth of the non-West in population, wealth and influence is only just beginning. The number of human beings alive is now increasing unimaginably fast. It grew from one billion in 1800 to two billion in 1930, and to three by 1960. By 2000 it was already six billion. And five of those six billion inhabitants of the world live in Asia, Africa and South America. The Islamic Middle East is already one of the richest parts of the earth. Japan has begun to exert a new order of influence. Now none of these draws predominantly from the Jewish and Greek sources which have informed the West so powerfully in the last 500 years. Even so, is their capacity to ensure that their peoples find profound meaning in life upon which to draw any greater than that of the West? It is noteworthy, I think, that over the last 25 years there has been a widespread concern in Japan for a higher morality. The "moralogists" in that country have been searching, with abundant financial backing, for what they imagine to be the former western secret of the relation of the right to the good.

In an extraordinarily perceptive essay, Erich Heller[41] points out that while Nietzsche's scientific and scholarly contemporaries thrived on the comfortable assumptions that first, there was such a thing as "objective", and therefore morally neutral, knowledge and that, secondly, everything that can be known "objectively" is therefore also worth knowing, he realised that knowledge, or at least the mode of knowledge predominant at his time and ours, is the subtlest guise of the will to power. And as a manifestation of the will it is legitimate to judge it *morally*.

II

In a period of wealth and confidence in the inevitability of progress there is a feeling that if there are problems we shall solve them before too long. With a slackening of the pace, and with more and more economies forced on us, new incentives are given to ask what is really worthwhile. A more meditative frame of mind is needed than at a time when the emphasis was on moving ahead without much regard for where we were really going. Theoretically, a tightened economy *could* intensify a search for sources of authority and of authenticity.

Whether it will do so is still an open question.

For most people such a search for authenticity will have to be prompted by practical problems uncovered by current developments. For example, among the increasing number of test-tube baby embryos as year follows year, is the choice of which to "delete" and which to foster, one to be made by the man in the laboratory "objectively"? If so, is he to decide that as far as may be only more and more normal or average people will be born? Or, to take another example, as man's control over the world increases how can he decide which are better ways of spending leisure and which are worse? What right has any leader of opinion to encourage others to follow the direction he indicates unless he has principles (and depths) from which to draw?

Today many people find it difficult to locate sources of meaning which matter. If the education they are given bypasses the problem, that education is, I suggest, insufficient in its sense of responsibility.

The traditional direction in which men have looked for guidance is of course a religious one. The outstanding anthropologist Clifford Geertz may not be a believer himself but he understands much of what religion is about. "Religious belief," he writes,

"involves not a Baconian induction from everyday experience – for then we should all be agnostics – but rather a prior acceptance of authority which transforms that experience. The existence of bafflement, pain and moral paradox – of The Problem of Meaning – is one of the things that drives men towards belief in gods, devils, spirits, totemic principles ..."[42]

The essential in any contemporary quest for any religious meaning in life is an inkling of the inexplicable, of a groping into the unknown rather than the adoption from the start of a creed as a set of answers given by other people for us to accept.

The search for meaning is a feature of forward-looking Islam and Judaism as well as Christianity; but it is from continuing development of the legacy of Christian insight that those in the West who are religiously aware are most likely to discover truths which matter. No one reading the classics of religion, or Father Zossima's discourse in *The Brothers Karamazov* or Pascal's *Pensées* or

Kierkegaard's *Concluding Unscientific Postscript* can be left in doubt that though a discipline and codification that is necessary may be brought to belief by the rationalising mind, there should be passion and imagination within both the search and the discovery.

There are many, however, who cannot find in the assumptions or manifestations of Christian belief as they have encountered them an authority which is acceptable. The same would probably be true for them of any other religion. Yet they, too, are deeply concerned about the vacuum and negativity of our age. "The essence of our real condition," said Saul Bellow in his 1976 Nobel Lecture,

> the complexity, the confusion, the pain of it, is shown to us in glimpses, in what Proust and Tolstoy thought of as "true impressions". This essence reveals, and then conceals, itself. When it goes away, it leaves us again in doubt. But we never seem to lose our connection with the depths from which these glimpses come. We are reluctant to talk about this, because there is nothing we can prove, because our language is inadequate, and because few people are willing to risk talking about it. They would have to say "There is a spirit" and that is taboo. So almost everyone keeps quiet about it ...[43]

But many who might object to using the word "spirit" know that among the sources of meaning to them are personal experiences which have come to them of beauty, of love and of the finitude of life. They may find neither safety nor authenticity in religious belief but they are sometimes rescued from solitude and anonymity by literature, art or music. To be awake to what novelists, poets and composers – Bellow himself perhaps, Iris Murdoch, Maxwell Davies, John Taverner, William Matthias – have been saying in notes or words is on occasion to be shown where meaning lies. But shown, not instructed; it is a mistake anyway to suppose that knowledge is restricted to what can be talked about. They want to be saved from the relentless self-seeking of the ego; but they do not want to be greedy for what they suspect would be an undeserved, as well as an incredible, immortality. They may find comfort in the perception that they are kin to other men and women now and in earlier centuries who have recognised that life has unaccountable depths.

For some who are secular humanists as well as for some who have religious convictions this sense of the past supplies a context to the passing moment, giving depth to it. So that the contemporary emphasis on the importance of the "objective" and the useful is put in its place with no denial of the need for both. Among both believers and humanists – and those outside either category – are many, too, who find in friendship a positive source of meaning. And a sense of human closeness brought by feeling oneself a part of a community, in which kindness and a sense of duty towards one's fellows are important, may be related to friendship.

Action that really involves us can also bring a sense of meaning at any rate temporarily – in political purposiveness for example, or in the skilled performance of a task; driving a car with delicacy, planing a piece of wood with exactitude, originating a computer programme cleverly or analysing a computer read-out with accuracy. These can be so absorbing that all sense of time is lost and the job seems self-evidently worthwhile.

All the same, the extent of the fulfilment to be found in the exercise of skill, in political involvement or in service to the community may be more transitory and shallower than that which is needed if men and women are to find sources of authority adequate to the demands of an age which has largely lost faith not merely in God, but is beginning to lose faith in progress and in itself. It is by no means certain that in the future man can develop, even keep, his humanity. What lies behind C.S. Lewis's Riddell Lectures *The Abolition of Man* (1943) and George Steiner's *In Bluebeard's Castle* (1975) is the fear that we may be carried willy nilly back into a more animal and less human existence than ours in the West has sometimes actually been – and still more has seemed to have the potentiality of becoming. The Club of Rome's famous report *The Limits to Growth* (1972)[44] dealt with the limits to growth threatened by population trends, by developments in agriculture, resource-use, industry and pollution. The limits to moral and spiritual growth which are imposed by our loss of depth and vision must be taken more seriously than any of these.

III

Among the fundamental human needs is a growth in man's power to evaluate his experiences. And this it should be one of the functions of higher education to give. Truths can be extensive or they can be deep; both sorts are indispensable to civilised living but the educated man is one able to differentiate between them. An almost wholly utilitarian concept of its purpose is patently inadequate as an answer to the problems man faces. It is not in context, unless the context is thought of as only short-term.

Higher education in the West, which caters for an increasingly significant proportion of the most intelligent young, needs to become newly aware of the scope of its responsibilities. This is not a matter only for those who are professors and lecturers. They indeed are apt to be more the servants of social forces, movements and trends than they may suppose. If major changes are to take place in the climate and content of higher education during the decades ahead these will be brought about by pressures from outside the campus even more than by promptings from those inside it. But those inside can help to encourage and clarify the social will as well as to put a new liberalism into the programme and content of their teaching.

The reiterated, present demand that there must be "education for capability" is undoubtedly justified, but by itself it is a very limited goal. What is normally meant by education for capability exercises chiefly one level of the mind, whereas what I have been suggesting is that higher education must keep its eye also on the more profound human needs.

Competence, both professional and technical, is indispensable: the world of work matters. But universities, in Stuart Maclure's words, should also be "centres of critical and informed comment on the changing state of civilisation". More than that, their teachers, if adequate, will inevitably be engaged in changing the perceptions of their students. This will include helping people to recognise their hidden assumptions, confronting them with choices between lines of action which involve different sets of values. There must be recognition that decisions may have to be made between levels of profundity as well as between quantities of evidence. The reductionism now prevalent in the teaching of so many subjects is a serious limitation.

Learning of the kind I am talking about is existential learning; it cannot, that is, be added to by memorisation or "hard work" alone. More self-involvement is required, more "depth and darkness". But for many people there is a connection between cognitive awareness, existential concern and actually doing things. Though it is important that higher education should "expand the moral imagination" there are limits to what can be done without throwing oneself into deeds.

Nearly all action, however, requires the crossing of disciplinary boundaries – for specialist knowledge, when applied, nearly always has consequences outside its own province. To foresee these and in addition to learn how to cope in the real world involves seeing some of the limitations of one's specialism. It also calls for recognition of human and moral problems. The need to cultivate farmland efficiently should bring into consciousness not merely the propaganda of conservationists but the moral issues which motivate these conservationists. Historians need to be aware of the effect of the victories of conquerors and kings not only upon the territories they capture but the people living in them and, more subtly, the personal development of those who were victorious. The surgeon, the economist, the business manager, all need an education which increases the range of their awareness while not reducing their specialist skills.

The scope of many subjects can be stretched by the use of biography in teaching them, either the lives of their past exponents or the personal experiences of the teacher. An international frame of reference can often enlarge the imagination, including the moral imagination.

Obviously among the influences which can be creative are not only those of the lecture room and library but the general environment in which the student lives – particularly its overall spirit. This is too complex a matter to be dealt with here, even if we could know with any exactitude the relative effects of residence, co-education, union activities, counselling, church-going, the existence of a foundation year, sandwich course arrangements, a unit-based course structure, forms of examination, etc. The impact of any of these can vary greatly from student to student. Even upon the individual their effects will probably be different at different stages of his or her development.

Not just once but many times during their higher education students need encouragement to work out the differences between the standards people use in their public and their private lives; and to feel profoundly the need for a philosophy of life of their own – personal experiences and insights being indispensable to its formation if it is to be genuine.

A highly departmentalised place of higher education, almost all of whose emphasis is on specialisms and the production of professional expertise, runs the danger of giving its students a reduced and limited concept of knowledge itself.

"Where is the knowledge we have lost in information?" asked T. S. Eliot. The shadow thrown forward by the question grows.

An Absence of Outrage: Cultural Change and Values in British Higher Education 1930-1990

Higher Education in Britain in the 1930s and 1940s

The far-off era of the 1930s seems to us now to breathe an air of largeness and leisure. One's university days, said Sir Walter Moberly at that time, should offer "the gift of an interval" and as, successively, Vice Chancellor of Manchester University and Chairman of the University Grants Committee (UGC) from 1935 to 1949, he was one of the most influential figures of his time. Like that of a number of his contemporary Vice-Chancellors, his academic training had been in Philosophy. He saw higher education as holistic in nature. He believed in the desirability of a period of residence for as many undergraduates as possible because he thought that a collegiate style of life would encourage both worthwhile discussions late into the night, and a growth of human understanding. In his view, universities had much responsibility for the moral and intellectual life of the nation as a whole. His *The Crisis in the University* (1949) voices this philosophy and also his fear that it was under threat. Above all, he was concerned that during their student days, men and women should be challenged to face some of the great questions: What is life for? What differentiates a good life from a bad one? How can one ensure that students emerge from their university days with a sense of what the present owes to the past?

Under his chairmanship, the monthly meetings of the UGC could spend the whole of the morning session discussing broad issues of purpose and policy, leaving mere money matters to the afternoon! Under his successors – from 1949 onwards – financial questions and problems loomed large. Until the early 1950s, however, two factors contributed to a continuing spirit of optimism in the country. One was the post-war determination to look ahead to a Britain which would be better educated and less socially divided. The other was the persistent confidence that the nation and its universities were *organically* related and that this relationship could be maintained without too conscious an examination of the elements that contributed to it. When members of the UGC (which itself had some elements of a club about it) and the representatives of the "customers" of the Committee – the Vice-Chancellors – met in friendly surroundings such as the Athenaeum Club, of which at that time most were members, there were opportunities for conversations which could be open, spirited and helpful. If the State threatened to be difficult about finance for universities, an authoritative leading article might appear anonymously on exactly the right morning in *The Times* giving what in effect was the UGC viewpoint. In other words, some of the features of a village society were still operative. Such a time of optimism and stability tends not to be one of disillusionment.

The 1950s and Early 1960s

From 1952 or so onwards, change began to be discernible in the prevailing winds, bringing clouds at first scarcely bigger than a man's hand. By 1970 rain was falling heavily. Causes of the change included:

• The exhaustion of the mood of euphoria and hope which had followed the ending of the war (a mood which has never returned).

• A new consciousness of the high cost of higher education in a country whose economic state was fragile.

• A sharply increasing awareness that material progress depends on technological and technical accomplishment and that competition from other countries was growing rapidly with many consequences for the kind of higher education called for.

• A new realisation that there were responsibilities that society itself must undertake, with higher education given a narrower remit and concentrating more upon tasks for which it was fitted, e.g. research and the training of professional expertise.

The national mood from the 1960s onwards was thus much more realistic than it had been. In the 1950s, however, many evidences remained of an earlier idealism. During that decade a number of new universities were being planned in Britain in addition to Keele (founded in 1949). Keele under Lord Lindsay – with 97 per cent of its students resident and a liberally-oriented, additional Foundation year for all students – incarnated many of the holistic principles Moberly advocated. The group of new universities built in the 1960s (the first to open its doors was Sussex in 1961) were, significantly, not sited in industrial centres but in cathedral towns (Canterbury, York, Norwich, or semi-rural places – near Lewes, Lancaster, in Wivenhoe Park, or near Stirling). And the new map of learning they drew gave little place to technology.

The Robbins Report and the Period 1963-1980

It was the government's awareness that we were at a watershed in national development which led to its appointing, in 1961, a committee under Lord Robbins "to review the whole pattern of full-time higher education in Britain in the light of national needs and resources". Today its Report (1963) seems to look both backward and forward. It recommended a vast increase of student numbers, a great expansion of technological education, and a far-sighted national planning of the whole system. But such policies were to be informed by principles which spoke with an earlier holistic voice – that what was taught should "promote the general powers of the mind"; higher education should transmit "standards of citizenship" and be responsible "in partnership with the family for providing that background of culture and social habit upon which a healthy society depends." The provision of much more residential accommodation for students was to be an important element in this programme. In the event, the government accepted only such parts of the Robbins proposals as were compatible with much more governmental control of the system. The relationship of the UGC with the Treasury was severed by the decision that money from the State to support university expenditure would, from December 1963, be channelled through the Department of Education and Science (DES). The significance of this transference is considerable; relationships of the universities with the Treasury had traditionally been close but henceforward they would tend to be more distant; the DES with its existing powers of influence over the finances of non-university higher and further education would now also gain power over the university sector.

The decade 1965-1975 saw a great increase in the control the government was able to exert not only over the quantity but the presuppositions, nature and types of higher education which the nation provided. And this with very little attention given to philosophic considerations (was this not anyway rather *passé*?) or non-utilitarian values. The times were hard, money was scarce, the nation needed a far higher proportion of young intelligence relevantly trained – and relevance was understood to mean for occupations that were useful or researches promising results that would not be too long in coming.

During the 1960s, a number of former colleges of technology were accorded full university status and put on to the UGC grant list. But a more significant development in this period was the building up, from 1966 onwards, of a "binary system" of higher education consisting of some 30 polytechnics not financed through the UGC but educating people to degree level. A number of cogent reasons can be put forward for ruling that the universities should no longer be the sole providers of education to degree level. The first springs from remediable deficiencies in the universities themselves. To many people in the 1960s – and later on too – universities appeared as stand-offish institutions, loving to draw their skirts about them. If universities no longer represent an ideology largely accepted within the nation as a whole, if many more experts trained in applied fields are needed than universities are supplying, the provision of such people must be under planned and flexible control for the requirements to be met. Must not in these circumstances the State have greater direct planning powers within the total higher education system than hitherto?

In the past, Britain may have unloaded more or less successfully upon the universities the responsibility for ensuring that a sufficiency of educators, scholars, nuclear scientists, administrators, economists and other fit persons was available, especially when there was no likelihood of a glut. But is not this an amateurish way of planning the fulfilment of national needs? The task anyway is going to be harder when cuts become necessary. The greater the proportion of the young having a period of tertiary education and the greater the tax burden involved, the stronger will be the argument for allowing the State more power to exercise control over numbers of entrants and standards of qualification.

Desegregation of British Higher Education

The changes of outlook manifest in places of higher education during the transition from 1965 to around 1990 are not to be understood, however, if they are regarded as wholly – perhaps even chiefly – due to economic pressures. A very significant element in them was a shift of values and perceptions in the national consciousness. To some extent this is to be seen in the attitudes of students, whose expectations and hopes influenced the character and content of the higher education they received more than it might have done in more elitist days. In the late 1960s, personal autonomy, fairness and equality of rights were ideas of paramount importance to the young, both in higher education and outside it. Many students wished to give priority to a common endeavour which unites rather than to a competition between themselves which at worst can alienate them from their fellows.

The widening social range from which students came, their aims and purposes in studying, and their lessened withdrawal from the world during their undergraduate years are among the factors making for a different experience of higher education from that obtained by their less numerous predecessors, even though entry standards were higher rather than lower. The growth of the habit of going away from their university or polytechnic each weekend during term; the far greater numbers of students living in lodgings; cafeteria-type feeding; and the co-educational schools from which the majority now came; these were all elements which made higher education a less segregated process than it had been.

Throughout the period 1965-1980, many students wanted to gain more control over the type and content of the higher education provided. A higher proportion, both men and women, had less confidence in institutions or the powers that be than had their predecessors. They wished to study subjects useful for furthering social and practical ends. Who, they asked, had been deciding what should be taught? The traditional curriculum in higher education had consisted of a body of knowledge to be passed on and disciplines to be mediated on the decision of scholars, experts and members of an academic hierarchy. Some of the student protests, which became fierce in some countries in

the later 1960s, were directed against the whole assumption, stem-
ming from medieval times, that the elders represent all that is fit in our
civilisation to be passed on. It was not right, they held, that higher
education should be so identified with the industrial-capitalist ethos,
that it should neglect the contemporary situation, that it should be so
abstract in its intellectuality, and that it should be so merely impersonal in its apprehension of significances.

But the lengths to which some students began to take their protest
against convention did much to puncture further public confidence in
the universities. It helped to build into governments a quiet determination that places of higher education should in future concentrate
more upon the production of specialists and practitioners of the hundred kinds the nation needed. There was also in the mood of students,
however, an inchoate disillusionment with contemporary society itself
and its values. That this was at odds with their material ambitions went
unrecognised. The criticism by American students of the Vietnamese
war was in large measure a moral one. The influence on the student
outlook of existentialist philosophers, including Camus and Marcuse,
was considerable. The threat of encroaching depersonalisation seemed
real – a threat voiced by Galileo in Brecht's eponymous play (trans.
1960): "With time you may discover all that is to be discovered and
your progress will only be a progression away from mankind. The gulf
between you and them can one day become so great that your cry of
jubilation over some new achievement may be answered by a universal
cry of horror." There is evidence that while the staffs' concern – often
exclusively – was the achievement of academic goals, the students wanted
their period as undergraduates to be much wider in its concerns.[45]

A powerful reason for the failure in the 1960s of the movement to
give more weight to general education was the manifest and increasing
prestige and financial rewards which specialist attainments brought.
Among the encouragements to offer degrees made up of modules or
units – an educational currency popular with students and one whose
payments students can take with them at the end of a year if they move
elsewhere – were the increasing mobility of society, student pressures
against authoritarianism and predetermined programmes, and the power

of international example. Part of the attraction of courses which are a collection of units lies in the increased freedom given to the students themselves to decide what they shall study. But the unit principle can also enable the choosers, almost without noticing, to postpone decisions about their career, about hard work and about a deep centre to their intellectual life. Both a preoccupation with what students want and their own anxiety to have their wants fulfilled tend to voice a naturalistic philosophy. Levels or depths of wanting are not involved. A course made up of modules, even with inbuilt prohibitions to this combination or that, still allows many bolt-holes into miscellaneity for those tempted to escape.

Students, by and large, came to approve of colloquia and discussion groups more than lectures, which were declared artificial and authoritarian. Seminars (even dialogues or confrontations as on TV) seemed more democratic. The danger is that while lessening the generation gap, they too often leave a number of the participants feeling that no one view has more authority than another.

In their attitudes to examinations, in the period 1965-1980, students were quite strongly in favour of continuous assessment rather than three-hour papers and of plain Pass/Fail divisions rather than finer gradings; that is, they preferred a reduction in the *distance* between themselves and their fellows (whether their seniors or their contemporaries) to being forced into a competitive stance.

The Period 1980-1990

This decade saw a great intensification of the pressures already apparent in the preceding 15 years – with more and more emphasis laid on short-term rather than long-term objectives; greater and fiercer stress placed on economic factors, on control of access and on the selection of research enterprises (with an eye to the main chance). The UGC, with such ability as still remained to it to act as a buffer between university interests and those of the government, ceased to exist altogether in 1989. Henceforward, the responsibility for financing both universities and polytechnics is that of Funding Councils more directly under the influence of the State. From 1991, significantly, these will be housed in the same building.

What becomes clearer and clearer is that the agenda for the discussion of issues in higher education is now one which the government itself has chosen. The larger and longer-term purposes of higher education are not subjects much attended to. The urgent questions include those of finance, student fees, student loans, the provision of minimum hours for those employed as lecturers to give to teaching, and plans for co-operation with industry and for constructing science parks so that higher education can in future aid national development more realistically.

An Absence of Outrage

Nowhere indeed, remarks a foreign commentator[46], does this dictation of the agenda for the debate seem more evident than in the question of the funding of research and development. The range of solutions seems to have been predetermined. Absolute freedom will remain for the cheap (i.e. unimportant) disciplines, but science and technology will be on the leash of business and industry; the only thing to be resolved is how long the leash will be. In the background is an absence of outrage at (if not tacit acceptance of) higher education being merely a means for manpower development and the creation of wealth.

The decade 1980-1990 saw – not merely in Britain but in France, Germany and Italy, to name no others – a rapid increase in the use of corporate management techniques, a process which, facilitated by computerisation, is likely to continue. In universities as in many other institutions, numbers of traditional values and relationships gave way to ones that were more technicist in character. Decision-making about priorities tended to be shifted to managers and administrators, sometimes rather unnoticeably even to themselves. It may be significant that today only one or two among the 100 and more Vice-Chancellors of British universities are philosophers; it now seems right to most universities not to appoint as their head even a graduate in the humanities but someone with managerial ability and a certain toughness, whether scientist, engineer, lawyer or economist. As in the country as a whole so in higher education; policy directives, taken centrally, affected and limited what could be done at the periphery – in individual universities and polytechnics, in their departments, even in the courses their departments gave. Autonomy for institutions of higher education, though preserved and (in the case of polytechnics increased), tended in practice to be more limited and circumscribed than before. Initiatives were possible only in authorised directions.

In this way, broad and deeper questions relating to the purpose and philosophy of higher education tended less and less often to be asked. The managers – including the civil servants of the DES – were not for the most part interested in asking them. And most of those further from the centre, even if they had been inclined to ask such questions, found themselves both lacking the necessary leisure and discouraged by the spirit of the age from indulging in so unprofitable an exercise.

An Absence of Purpose

In these circumstances, it has become more and more difficult for higher education to think in terms of overriding purposes at all. It belongs to a past age to regard higher education, as Robbins did, as having among its responsibilities the transmission of "a common culture" or even "common standards of citizenship". We no longer talk in such terms. Our society itself anyway is rather lacking in purposes that can be called overriding. We are all emotivists now, to employ the term used by Alasdair MacIntyre in his seminal *After Virtue* (1981). In it, he characterises the "emotivist" as a person without ultimate moral criteria. "Whatever criteria," he says, "or principles or evaluative allegiances the emotivist self may profess, they are to be construed as expressions of attitudes, preferences and choices which are themselves not governed by criterion, principle or value."[47] The individual, left with the freedom to choose but no hierarchy of values, is likely in his business or professional life to be a follower of its conventions and in his private life to lack any beliefs for which he would go to the stake. But though we live in a world which fosters individualism it has become harder for people to find any unifying meaning in things, or perhaps even to want to find one. The higher education they receive is not expected to help much in this matter and it can hardly be said that for most students it does.

The idea that education in a university can and will affect not merely technical advances in the world but also its moral climate is now scarcely taken into account. Adjusting a course to face economic, industrial or even environmental facts is one thing; interfering with a social climate which encourages emotivism and the freedom of individuals to do what they like is quite another.

Yet such fostering of a detached individualism has widespread consequences. The example of the West, powerfully reinforced by the technological and monetary rewards which following that example will bring, spreads its influence everywhere. Ours is an amoral world. Technology and professional expertise are instruments for the conquest and consolidation of power. Amoral multinational companies in manufacturing, telecommunications, transport, banking, and financial and insurance services are today immensely influential upon life worldwide. Such questions as, What for? and What happens to human potentiality in the process? are hardly glanced at.

In this kind of social climate, chances abound of escaping into an existence that lacks meaning altogether. Universities and polytechnics are hardly less free from problems of drug addiction, alcoholism, sexual promiscuity and careerist ambition than the world outside. It is not easy to blot from the mind the television pictures showing so vividly serried ranks of intelligent, highly paid, young Japanese employees (some of them university graduates) in car factories spending their leisure time with eyes glued to pinball machines into which they insert coin after coin in competitive quest for a bigger harvest of ball-bearings than their fellows.

But there are elements much to be reckoned with in humanity which simply will not accept escapism as an ultimate stance. A whole dimension of truth seems somehow to have been left out, if we kid ourselves into being content simply to spend our time unnoticeably. To assume that "all moral judgements are nothing but expressions of preference"[48] is close to declaring that all values and morals are forms of self-deception and self-interest. Standards of detached objectivity and impartiality are invoked to show how admirable is our lack of standards of importance.

Higher Education as Instrumentality

As we have seen, higher education has tended to become more and more confined and, let us say, instrumental in character and more and more subtly so. If its only significant aim is to produce and equip professionals to run a managerial, electronic and consumer-orientated society, what reason is there to think that such a society will take us in the long run where we really want to be? Contemporary society, left to itself, will set neither limits to its use of technology nor boundaries to growth except those which shortages of raw materials or skills arbitrarily compel. We cannot in the long run avoid more ultimate questions of objective than those which additional knowledge or training will provide. What is really meant by the term "a better social future"? What does "better" involve? Even if we develop new and powerful types of control over the world that seem to be called for, that still leaves largely undecided the direction in which we want civilisation to go.

It is difficult to see what is to guarantee that a merely unconsidered future will necessarily be worth living in. The more that men or women go on simply using technological devices as ends in themselves or go on being hung up by them, the more the motive for living a life that has scope or depth is weakened.

It certainly cannot be said that higher education now is conspicuously successful in producing more than a percentage of graduates who are "all round" men and women; sensitively literate, numerate and civilised. That indeed is one of the causes of the decline of public enthusiasm for it. There is no doubt at all that the training of people with a capacity to analyse situations and high expertise of a variety of kinds is indispensable to modern life. But by themselves, these are not enough. A widened and deepened awareness, and a sense of direction for human life are also called for, and places of higher education cannot leave to other institutions all the responsibility for educating them. What others anyway? The family? The churches? Big business? Schools?

The political parties? Parliament? The retort of course may be that it is the responsibility of individuals, not of institutions as such, and that many responsible people can be found in universities. As Martin Trow has percipiently observed, the colleges with the most effect on students are those with a sense of their own uniqueness. But a sense of uniqueness comes from the influences built by individuals *into the institution*: it does not leave them operating just as individuals.

During the period 1970-1985, two highly responsible investigations into the state of higher education were made – one regarding the United States under the leadership of Clark Kerr; the other regarding Britain under the leadership of Gareth Williams[49]. Both were action-orientated; neither was much concerned with how higher education could cope with a shifting moral climate and the need of society for orientation. What makes it the more significant is that in 1989 Clark Kerr published a powerful paper rejecting the idea that academics can any longer trade out of ethical issues by treating ethics simply as a matter of personal taste. If institutions of higher education are in some vital ways to be "the conscience of the nation", university teachers must take their collegiate responsibilities seriously. Regrettably, they have become "more reluctant to serve on committees, more reluctant to make time readily available when they do, and more reluctant to accept the responsibilities of writing good reports on institutional matters. They wish to concentrate on their own affairs and not those of the institution"[50].

Yet the situation in 1990, outside as well as inside the universities is, as we have seen, challenging. Threats caused by pollution, by the escalation of the world's population, by the certainty that genetic engineering involving human beings and the human species is going to be possible on a wider and wider scale – these need to be taken seriously by every intelligent man and woman. And they all impose not merely technical dilemmas but dilemmas for the conscience, and not merely nationally but internationally. There is little evidence that universities or polytechnics are paying them attention to any depth. The sectional, departmentally self-interested, approach most common where there is interest at all is ludicrously inadequate to meet the challenge. It is not enough for the intelligent to be taught the techniques of architecture, engineering science, animal farming, computer theory, musical counterpoint, managerial science, anaesthetics or economic planning without training of the introspective imagination and with no discipline of foresight and insight to help them to realise the consequences worldwide of their knowledge.

It is not irrational to feel the importance of beauty, or of caring, or of life itself. The plotting of the future, if it is to serve mankind and not destroy it, requires many individual perceptions of what is worthwhile. No subjectivity, no standards. But the individual to whom they come will depend greatly upon traditions of what to look at and what to value, which they have acquired through their upbringing and education. Their insights, however, when they arrive at them, will be personal ones which need to be "placed"- that is, realised and judged – if they are to matter more than transiently.

This process is not essentially different whether the insight results from the success (or the failure) of a scientific experiment, the appreciation of a poem or sonata, the making of a moral judgement. What is called "decision-making" is often only the final step in a process which will have involved listening to the evidence according to some tradition of selecting what is really evidence, internalising it (which may involve feeling its power), and evaluating its worth as objectively as possible.

While the content of higher education must be closely related to students' professional needs, too narrow a concept of what is relevant to those will certainly prevent the production of the kinds of professional most needed. Students need to consider some of the consequences of the very rapid growth of opportunities for control over other people which the advancement of human knowledge and powers of communication are bringing about. The question of the concept, or norm, of the man or woman upon whom those controls are to be exercised will not go away. We have clues to the norm and how it is to be sustained in, for example, the expression of mind and desire in literature, music and art; in the concepts of human potentiality which have been seen and clarified in philosophic and religious exploration; in some of the medical and psychological discoveries of the past 200 years. But to follow these clues requires a developed sensitivity and imagination, some sense of history, and a capacity to judge human nature informed by an experience gained interrelatedly from life and books and the media. It requires that students shall not be specialists only but be able to estimate the relative importance of the factors, moral and spiritual as well as physical, which contribute to the real evidence. Only in this way will they be able to counter the threat inherent in going further and further ahead with small concern for the direction in which we are going.

La Préoccupation des Clercs

A problem with most specialists is how to get them out of their protective shells. To a few it may be insoluble: some find it possible to show excitement easily within their specialist field, and very occasionally can be persuaded to reveal why it absorbs them. But if they are required to venture into wider questions – even, say, its place in university education as a whole, or the moral or social consequences of research into it, or of applying its findings – they will declare that these are matters beyond their remit. And anyway there certainly isn't time! Their social and moral responsibility, they feel, is somewhat limited. The claims of their subject are paramount and this is indeed their proper territory. Other, less important, subjects perhaps may be able to "take the strain".

But this is to make oneself content with educating knowledge, and reason too, in one dimension rather than holistically. Granted that there is a distinction between knowledge which is, as it were, external – concerned with facts, measurement and the apparent behaviour of things – and that which is more subjective and includes feeling and evaluating. Both kinds are indispensable to a properly human and properly humane life. The kind of personal and moral commitment which is the mark of civilised people is not an irrationality.

How do we help students to recognise any authority other than that obtained from knowledge or the logical reason? There is of course something absolute, something implacable in those, but to acknowledge no other authority is to be left with an existence which has far too little direction in it. Much that is essential to all-round learning involves experiences which detached or technical study neatly avoids: personal suffering, personal happiness, the actual experience of cruelty, of good and evil, commitment, the mysterious, the tangle of human motives. To seek to educate people to be experts in a world that no longer has much meaning to it is a kind of madness and needs to be recognised as the madness it is.

Conclusion

In his Inaugural Lecture at Southampton University on *The Good versus the Interesting* (1987), Professor Alan Bance argues that Thomas Mann by virtue of bringing into the open his subjective experiences, "transfers knowledge from the private to the public sphere". What he writes is thus not just "interesting". It diminishes the sum of human ignorance and therefore the sum of unconsciously motivated action. Really to enter into the experience which reading him can bring is to be saved from the cultural nihilism which once almost overwhelmed Europe and could do so again.

Earlier I made it clear that the concept of education which informed the thought of Moberly, which played an important part in shaping the new universities in the 1960s and which was still influential in the Robbins outlook, took it for granted that higher education had a holistic and organic, as well as an instrumental, character.

The direction in which we have been going in the last two decades, under financial pressures growing more and more severe, and governmental directives more and more compelling, may produce for us thousands and thousands of graduates able to solve technical problems disinterestedly. But they may well regard larger questions which cannot be made into technical ones as if they were quite marginal. Such refusal to face the truth could, I suggest, in the long run destroy not merely the university and higher education but, essentially, humankind itself.

A Diagnosis

Introduction

One of the most fundamental of all the insights which came to 20th century thinkers was published in a very obscure place as early as 1916. It was in a journal with a tiny circulation called *The New Age* in February of that year that these words from T. E. Hulme's *Notebook* first appeared: "In order to understand a period", he says, "it is necessary not so much to be acquainted with its more defined opinions as with the doctrines which are thought of not as doctrines but as FACTS. (The moderns, for example, do not look for their belief in Progress as an opinion, but merely as a recognition of fact.) There are certain doctrines which for a particular period seem not doctrines but inevitable categories of the human mind. Men do not look on them much as correct opinions, for they have become so much a part of the mind, and lie so far back, that they are never really conscious of them at all. They do not see them, but other things *through* them."[51]

A recognition of the influence upon us all the time of presuppositions we have imbibed, without in the least knowing it, underlies much of what follows. Our debt to what we take for granted is immense – not only in regard to our physical existence (for example, that we have two legs, not four; that night inevitably follows day; winter, summer) – but to the mental and spiritual climate whose air, as it were, we have no choice but to breathe. The period we are alive in today has many secret influences over us, some of them hard for us to recognise however hard we try, some of them quite impossible to recognise.

This chapter will be divided into four parts. First, a short historical recap of where we in the West have come from doctrinally and ideologically in the last few hundred years. Second, thoughts on some of the background influences which, mostly without our awareness of the debt we owe to them, have come to affect the education we can give to those now largely regarded as consumers of it: children, adolescents, but particularly the many now going on into higher education. Third, reflections upon the consumer ideology which energises and impels the globalisation movement of which we hear so much. Is escape from this even possible? What hope is given for such an escape by the arrival of post-modernism and the presuppositions it brings with it? Fourth, an outline of where I think the frontier now lies, both for society and the individual, between what may roughly be called belief in the human spirit and loss of such belief.

I

First, then, the background question. Where in the last few centuries has our society come from? For, as Nicholas Boyle[52] suggests in his penetrating book *Who Are We Now?*, we can be helped in answering it by looking back at our past with as much understanding as possible. It may be harder for us in the West today than perhaps it still is for the inhabitants of Islam to imagine ourselves back in a medieval world where individualism mattered such a lot less, in which the community exerted so much control over what one believed, in which the existence and influence of God were taken almost completely for granted – with Church more powerful than State. A Catholic *type* of religion, Christian or not, Muslim or whatever, seeks to sanctify all aspects of the life both of the individual and the community – eating, drinking, religious observances, sex, the passage of the seasons (Lent or Ramadan), welfare and war.[53] The Renaissance brought with it a new emphasis on the *individual*; and the Reformation, which it made possible, brought to many a conviction that one could have a direct relation to God. A personal faith indeed was essential to salvation: the church and the community no longer had final authority; individuals, guided by scripture, could and should stand on their own feet. The Enlightenment movement of the 18th century in Europe, inheriting the mental climate which such trust in independence brought with it, vastly encouraged individuals to explore, to analyse the world they lived in, to question without fear whether God existed at all, and if He did or didn't whether belief in Him mattered all that much. One was free to eat and drink even (if one wanted) to be merry – and what a relief! But too much merriment was frowned on. For the legacy left by the seriousness and conscientiousness for which both Catholic and Protestant traditions had stood, found a new home in widespreading assumption that progress was what was called for – a progress in welfare, for instance, would bring with it better health, longer life, more comfort. But it had to be earned – earned by concentration of mind, by courage, hard work, initiative and enterprise – maybe to the near exclusion of a life of feeling. These were all qualities which, in Britain, the Victorian age, and to a considerable extent its immediate successor, exemplified. People largely believed in morality, whether they had or had not much use for religion.

It was not until comparatively recently that this mental climate began slowly to give way to another. Social climates do not change rapidly. The one at any time currently predominant goes on being interpenetrated by its predecessor. No past period indeed has ceased altogether to exert an influence, however small and diminishing, on all its successors. The post-modern age which we may be coming to live in has lost a lot of the conviction its predecessor had in the Victorian virtues; it is not so sure that material progress, though likely to continue on large scale, is going to bring great happiness to humanity; it is not so certain that knowledge or conviction or even belief in oneself are unmitigated goods. We must learn to live in a world full of uncertainties with questions which can never be answered, hopes that can never be realised. Is post-modernism a sort of sun-lit cloud which the winds will quite soon blow away? Maybe it is; but the effect of the sunshine and the rain it has already brought with it seem likely to have fertilising effects which are going to be felt for some time ahead.

II

The content, kind and quality of the education we shall find possible to give our children in any period must be influenced by the presuppositions affecting the outlook and climate of that period. We do not see these, we see things *through* them. The formal institutions we provide and look upon as responsible for training the young are of course only some of the sources from which they will be receiving an education. That will have begun long before they enter any school – which particular language they learn to speak, the range of their vocabulary within it, the accent in which they speak it, are intimately part of the education they will be receiving, long before the age of three, from home, TV and their friends. But their presuppositions, the selection of their prejudices, their standards of morals and behaviour will also be in daily process of being acquired with nobody very conscious that this is so. Which of the following will they have come to take for granted today by the age of five and which of them not? – electric light, mobile telephones, pop music, cars, travel by plane, *The Sun* or *The Times* as a daily paper, the inside of a church? One could go on with the list almost indefinitely. And though the school can use the material which this environment and a collectivity of attitudes provide, its actual control over such material is quite limited. Literacy and numeracy can of course be vastly improved by deliberate manoeuvres perseveringly employed. It is far more difficult to eliminate racial prejudice, to suggest in what ways Sunday could be, or even used to be, a different sort of day feeling-wise from Saturday. And it is quite impossible not to be carried along with the stream of technical advance on which we all float. To foster expectation is among the most potent of educational tools. But we have largely to fit in with the *kind* of expectations alive within our period. The other day I saw a little girl of seven or so busily tapping the keys of the computer in the local library to find the information she wanted. We've no choice but to accustom children to live with the computers and the internet, to absorb the idea that success in competitive examinations matters, whether or not they can pass in them, that in due course earning big enough money to buy not merely healthy food is OK but hopefully a bike, a motorbike, a car.

Throughout large parts of the world, from the far West to the far East, the enormous influence of ideals of material success is not to be doubted. Prosperity matters: attaining the level of wealth required to service our consumption of products. And if to secure this state of affairs we need many people of enterprise, inventiveness, trained technical expertise, we must see to it that our educational system provides them for us. The managers, the professionals, the technicians, those who can repair the complex aircraft engines, hi-fi sets, computers, when they go wrong – these are indispensable and needed not merely in greater numbers from our technically equipped young but from a fast-increasing proportion of the total. Not to produce them would mean a rapid descent in the league table for any country – but, more importantly, a rapid descent in the power it could exercise. Maybe that doesn't matter – but at least self-respect, national and personal confidence, ability to hold the head up, suggest that it may.

There is little doubt that the most powerful nation in the world, at any rate for the time being, is the USA. And the one which has in the past half-century been most effective in lighting within the western mind presuppositions regarding the immense importance of material success, of wealth and of a forward-looking technology. There is a constellation of reasons to account for the current dominance of the USA. One of them is a temper of mind owing something to the mental attitudes of the Pilgrim Fathers centuries ago and to the Calvinist streaks within Puritanism. For Calvinism was by and large "pro-wealth and anti-luxury". Hard work leading to achievement and increased prosperity was much approved by those early settlers – and it is a combination still thought rather well of by big business in the States.

The debt owed to the USA by our formal system of education at all stages has increased by leaps and bounds in the last 30 years: its example has influenced both the direction and pace of the development in our school and higher education systems. Defining one's short-term ends, practicality, bringing the analytic mind to bear on problems – these are among the necessities which pragmatic America emphasises.

It is the influence of the US example and mentality, particularly upon the development of higher education over here since 1980 or so, to which I want now to draw attention. Among the people who affected more than most the quickening of change in the direction in which higher education in the USA was already very definitely going was Clark Kerr. His seminal little book *The Uses of the University* was published in 1972. Clark, who is still alive, was perhaps the greatest leader which the enormous University of California has had. Today it is a rival to Harvard in a way it certainly was not 40 years ago. In the mid-20th century, both Harvard and the enterprising University of Chicago under Robert Hutchins had stood for a less utilitarian more human concept of what a university was for. But it is what I might call the Kerr, not the Hutchins, tradition which is triumphing.

The study of higher education – with philosophic, historical, sociological and political contributions of quality made to it – has involved over the past 25 years a number of very able American scholars – including Martin Trow, Sheldon Rothblatt, Burton Clark, to name three of the most distinguished and even, it may be, influential. But it is of course the places of higher education themselves (often consciously or unconsciously shaped by and incorporating the ideas which such authors have examined and about which they have written) that have been determining the suppositions their students come to take for granted. The immensely wealthy Business Schools of American Universities – with their close links to advanced, technically sophisticated industries – and the highly resourced American University Institutes for research into the applications of science have a potent and increasing influence world-wide. Is it not with M.I.T (founded 1861) that Cambridge University (founded in the 13th century) established in 1999 an intimate, degree-awarding, relationship?

In Britain, the example the USA has set is one of the factors that has affected not merely the enormous expansion of our higher education provision, but to an unexamined extent the intellectual and social climate of the universities, new and less new, in which a large majority of our students are now studying. The thinkers who continue to energise the policies these universities have adopted and to encourage the extension in the range of subjects they offer are often people who have been, or still are, very much within our university system themselves but with many American and international contacts. Both our present government and its predecessors – with their civil servants – have relied not merely upon such people from academia but many others direct from the business world to give them advice on policy. Jarrett, Dearing and company, however, have all been well apprised of the US, its industries and its higher education provision. Their recommendations in almost every case show that to be so.

It is of course the States and those who have graduated from its universities who are among those most responsible for the rapid and relentless evolution now taking place in most parts of the world in commerce and industry involving a vast enlargement of their technical capacities. This globalisation movement is on a massive scale. And it affects not merely the still growing dominance of the wealthy West and Far East but, more subtly, the mental attitudes of the majority of their young inhabitants. The doctrines involved "become so much a part of the mind," as Hulme said, "and lie so far back, that they are never really conscious of them at all. They do not see them, but other things *through* them."

The higher education we are providing in Britain, for nearly a third already of the 18-21 age group, is more and more being adapted to fit in with this orientation, the cost to universities and colleges for not following the trend being penal. Most however are following it readily, especially if they are ambitious. Their applied Departments in many fields flourish – their newly developed Business Schools are immensely popular and expanding fast. Their Theology and Philosophy Departments are today minor parts in most of those universities which still have them. Many of our new universities have neither.

Finance has started to pour in for the creation of regional "centres of enterprise" in our country, with universities encouraged to play a vital part in their development. (Bristol University, for example, was in 2000 granted an extra £2,600,000 to forward the work of such a centre.)

Much of all this is of course to the national and our personal benefit. But the inbuilt emphasis on material prosperity, including the concentration on research which promises to yield a relatively early "pay off", has far reaching consequences.

III

The globalisation movement to which I have referred essentially belongs to an age of confidence, of one which firmly believes in progress. Without the sheer self-confidence of the entrepreneurs behind the inventiveness and marketing skills of Microsoft, Ford, Kelloggs, Coca-Cola, McDonalds and a score of other firms, it would have got nowhere. They rejoice in being modern, practical, people who face facts, hazards and problems objectively.

But increasingly, from the mid-seventies onwards, a post-modernist and post-structuralist frame of mind has been coming into the picture. Those to whose thought and writing it owes so much are typically from Europe not the USA. Lyotard, Derrida, Foucault, Lacan, are all Frenchmen. The presuppositions they voice (not entirely absent from the student demonstrations in Paris of the late sixties of the last century) are ones of disillusionment with authority, of the need to suspect mere objectivity, and too much planning at the expense of personal freedom. They want people to have the maximum degree of freedom that is possible. They have given up hope that a detached objectivity will provide us with answers to many of the questions that matter and have given up belief in most kinds of certainty. There are no absolutes. We should not look to "grand narratives" – objective systems of thought – as means of escape from the inexplicability which is inherent in life. Metaphysical explanations ("metanarratives") are to be shunned, as are pretensions of every kind. Informality in dress and in manners is to be welcomed.

We are free to believe in what we find personally satisfying, to reject creeds we don't find credible and to live as happily as we can, surrounded as we must be by uncertainties. We can take pleasure in personal relationships, in closeness rather than standoffishness, calling others by their first names at as early a stage as possible. We can take pleasure too as consumers rejoicing in the astonishing variety of commodities from which to choose in supermarkets and in the variety of experiences from which to choose in the greater supermarket which life itself offers. Such pleasures will help us to escape, to cope and to survive, even with the uncertainties that are on every side.

Such an outlook – exemplified in enthusiasm for charismatic renewal, for abolishing as many hierarchies as possible – has little confidence in the finality and so-called objectivity of science. We must learn to live in a world full of uncertainties, not pretending that we know the real and final truth about much at all, taking pleasure in being able to feel, and not only to think.

One of our foremost writers on higher education, Ronald Barnett, argues that the most important aim of the university today is teaching its students how, in a world of complexity, growing almost daily more complex, to live with uncertainty.[54] To live effectively like this calls for many virtues: courage, resilience, risk-taking, persistence, self-irony among them; but doing so is the only way in our time to retain professional competence on the one hand and personal integrity on the other.

We may have to put up with globalisation, with the spread throughout the world of a consumer ideology – with ourselves among those adopting it – but at least on occasion we can trade out personally from some of its presuppositions and consequences if we submit to a post-modernist philosophy of non-committal.

I would agree that there is much to be said in favour of a philosophy which gives scope again to the subjective, legitimises emotion, queries the goals of an endless quest for more and yet more knowledge. The degree of dependence upon uncertainties which seems to be advocated however, is, I should have thought, unlikely to satisfy for long more than part of our nature. In any case, the assumption of post-modernism that we must do without appeals to authority, do without all certainties, is not really something it quite believes itself. Are not Lyotard, Derrida and company being looked to as teachers whose words carry a lot more authority with them than those who suspect their gospel? Moreover, if people have to learn to live with uncertainties at least a desire to go on living is implied – a belief in life itself as quite certainly worthwhile. And concealed in the very quest for freedom – freedom from imprisonment in an objective world alone, freedom from being confined to formal dress and formal manners, freedom to be informal in speech and behaviour, freedom even from having to have definable, unchanging beliefs – is not there somewhere concealed in this shining quest a conviction that genuineness matters, that pretentiousness is out? Such conviction is in itself, in a subtle way, a kind of certainty.

As Brenda Watson has pointed out, it is certainty that provides the dynamic for action. "Without some kind of certainty," she says, "it is difficult if not impossible to react responsibly, or to take initiative. Doubt operating at a basic level is debilitating."[55]

IV

In fact, we just cannot do without some certainties – even if, in this 21ˢᵗ century, we must also live quite unavoidably with many uncertainties too. Humanity is not soon, perhaps ever, going to find answers to many of its problems. But at least the climate post-modernism brings with it frees us from taking it for granted that the scientific and research routes to knowledge are the only ones worth treading.

My basic doubt about the sufficiency of the assumptions of postmodernism is whether among all those uncertainties and informalities it also faces with any adequacy the existence of the realisation which may come to us at times that there are *dimensions,* or *levels,* in our experience of life. We live in a world not only of clocks, computers, events by the hundred, sleep and awakeness, but of birth, death, suffering, joy – that is of experiences which can bring us moments of depth, confronting us with certainties which are at a different level. Watching or reading *King Lear* for example may be more important to us somehow than a novel by Doris Lessing; listening to Mozart's *Requiem* more important than to *The Mikado*, unfailingly entertaining though it is.

Quite a lot of poetry, a small part of it in use in schools, has dealings with this deeper level, whether it was written by those with a religious faith or not. Was Shakespeare a believer? No one knows. Hardy certainly was not. Perhaps Paul Celan, obsessed with death, hardest to understand perhaps of all the difficult 20th century poets, retained remnants of a Jewish faith, but if so it was no orthodox one. Seamus Heaney, yes, but he remains a very secular sort of Catholic.

All these however were, at least occasionally, on the side of the frontier which divides them from those who find living a life without much meaning enough for them. George Steiner in the last pages of his autobiography, written in his formidably articulate style, adumbrates his defence of his belief in the transcendental. Agnostic though he is, he is sure that a non-empirical dimension to reality exists. Evidence for what he calls a "God presence" is profoundly there in the work not merely of Augustine or Dante but of Plato, Pascal, Kant,

Tolstoy and Dostoevsky. The level at which logic and argument are carried on is therefore not the only level with which education or life should be concerned. "The often unexamined arrogance of reason," Steiner says, "notably in the sciences, seems to cut off ascertainable experience from what may be essential. It is to know everything but to know nothing else."[56] If there were no Bach, no Beethoven, no Michelangelo, the deprivation would leave "the greater part of our civilisation vacant".[57] So there is little doubt on which side of what I have called the frontier Steiner would put himself.

I do not think that the boundary of such a frontier runs today between churchgoers and non-churchgoers, those who repeat a creed and those who would hesitate – but rather between those who have inklings at times that there is some sort of meaning to human life and those not concerned with such matters. This is not to say that I regard having a religious faith, with doctrines which are basic to it, as unimportant, holiness and worship as dispensable items for very many who are on the Steiner side of the frontier. Today, perhaps because of the very spread of consumerism and the secularisation which tends to go with it, there has been a revival in many countries of religious adherence in opposition to those advancing threats. The passion and the strength of an ardent fundamentalism, whether in Christian, Muslim, Jewish or Hindu territories, are obvious. But the use of appeals to unreason, to the miraculous, to support for campaigns semi-military or military in nature, only too often, too soon, activates anti-spiritual, primitive, low-level states of mind in those fundamentalists involved, whether they started from a higher level or not.

The state of Christianity and the churches in this country today pretty clearly shows that the presuppositions of post-modernism are exerting their influence. There is plenty of evidence that both the uncertainties and the certainties still depended upon underneath them are powerful.

It may be that in coming centuries Christianity will not find itself best conveyed through the credal statements regularly repeated in many places of worship, though by no means all, today. But the faith in God and in humanity which is so intimately a part of Christianity is more than a matter of external interest, more than an evanescent, subjectively felt, affection of the heart.

I have already said something about the differences of *level* at which we have to live our lives. Our deepest insights, if they should come, may be followed immediately by the need to attend to some quite minor matters. Living at one level is no substitute for doing so at several.

One of the greatest passages in literature comes, as you will know, towards the end of Shakespeare's *Lear*, where the King enters with Cordelia – the incarnation of all goodness, all virginity, the feminine itself – dead in his arms. The "never", five times repeated, which he utters is a lament for the mortality of us all, and also for the removal of all meaning from life, all that makes it worth living or enduring.

But those "nevers" are followed by "Pray you undo this button" – most mundane of requests for a tiny technical deed. All our modern technology, compared with our high moments, is in a way an undoing of buttons – though now it is usually a matter of pressing, rather than undoing, them. But the level at which men and women tap the keys of their computers or attend to the firing of a rocket into space from Cape Canaveral makes no spiritual demand upon them, as does Lear's admission of the reality of death. And death is a matter which curiously the post-modernists barely mention.

We may have to wait, or hope, for a different set of presuppositions through which to see the universe we live in from those which post-modernism grants us. For the assumptions that subjective experiences, however deeply penetrating, are the most we can ask for, that there is no philosophy which can hold them together, no resurrection of body or spirit, no tradition of fundamental beliefs we can draw upon or trust, are in the long run questionable, less than satisfying, assumptions.

Doubt Versus Belief – Now

I

Today very many have abandoned belief in God – sometimes with regret, sometimes with pride, often with a touch of both. Of these some have lost their faith gently, hardly knowing they have done so. And there are great numbers who never had a faith to lose.

Loss of faith in God, or, as Adrian Hastings says, "something more ultimate than ourselves", "something we cannot alter", tends to be accompanied by a loss of certainty that anything in human life matters quite essentially. Can we go on any longer believing that there are saints or heroes? Aren't heroism and holiness at bottom just sadly misjudged illusions? It may well be that in the last resort there is nothing which has meaning.

Losing faith in God and losing certainty that life itself has any great meaning or significance may perhaps be inextricably linked – though we can of course easily help ourselves to forget that we lack anything fundamental and try to escape, even with superficial parts of ourselves, into money-making, fun, the excitements and pains of sex, into drink or drugs, into intense competitive effort, into sheer, interesting, technological professionalism.

But why such a widespread turning away from belief? There is a multitude of causes, and hope of a return to believing depends upon our finding answers – and counters – to some of the more important. For more than 200 years now a temper of mind has been growing in its dominance over us which looks upon objective facts as the only realities, the only things to be trusted absolutely. The quest for them can fascinate certainly – and point a way ahead. For immense numbers of facts about the universe and its behaviour, about our own bodies and minds, in fact everything finite, remains to be discovered. The quest can be exciting: as yet we may know comparatively little, but with resolution and research (aided by the new intriguingly sophisticated instruments putting themselves almost every month at our disposal) we shall be able to conquer more and more knowledge about how everything works. So the best way forward for rational human beings would seem to be the way of intelligently applied brain power – a way indeed which we have been following already with splendid success. Following it has already brought us longer life, better health, more leisure, ability to travel faster and faster, more interesting food and drink, a greater chance of a peaceful death. This is the way forward sought by those who think they are sensible enough and clever enough to recognise a fact when they see it and detached enough to take it objectively, and thus properly, into account.

Such a temper of mind certainly tends to be unfriendly to religious conviction: for religion often seems to fly in the face of facts. The very existence of a supernatural God cannot be proved; and belief in so hypothetical a being can seem at best superfluous. Isn't such believing simply self-interested, even culpable, self-deception – a distraction, escapist?

An additional cause for the turning away from religion, at any rate in the West, is the progress made, particularly in the last 100 years, of a critical approach to the contents both of the Bible and the scriptures of other religions too. The inconsistencies in these writings have shown up the credulity of those who, writing long ago, mistook myth for truth and legend for history. For who now, to look at the gospel records only, can really believe in a star guiding men – wise or not – to any exact location? Or water being changed into wine in the twinkle of an eye? Or the birth of a child inheriting no genes from a human father? Most people today don't read the Bible anyway. Such authority as it once may have had seems to have been undercut. They do not any longer look for a lead from such a source.

A third factor in the decline of faith is different in kind. Because the world in which we live is now so busy, so noisy, so full of things to attend to, to actuate, to listen to, times of quiet in which we might come to know ourselves are simply not to be had.. The very kind of concentration which manipulating instruments demands, is alien to the kind of attention an inward glance calls for. And a media world filled with happenings and confrontations one after another is an antidote to quietness.

Alienation from religion in the time immediately ahead may be encouraged further by the permeation of post-modernist lack of hope. At first sight post-modernism, with its teaching that objectivity is a myth, its call to everyone to make use of his or her own kind of freedom, seems at odds with the trust in sheer fact and resolute logic which has been one of the main factors in causing a decline in religious belief. That may seem so. But though it queries some of the certainties of science, post-modernism is at least equally unfriendly to the presuppositions of religion. To the post-modernist, endlessly waiting for Godot, there are no absolutes whatever. To escape from despair every society may well have to indulge in fictions and fancies. Freedom to choose between art forms, religions, architectural styles and a succession of partners to live with is ours. The world itself is in some ways a great supermarket. We can get along and live lives that are interesting enough without God and we can help others of all races to do the same. Humanity anyway is left with no long-term future and no hopes except those it invents for itself. All this contributes to the collapse of any truly credible, trustworthy, authority, not least in religion.

II

It is clear enough then that the widespread decline of religious faith today has a variety of causes. I have mentioned some of the more influential. It is not going to be possible to counter any of them effectively for long by the simple preaching of a gospel. Nothing is going to be effective which does not take into account the deep presuppositions which inform and motivate those who don't believe that a God exists and are convinced that religious belief is a deception. What can be said in reply?

One of the presuppositions to be challenged is that the evidence provided by our senses is an adequate guide to the real nature of things. Why should anyone suppose that human beings have anything like all the equipment to be sure that there really is nothing outside the range of our senses and powers of mind? Does not the utter lack of humility in such a stance, once we look it in the face, rather take the breath away? We are in fact very finite creatures, dependent for our apprehensions upon the data given us by the small range of senses we possess. We have five of them – sight, hearing, touch, taste, smell. Why assume that no being could conceivably have eight, nine or ten? Even some animals and many species of bird seem to be equipped with powers of finding their way not dependent upon the senses they possess in common with ourselves.

Our limitations, however, are not only in the range of our senses. We cannot conceive of time except in limited ways. We find it impossible even to conceive of years passing or events occurring except within a sequence; language itself for us is a succession of words, sentences and paragraphs, and music we largely apprehend as a succession of notes, phrases and movements. We have a word for eternity, but conceptualising it is beyond us. Space we visualise three-dimensionally; it seems to us largely nonsense to suggest that it may have other dimensions. Certainly we can't visualise them. Our capacity for remembering events and experiences is limited. No one can recollect even the experiences of high significance he or she had in the first months of life. Our limitations of sense and of imaginative capacity may have in the main simply to be accepted. But it is far from easy to bear in mind how intimately and actively they are parts of us.

Besides such inbuilt limitations of sensing and conceptualising, there are others of sheer intelligence. Those who believe that it is possible to measure intellectual ability take the average human IQ as 100. On this scale the most "intelligent" beings can score 160. (Richard Dawkins may perhaps even score 170!) But on any scale a score of 300 is unimaginable. Does that imply, however, that no other creature could conceivably exist and be so gifted? We live on an earth which is part of a universe whose extent and size are immeasurably beyond our apprehension. For all we know there may be other universes than "ours", distinct from all the stars and suns and nebulae whose existence we know of. Indeed many astronomers today think this probable.

What are we to make of a creative energy so stupendous both in space and time that the light from even some of the stars we can see was emitted by them two billion years ago? Such immensity of originative power is not necessarily to be attributed to a God who can – or should

– be worshipped. Additional and very different considerations would need to be brought into the reckoning for that to be the case. But what the implications are of the very existence of energy at this potential we can realise only with the greatest vagueness.

It is not though only our ability to look outside ourselves, whether near at hand or incredibly far away, that is limited, but our capacity to look within. The mixture of our own motives can fox us with the utmost ease. Even some of the ablest of human beings – including scientists, economists, highly enterprising men of business – have been curiously lacking in self-knowledge. The depth to which most of us can delve with any confidence into our unconscious minds is not great.

In the light of these ignorances and many others, I would have thought that immense humility was called for in our attempts to probe and understand creation. We shall certainly not be able to discover, whether by reason or revelation, more than some of the truth either about the universe far outside or that far within ourselves, maybe cannot as yet even begin to recognise some of the clues. The presupposition of contemporary secular man that facts and reason are, or ever can be, sufficient keys to understanding the universe, let alone the meaning and purpose of human life, is wide open to question.

But even though the capacity of our senses and minds is so limited, no one's life is really as confined by what fact and objective knowledge convey as is now so often presupposed. Do we not need to pay greater attention to the significance of experiences which come home to us, freeing our spirits, taking us inside life as it were instead of leaving us its observers only? Music can do this for some of us. So can the beauty and terror of nature. So can love. The love of parent for child is not quantifiable, is often simply taken for granted, but can be of incalculable influence – the love of man for woman and of woman for man can be profoundly seminal in both senses. Meaning when it comes always seems to do so as something experienced. We may observe acts of courage, acts of sheer unselfishness, but they will have meaning for us only if we can enter into them imaginatively and see that they are not simply ways in which somebody is behaving. They are of course that too. There is always an outside as well as an inside to human action. There is truth of fact and truth of experience.

Truths of fact can frequently be tested by measurement; experiments of a scientific kind can often be repeated more or less exactly time after time and observations made that are verifiable because this is the case. An experiment is as it were an event which can be controlled. But personal experiences are not under such control; quite often they are not exactly repeatable at all. Meaning is not to be commanded and does not come when you do call for it.

A life without flavour, without depths and shallows, one that is a mere series of unfelt happenings would indeed be a life without meaning. Any understanding of life that is adequate must take into account experience and experiences which involve emotion. A concept of reason and the reasonable which does not do this lacks a dimension. Granted it may sometimes be difficult, even impossible, to judge the worth of an experience, even how deeply it really moved us, does not deprive it of truth. Some experiences can be transforming – though it may be a long while after they happened before this becomes apparent, if it ever does. A death, a sorrow, a failure, may educate us and do so profoundly. Nor are these experiences whose truth is to be denied, but it is a truth not arrived at by calculation or even to be put into words.

So far I have been contending that the loss of faith in religion which is so widespread in our time may in part have come about through two types of presupposition, both of them defective: (i) our over-confidence in the sufficiency of the evidence yielded to us by our five senses and powers of deduction, and (ii) our under-confidence in the profound truths which living itself can yield to us.

I do not contend for a moment that we can live without presuppositions, but those which dominate our secular society are far from capacious enough. Their dominance inhibits the development of parts of our nature which ought to be allowed scope. But even if the prevalence of the two types of inadequate presupposition with which I have been dealing does go some way to account for our loss of religious faith, it does not follow that regaining such faith is desirable even if it were possible. What would make it desirable?

In the past religion has been within communities a binding force of immense strength – whether for good or evil. A taken-for-granted religious faith gave the majority of people confidence that there was a fundamental coherence and a final meaning in things. Believing and belonging went so closely together that it was often impossible to separate them. For the sake of a sure sense that they belonged to an animated, spiritually encompassing world, men and women endured sufferings beyond description; many were slowly burnt alive at a burning stake.

Can a society remain human, even survive for long at all, in which no one is willing to go to a stake about anything, in which all who belong to it believe only in success – and having fun? Is a society with no religious beliefs sustainable in times of long continued suffering or failure? I wonder. Certainly the immense progress which has been made in the past half-century in providing comforts, technical services, even welfare, does not seem either in the West or east to have brought happiness or contentment with it. Indeed Japan, where such progress has perhaps gone furthest, appears to have a higher incidence of mental illness than almost any country for which statistics are available, and in the USA the growth of dependence on drugs of so many of its citizens could threaten its very future.

But what now can give us again a faith at depth in a religion which has profundity and the hope which might spring from it? It is not going to be possible to understand or get inside a religious faith without escaping from some presuppositions which may inhibit us and are pretty pervasive within us largely without our realising that that is so. And this may well involve an alteration of viewpoint almost impossibly hard for us to make, a rediscovery or new discovery of ourselves which cannot be made wholly in detachment – though detachment will be needed to examine with some rigour the new convictions we arrive at.

A religious faith which will stand the test is one that is open and able to cope with truth shot at it from any direction, with suffering and dread, with injustice, with failure, with the inexplicable. Our feelings of awe at the sight of the stupendous in nature – giant seas, majestic mountains, vast cloud-tossed skies – are not ones we often mention. Yet they are real to most of us. We need to acknowledge the fact and that to each of us life itself and birth and death have insoluble mystery about them. Religions at least try to accept these things. That is why they all put to question the adequacy of an outlook which only includes a limited range of our actual experience and which discounts those sensings of "something far more deeply interfused" which come momentarily to so many of us. We all, I suspect, know very much more than we say or may even be conscious of. Faith of a religious kind is in some ways less, not more, escapist than a secular one.

We have to come to terms with the knowledge that our experiences of awe, beauty, love, the promptings of conscience and of the inward light are real; and we must take them into account and take into account the dimension of depth they open up for us.

Clearly, whether we grow up more favourably inclined to secularism or to religious belief will depend to a large extent upon the society, and particularly the social group within it, to which whether consciously or not we feel we belong. And clearly, too, it isn't going to be easy for us, however clever we are, to be as critical as we might wish of the adequacy of what we are taking for granted.

In the Christian tradition God is seen not only as a professional, as it were concerned with the making of worlds and universes outside us, but as a person, concerned with the making of us from within. There does come to many believers occasionally a conviction, fleeting, evanescent perhaps but not to be doubted, that there is a light within us to be trusted. The outcome of obedience to that trust may not be what was expected. But it will, however unexpected, if accepted in faith, lead to a conclusion whose rightness may later become clear. "And he went out, not knowing whither he went" (Hebrews 11, v.8).

The future of humanity, its rescue from contentment with little more than a happy animal existence, is dependent, I believe, upon its having a larger faith and a longer hope than secularism and doubt are capable of providing. Sanity and truth have depths as well as surfaces.

The Challenge to Evolution

I

Can humanity evolve further? "Yes, of course" is likely to be the response. But more reflection may prompt further questions: What direction are we going in now? What control have we over it? Should we *want* to evolve further anyway?

We probably, if not certainly, do have more control in some respects over the future of humanity than any previous generation has had. Though problems remain, our technological expertise, advancing year by year, makes worldwide communication – physically, financially, informationally – increasingly rapid, easy and efficient. But as individuals or as societies we seem to have astonishingly limited control over the direction in which such progress is taking us. People in many countries can no doubt expect on average to live longer, with greater comfort, better health and more free time. They can expect their education to make them more literate, more numerate, than any of their predecessors – prepared to use a wider and wider variety of devices and machines skilfully: cars, refrigerators, phones, computers, TV, lasers, fibre optics, contraceptives, and many others. So that, willy nilly, the world's inhabitants, at least if they live in the more developed countries, are on the way to achieving mastery over many a situation which would a few years ago have confined, even enslaved, them. And these benefits will have been gained with hardly any effort on the part of quite a high proportion of the beneficiaries. They may have had to spend some of their money perhaps, to choose which advertisement to answer, which course of instruction to follow, and so on; but for the most part the recipients of the benefits will have been carried along by the stream – simply following what their neighbours were up to. They may hardly notice the different way in which they have come to employ their labour, the many hours that now they spend each year in their cars or in watching TV. Theoretically the way they live *is* under their control; in practice they do for the most part what has become "normal". In many respects this direction of progress, whether we have much control over it or not, seems good. But we need to take into account that one of the compulsions is to make us concentrate our minds for a higher proportion of the time than before on the acquisition and practising of techniques. For lack of such directed concentration can be disastrous – a car accident; too high a dosage; interpreting a message from a computer wrongly; simply not being aware of this, that and the other.

It may however be that the *level* at which we are thus compelled to exercise our minds for much of the time will make it more difficult for us to exercise them in a different one. The global spread of technology may make it less rather than more likely that people will even want to explore their deeper selves. It is so easy to find our leisure hours catered for with the same splendid technological ease as our working ones are – with cruises, pornography, Imax films, competitive sports of a hundred kinds readily available. We can escape with delight. And the resources of the internet are only at the beginning of their potential for giving people all over the world not only information but entertainment that is engrossing, consuming time pleasantly from childhood through to old age. If one's working life ends soon after 50, with pension and maybe a bonus provided, how indeed is one to pass the time if before retirement one has had no practice in reflection or in anything but being practical, skilful or entertained?

"Irks care the cropful bird?" asked Browning. Contentment with happiness and progress at one level may make it harder to credit that we may be sacrificing capacities at a different one and which are at least potential – capacities perhaps for insight, faithful love, unselfish hope. But these may no longer appear much called for in a world where achievement is so often thought of in terms of possession, fun or escape.

So that the question, What kind of human nature should we think of as most essentially human? tends to seem rather a nonsense question anyway. Can we preclude the possibility that the civilisation we are fostering is a meaningless emancipation? This was a question put to himself by Jurgen Habermas in his German way. "Is it possible," he went on, "that one day an emancipated human race could encounter itself within an expanded space and yet be robbed of the light in which it is capable of interpreting its life?"[58]   A world which regards truth as to be discovered only through attained mastery of some kind of technique, may regard the search for truths at a deeper level as foolish, an entertaining irrelevance – even an enemy to be conquered. Indeed it may well tend to think that even to *expect* life to have a meaning is a wrong kind of expectation.

And yet this contradicts much past human experience, the world over, involving innumerable men and women great and small. The truths with which we are bidden to be content seem to be only those of which we can be conscious. But the limits of human consciousness which Coleridge subtly referred to as "necessary to us" are very real. He pointed out the significant fact that "the furthest distance our recollection can follow back ….. never leads us to the first footmark." Some of our limitations are absolute ones. "What we cannot imagine we cannot in the proper sense of the word conceive."[59]   And he goes on to say that mysteries are neither under the direction of the reason nor in the same *plane* as it is. "The life we seek after is a mystery to us both in itself and as in its origin is the life we have."[60]

But here of course Coleridge is assuming that we *do* seek after a life that has meaning. And in our own age of complexity and supercomplexity, so much of the concentration is on the spread of technical accomplishment globally that this is more of an assumption than it used to be or was in Coleridge's day. So that if we want people to believe again that life has meaning and importance, we have somehow to break into them – to make them realise that they, actually within their own lives, know more than facts and skills and pleasures; that their moments of genuine love for wife, husband, a sexual partner, children – even if once upon a time – were drawn from some deeper level within them than facts or skills. Failure at something indeed may perhaps matter more intimately to us than success. Remorse for a crime committed or defect endured, may drive people to a deeper level of existence for a few minutes or hours. All such happenings can bring meaning with them. But of course they have to be *recognised* as mattering and to be remembered long enough to be brought into a reckoning. Something very like a surrender will have been asked for by each – a surrender not evasive of argument but which puts us into touch, however momentarily, with a dimension within ourselves which for most of the time we hardly know exists.

And if the retort of the detached observer is that this is just self-deception, he needs to consider whether there may not be an element or kind of self-deception in detachment too; to realise that every mind, including his own, depends all the time on a vitality and spirit which is far from detached and a prime, primitive, source. For primitive here does not mean jejeune, but fundamental – basic to our ability to discern and understand. Coleridge, in touch on occasion with his unconscious mind more profoundly than most of us ever are with ours, remarked that in matters of such discernment "to believe and understand are not diverse things but the same thing in different periods of its growth."[61]

In fact unless we do believe in life in some real way, in spite of our escapes into work and leisure, we cannot go on living at all – entirely unconscious though that belief may be. The fact is that we are all inside life, not only observers of it, and the world is outside us however clever our observation of it. Indeed to realise the meaning of many of the observations we make of it does actually call almost moment by moment, without our being aware of the matter, for reference to our knowledge of what it is *like* to be alive – reference, for example, to our intimate knowledge that listening intently is different from listening casually, that trusting people is quite different from observing them detachedly, that conformity is not the same as allegiance, that hope can utterly transform an outlook. A world made up of outsides only would be one cut off from meaning.

II

Whether or not humanity evolves further or only progresses in affluence and technical achievement is very much an open question. While such progress gives us much we should be grateful for and is to be welcomed, the evolution of humanity to a new stage of understanding and self-understanding may not happen unless something more central within human beings becomes more involved.

And within the next 50, 100, 300 years we are going to become – perhaps by leaps and bounds – able to control our choice over what kind of descendants to have to a far greater extent than we can now, and this whether or not the cloning of human beings is permitted in any or every country or in none. For the desirability is obvious to many people that a higher proportion of children should inherit genes which offer them a hundred advantages mental and physical. This has only been brought about so far in a random way – e.g. the tendency of intelligent men and women to marry others of roughly equal intelligence; of some physically adventurous people to mate with others with a fairly similar degree of physical adventurousness. But the greater our knowledge becomes of how to prophesy with a fair degree of certainty the attributes of our successors, the greater our already fast-increasing control over conception, the greater becomes humanity's freedom to choose what kinds of human beings to propagate.

If we are going not merely to have within our control growth of our descendants from babyhood onwards but increasingly to be able, before they are born, to determine to a considerable extent the kind of human nature they are likely to develop, what qualities should we most want them to have? Without doubt we shall wish to breed children who will become men and women of high intelligence, heterosexually inclined, having genes which endue them with a reasonably good chance of a long life. But how important are sensitivity, introspection, capacity for sympathy, ability to love, ability to imagine, spirituality? Such choices – and at least some control over predispositions to them may probably be awaiting us – involve a philosophy of life, ideas about the qualities of the human race we would like to see not merely progressing but evolving.

The choice before us whether or not humanity is to evolve in capacity to understand, to enter deep places in life, rather than remain contentedly and somehow innocently in the shallows, is, I suggest, a real one. No one who has loved has any doubt that love is deeper than liking; no one to whom the profoundest music of Bach brings meaning has any doubt that its appeal is at a different level from that of a Gilbert and Sullivan opera, however entrancing.

Whether we *want* to evolve as well as progress may be the question. The greater the number of options humanity has, however, the greater the need for deep sources for guidance in choosing between these options if it is to evolve as well as to progress..

III

Religious and, in particular Christian, traditions have much to offer by way of guidance. We may indeed catch ourselves out interestingly by finding that we regard some of the latter as more Christian than others. In essence Christianity teaches, as David Jenkins has emphasised, that God is as He is in Jesus. But it is a Jesus conveyed to our understanding by a Spirit which selectively interprets the gospels and teaches those who listen more and more of the real meaning of his birth, ministry on earth and death.

The objectivity of God in Christian belief is of one who in Rowan Williams's words, "does not compete, with whom I don't and can't bargain" ... who "is neither created nor extinguished by our own will".[62] There is an ultimacy about such a Being, faith in whom cannot be held at a superficial level, only at a number of deeper ones which call for attention and silence; and, if that faith is to be held with profundity, perhaps for holiness as well. Something like this may well be true for many advanced religions as well as for the Christian. And most carry with them an important element of accountability for those who seek and find the truths they contain – accountability for conduct, for a moral way of life, not only for belief.[63]

Such fundamental accountability is not really much called for in our post-modernist, leisure-dominated society, with its manufactured concepts of what maturity means – though an awareness is growing that we all have responsibility in some degree for the future of the natural environment both in its high atmosphere and on the ground. But most people have no really deep conviction about the matter and anyway limit their conception of the environment we live in largely to a physical rather than a mental one. So that Walter Benjamin's observation remains largely true: "The construction of life is at present in the power of facts far more than of convictions, and of such facts as have scarcely ever become the basis of convictions."[64]

Immanuel Kant, in a famous and very personal passage near the end of his *Critique of Pure Reason*, wrote: "Two things fill the mind with ever increasing wonder and awe, the more intensely the mind of thought is drawn to them: the starry heavens above me and the moral law within me."[65] The existence of neither is due to ourselves but our civilisation depends upon both of them – and depends intimately. There is widespread conviction in the developed world that justice is one of the fundamentals and that awe and beauty are of profound – unsought – importance. And none of these belongs to a realm that is only utilitarian – or indeed progressive. If humanity is to evolve further, as well as to progress, it has to accept the reality of that realm's eternal existence and reckon increasingly with the significance of the fact.

It is not uncommon in our time for people who early in their careers have been "successful" to find life already growing stale. And the excitements, the thrills, the plays, the concerts which refresh them do not solve the dilemma. It may indeed not be soluble at the level which progress demands – any amount of progress, progress going on and on far into the future. Nothing may be the answer save an evolution which demands a deeper involvement in life, a more resolute facing of truths than success or progress require. What may be needed are explorations of spirit and holdings of belief at a level with which progress is not concerned, for which it does not ask.

A Modern Samaritan

If in heaven rejoice the redeemed and good,
The forgiven, the saints – but not dear you
Shall I even want to go there much?
It was *you* who understood.

Understood and entered profound and whole
Into my loneliness and grief
For friends new lost and vanished hopes
Gave me deep of yourself, restored my soul.

Yet you, unbaptised, unaware
Of God within you or without –
How can it be that you should bring
A message from Him, one I'd share?

A Comment on A Modern Samaritan:

Among the implications of these verses may perhaps be:

i) the one to whom the experience has come which is the subject of the poem has been open to receive it as meaningful;

ii) he or she possesses a background of traditional beliefs into which this experience can be fitted;

iii) these beliefs include a faith that God exists, that He is not merely interested in human beings but approachable by them;

iv) credal statements of belief are not primary.

To generalise: An experience received with some humility by an individual or community which seems to them meaningful will in many cases also be seen to be compatible with – and fitting into – a tradition of beliefs religious in nature. The greater in its comprehensiveness and spirituality that tradition is, the fewer the experiences felt by their recipient to be meaningful will it find no place for.

It is not possible for most people whose beliefs have found a home in one religious tradition to change easily to another, enriched as both traditions may well have been over the centuries by national and family loyalties, art, architecture, music, poetry and ceremony. But this does not by any means imply that all such traditions are equally profound, equally comprehensive, willing to explore to the same extent the many dimensions of human need, equally able to evolve so as to make it possible for them to cope adequately with the human future – a future certain to change rapidly in the conditions it imposes on everyone.

Religion – Can We Do Without It?

It is tempting to think that the multiplicity of technological devices now available, with an endless stream of further ones in the offing, may enable us to live more and more richly – without need for receiving guidance other than that which self-interest and a happy autonomy provide. Experience though has already sown seeds of doubt whether we are finding the degree of happiness we had been hoping for from new amenities showered upon us. And there are not merely new but increasingly skill-backed and highly sophisticated ones – TV, video, the mobile phone, the internet, drinks, drugs, clonings and cures in amazing variety. Appetites have been raised higher and higher but for many people now it seems that they can only be placated by the provision of more and more speed, more and more comforts, a choicer variety of delicious food and drink, more cruises into the sunshine and the where-with-all to take them. All these may be very welcome but their possession somehow rarely comes up to expectation, let alone satisfies.

But if this is so, is there any hope that the direction in which we are going can be altered? Where is the guidance to come from for the painful changes which may be needed – guidance powerful enough, commanding enough, to compel?

One tentative source might conceivably be for us to look again to traditional codes, codes incorporating rules that have served our ancestors well or at least reasonably well. These do, however, seem dated and one-dimensional when what we need is guidance that is multi-dimensional, imaginative, forward-looking, which takes into account modern technology and market forces The guidance offered by straightforward, reasoned argument also seems likely to prove ineffective – for most of us far too weak in its impact. It might conceivably be that intellectuals would attend to its counsels, but few people are intellectuals anyway and even intellectuals are by no means always consistently reasonable beings.

So it may well be the case that more hope is to be found in experiences which have come to us feelingly. Joy, suffering, failure, beauty, a death, may bring us face to face with truths which matter. They can reach us embodied in music, great poetry, majestic mountains. Their reception however may require from us a certain passiveness, difficult of access in a technologically dominated world, but which we may for a few moments be compelled into almost against our will. Whether though such truths, even if realised, will be lasting in their effects and able to ensure changes in the direction of our outlook depends upon not only our receptivity on the one hand and their genuineness on the other but whether we can *recognise* their authority, see and feel them not merely as compelling but as reasonable, too. And whether we are willing to submit to change as a result of them.

Facts, scientific theories, technical accomplishments, though they must certainly be taken grippingly hold of, deal in two dimensions only: there are other dimensions to our lives than they reckon with:

> The sun has burst the sky
> Because I love you
> And the river its banks
> Far down the river ships sound their hooters
> Crazy with joy because I love you.[66]

Both facts *and* experiences are essential ingredients to vitality, to any confident understanding that there is meaning in things.

Such a discovery, if it comes, will have involved a certain humility on our part, a willingness to enter into things, even if temporarily, more deeply. Our determination to go on examining them from the outside, with objectivity and detachment, is entirely right. But that is not all. To be able to experience them from the inside as it were, is inseparable from a delight in music or art or poetry, even to knowing what they are about. They are not mere arrangements, however pretty, of words or paint or notes, but records of their creator's experience and invitations to share it.

Now I would contend that it is in this field that religion operates, particularly the one I know best, Christianity. The things which are important in the Biblical narrative are often, in fact usually, the outcome of experiences which have come to this prophet or that, to

Hosea, to Job, to a psalmist, to Jesus, to Peter, to Paul – though their meaning, however creative the guidance it gives, is by no means always immediately clear to their recipient. And one suspects that their effect could be evanescent unless added to a body of beliefs already held, whether unconsciously or not, within the mind of the one receiving them.

Experiences are organic in their nature, begotten not made, having, if they are deep, the potential to energise and re-orientate the recipient whether it be an individual or a whole society. But this may only be, provided that they are able to put that individual or society intimately into touch with a warm tradition of belief, capacious and profound enough to be able to incorporate them. (As Wittgenstein pointed out in his *Culture and Value*, wisdom is cold: you can no more use it for setting life to rights than you can forge iron when it is cold.)

But traditions of the kind of which I have been speaking will not, if they are vital, be closed-up bodies of once-upon-a-time truths but able to grow, now slowly, now faster, fed century after century by the insights and experiences of living beings. In the past, many have contributed tellingly to such inheritances, not always in ways limited by creeds externally imposed. So in the case of Christianity have thinkers and doers from Paul onwards, some of them not even members of a church. Today we live at a time when an evolution in the Christian tradition may be needed, creative incorporations made within it so that newly perceived truths by a society more and more expertly equipped technically can be included – truths both about the universe and about human beings.

Who knows whether the churches will be adequate to create in our society a sufficient responsiveness to so ongoing a tradition? Or that a more responsive society will succeed in gaining from a vital Christianity in evolution the guidance and direction it so imperatively needs? If a Christian faith is to remain acceptable and personal it must be one which takes into account everything science can find out about how things work, the outcomes as they become available of many of the new probes and instruments for our use with which science provides us. But it must also draw daily upon the joys, the sufferings, the hopes, the loves, the fears our lives actually bring us. Without hope and love children shrivel; but so do adults, so do societies. I wonder whether, over the generations, we can continue to be, and develop as, human beings without the unconquered stability which faith in something far greater than ourselves makes possible.

When belief in a religion – or faith in God – reaches a low ebb the civilisation of which it formed a part comes under threat. A vital dimension has been removed from it. Can a substitute equal in its permeating power be found? Is there any way in which the disintegration of the culture once penetratingly informed by religious belief can be prevented when that belief has been lost? Can its unity be preserved? its sense of long-term purpose? its hierarchy of values?

It may be argued with point that in past centuries there was a good deal of merely exterior conformity even if religious adherences were so widespread – and much less real and interior belief than appeared. And this is surely probable: it seems unlikely that there was for instance among the majority any great understanding of the doctrines encapsulated in the creeds they obediently repeated if and when they went to church. But this does not mean that a high proportion were without faith implicit somewhere deep within them that God existed, that Christian values were right ones, that a life after death was probable. In other words a religious dimension was embedded in the mind, even if often at a sub-conscious rather than a fully conscious level.

And to have such a dimension removed, even if gradually, seems bound to have consequences – a subtle deprivation of confidence; a search for other dependencies – success in world marketing, the lottery, sex, escape through drugs or the adoption of a new religion instead of the old.

There can, I would argue, be no adequate replacement for a profound religious faith intelligently and comprehendingly held. And if a change in the social climate threatens such a faith with disintegration, what is essential is not its abandonment but an evolution in understanding of its meaning and potential. For some Christians this may entail the sacrifice of items in a creed which they are reluctant to part with; giving up membership of a church whose services have lost their potency. It may involve following unafraid the leading given to them by some of their moments of insight – though this will still need testing by common sense. What it will certainly not entail is ceasing to love one's fellows whatever their own loss of religious faith; or imagining that an analytical frame of mind by itself is ever going to yield answers that satisfy.

If this is a Christian faith, entering into it so as to discover something of the central permanencies within it will be a *sine qua non* if it is to go on bearing fruit either for individuals or societies. The guidance it can offer will involve sharing in at least some of its essential tenets and perceptions – among them those of a God who has standards and the immensely creative power of love and forgiveness. It may indeed well be that the mental probity and the control over our social future which are so necessary to us are only compatible with Christian beliefs if there is a continuing evolution in our understanding of all three.

The central message of Christianity itself is that God, creator of the universe and all things, shares in their life from the inside. He lives within all human beings, did so long before the coming of Christ and will go on doing it. In the life and death of Jesus, so Christians believe, He was manifest with a directness that is unique.

To accept this to be true asks for an outlook unusual in our time. It does not, however, require us to credit Jesus and his disciples with the kinds of knowledge, factual, medical, geographical, which the limitations of their time and culture would have precluded – as the limitations of our own prevent in ourselves but which we readily accept, hardly even noticing. Jesus was, after all, a Jew living 2,000 years ago, not aware that the earth was a ball circling its sun, not aware of the very existence of Buddhism already five centuries old, taking for granted a number of the theories of his day regarding demons and evil spirits and maybe believing that the earth itself would soon be coming to an end.

His divinity lies elsewhere: in the knowledge which his own faith, holiness and dedication gave him and which eventually brought him to the realisation of his identity with the God he worshipped. So that his death on the cross became not merely the sacrifice of his life as an individual, but a revelation of God's own suffering and self-sacrifice on behalf of all humanity. There is an ultimacy about such a perception.

Humility and a certain silence can help us to accept our human finitude; to accept' too, that Christianity itself is not a rigid, complete or completed system of doctrines to be held on to. A faith that there is much beyond human limitations of mind and sense, beyond human knowledge, will help to bring us hope; to bring stability and confidence into our lives – and into the life of 21st century Britain. It could bring meaning too, a growing conviction that we are in God's hands and that we do not need to have all the answers.

Reliance upon where market forces will take us is not enough. Nor even by themselves the impulses driving us ahead in one direction or another given us by scientific exploration, music, our daily experiences of love or failure. The stability, forward-looking, directed guidance we need must spring from a deeper level which makes use of the others. And that, it seems to me, will essentially be one that is both enlightened and religious.

End Notes

1   T. S. Eliot, Burnt Norton III.
2   Later Headmaster of Tavistock G.S.; Stockport School and Hampton G.S.
3   Later Professor of Theology, Nottingham University and Dean of York.
4   Later Nobel prizewinner (Chemistry) and Chancellor of Bristol University
5   Later Professor of Education, Bristol University.
6   Later Headmaster of Lancing; Master of Marlborough and Professor of Education, Exeter University.
7   Later Headmaster of Leighton Park School.
8   Headmaster of Shrewsbury; later Lord Wolfenden and Chairman of the U.G.C.
9   Professor of Comparative Education in the University of London Institute of Education.
10   Canadian literary critic; author of *The Great Code: The Bible and Literature.*
11   Historian. Later, Lord Briggs. Vice Chancellor, Sussex University. Provost, Worcester College, Oxford.
12   Historian. Later, Lord Bullock. Master, St. Catherine's College, Oxford. Vice Chancellor, Oxford University.
13   Professor of Economics, L.S.E.
14   Historian. Later, Warden, Nuffield College, Oxford. Pro-Vice Chancellor, Oxford University.
15   *The Scope and Use of Research in Higher Education.*
16   Sir Toby. Deputy Secretary, D.E.S.
17   Cf. *Between Man and Man* (1973). For a later annotation by Buber of the same theme see his article "Distance and Relation", in the *Hibbert Journal* for January 1951, especially pp. 111-13.
18   Marcel has asked not to be called an existentialist. But that is because of the vagueness of the term, not because of any retraction of view.
19   *The Mystery of Being*, I (1950), pp. 203-4, 215.
20   Marcel: *The Philosophy of Existence* (1948), p. 5.
21   *The Mystery of Being,* I, p. 193.
22   Jaspers: *Man in the Modern Age* (1951), p. 154.
23   Jaspers: *The Perennial Scope of Philosophy* (1949), p. 172.
24   Cf. *The Mystery of Being*, I, pp. 191-6.
25   *Man in the Modern Age*, p. 47.
26   Op.cit., p. 8.
27   *Man in the Modern Age*, p. 108.
28   Ibid., p. 108.
29   *The Mystery of Being*, I, pp. 114-16.
30   Cf. for example, Coleridge's brilliant distinction between liking and love. "Liking in the highest degree never *becomes* Love. All in a moment Love starts up or leaps in and *takes the place* of liking. The same individual moment, as the expression *in* time of an act *out* of time – the same instantaneity I find in the revolutions of Religion and of Moral Conduct." (MS Egerton, 2801, f. 106. Watermark 1825).
31   *The Prelude* (1805 edition), xiii, lines 114-19.
32   See official figures given by the Postmaster General (*Hansard*, 3 Feb. 1954).
33   *Tragedy is not Enough*, p. 110.
34   As Marcel has pointed out, man has a technique against birth but none against death.
35   *The Prelude*, xii, 11, 58-9.
36   Marcel: *Being and Having* (1949), p. 134.

37   *Report of he National Committee of Enquiry into Higher Education.*
38   *Real Presences*, p. 229.
39   Cf. his essay in *Soundings*, Vol. LXIV, No. 2 (1981), pp 118-31.
40   *The Coming of Post-Industrial Society*, p. 480 (New York,1973).
41   Heller, Erich (1965) *The Artist's Journey into the Interior* (an essay on the importance of Nietzsche), p. 184.
42   Geertz, Clifford (1975) *The Interpretation of Cultures*, p. 112 (London).
43   In *It All Adds Up* (1994) pp. 96-7 (London).
44   Meadows, D. H. *et al* (1972) *The Limits to Growth* (New York).
45   Cf Becker, H. *et al.* (1968) *Making the Grade.*
46   Edward Foster, Acting President, Whitman College, Washington.
47   MacIntyre, Alasdair (1981) *After Virtue*, p. 31.
48   MacIntyre, ibid. p. 11.
49   Professor of Educational Administration, University of London Institute of Education.
50   In *Minerva* (1989) Autumn pp. 139-56.
51   Hulme, T. E. (1998) *Selected Writings* pp. 210-11.
52   Boyle, Nicholas (1998) *Who Are We Now?* Chaps. 2, 3, 4.
53   Cf. Sacks, Jonathan (1991) *The Persistence of Faith*, p.4.
54   Cf. Barnett, Ronald (1999) *The Realization of the University.*
55   Watson, B.: *Theology* (May 2000), p.189.
56   Steiner, George (1997) *Errata: An Examined Life* p.167.
57   *Ibid.*, p.163.
58   Habermas, J. (1990) on "Walter Benjamin" in *Philosophical-Political Profiles.*
59   Coleridge, S.T. *Aids to Reflection*, edited John Beer (1993) p.79.
60   *Ibid.*, p.204.
61   *Op.cit.,* p.194.
62   Williams, R. (2000) *Lost Icons: Reflections on Cultural Bereavement*, pp. 186-8.
63   Cf. MacIntyre, A. (1981) *After Virtue*, particularly pp 9-12.
64   Benjamin, W. (1979) *One Way Street*, p.48.
65   *Op.cit.* (1781) conclusion.
66   Joseph, Jenny (1992) *Selected Poems*, p.46.

Appendix
Some Writings by Roy Niblett

1933 The Disarmament of the Mind, *The Congregational Quarterly*, Vol. XI, No. 3, July, pp. 313-19

1936 Personal Belief and the Teaching of Scripture, *Religion in Education*, Vol. 3, No. 1, pp. 31-6

1937 Hazlitt Revisited, *The Congregational Quarterly*, Vol. XV, No. 3, July, pp. 337-45

—— Purpose and Belief, *Community*, Vol. 1, No. 3, November 1937, p. 29

1939 Educating for Democracy, *Community*, Vol. II, No. 9, July, pp. 102-3

—— Wordsworth and the Child, King's College Education Society, Newcastle-upon-Tyne, *Education Papers*, pp. 56-63

—— Concerning the Objective Teaching of Religious Knowledge, *Religion in Education*, Vol. 6, No. 4, pp. 191-4

1941 Education and the Future, *Community*, Vol. IV, No. 3, May, pp. 22-3

—— Hazlitt's Literary Criticism, *Durham University Journal*, Vol. XXXIII, No. 3, pp. 211-22 (New Series: Vol. II, No. 3)

—— Some Thoughts about Teaching, *The Parents' Review*, Vol. LII, No. 4, April

1942 Christian Discovery, *The Modern Churchman*, Vol. XXXII, Nos. 4, 5, 16, September, pp. 163-8

1943 Aims and Means in Religious Education, *The Modern Free Churchman*, No. 24, March, pp. 1-2

—— A Defence of Education in the Arts, *New Era*, Vol. 24, No. 4, pp. 55-8

1944 The Needs of the Child, *Durham University Journal*, Vol. XXXVII, No. 1, pp. 28-33 (New Series: Vol.VI, No.1)

—— Wordsworth's Study of Childhood, *The London Quarterly and Holborn Review*, January, pp. 44-50

1947 *Essential Education*, London: University of London Press, 100pp.

—— My Faith and My Job, *The London Quarterly and Holborn Review*, April, pp. 143-6

—— Focus in the Teaching of English, *Studies in Education*, University College, Hull, June, pp. 45-52

—— The Personal Touch, *Now*, Vol. I, No. 4, pp. 3-6

—— The Grammar School in a Changing Society. Address published by the Association of Assistant Mistresses, Yorkshire Branch

1948 Gli Sviluppi della Preparazione degli Insegnanti, in Inghilterra Dal, *I Problemi della Pedagogia*, Rome: University of Rome

1949 The Education of Understanding, *Researcher and Studies*, No. 1, December, pp. 7-12

—— University Institutes of Education and Their Function. Address to the 36th North of England Education Conference, January: Conference Report

—— The Responsibility of the University, *Fortnightly*, September, pp. 165-171

1950 The Need for a Christian Philosophy of Education, *The Modern Free Churchman*, No. 45, March, pp. 1-3

—— Co-education, *New Era*, Vol. 31, November, pp. 198-200

—— The Function of the Teacher, *Schoolmaster*, November and December, pp. 528-30, 572-3, 608-9, 633-4

—— Reading and Living, *Broadsheet of Christian Thought and Action*, No. 28, pp. 8-11

1951 The Christian Tradition and School Discipline, *Religion in Education*, Vol. 18, No. 3, pp. 86-9

—— Tendencies in Adult Education, *Fortnightly*, April, pp. 245-8

—— The Meaning of Discipline, *Schoolmaster*, Vol. 160 (New Series), October, pp. 403-5

—— Education, Conscious and Unconscious, *National Society for Art Education*, Vol. 2, No. 1, May, pp. 16-19

—— The Grammar School and Its Function, King's College Education Society, Newcastle-upon-Tyne, *Education Papers*, Vol. 7, No. 2, pp. 5-10

—— The Training of Teachers, in *Report of the 79th Meeting of the Headmasters' Conference*, 26-7 September

—— The Universities and Research: The Valuable and the Invaluable, *Universities Quarterly*, Vol. 5, No. 2, pp. 117-23

1952 Authority and Education, *Journal of Education*, Vol. 84, pp. 5-8 and 56-60

—— Education and Indoctrination, *Question*, Vol. 5, No. 1, Winter, pp. 69-84

—— The Development of British Universities Since 1945, *Year Book of Education*, London: Evans, pp. 175-6

—— Religious Education Today, *Journal of Education*, Vol. 84, pp. 506-10

—— What Are Universities For?, *Fortnightly*, No. 1023 (New Series), March, pp. 1975-6

—— The Training of Teachers in England, *Universitat und Berufsarbeit*, Königswinter

1953 Character Training and the New Education, *National Froebel Foundation Bulletin*, No. 82, pp. 2-7

—— Education and Individuality, *Educational Forum* (USA), Vol. 17, pp. 269-78

1954 *Education and the Modern Mind*, London: Faber and Faber, pp. 155

—— On Existentialism and Education, *British Journal of Educational Studies*, Vol. 1, No. 2, pp. 101-11

—— Teacher Training and the Graduate Today, *Journal of Education*, Vol. 86, No. 1014, pp. 10-12

1955 Area Training Organisations and the Serving Teacher: A Policy, a Programme and Some Questions, *A.A.M. Journal*, Vol. VI, No. 1, Spring, pp. 24-31
—— *Education – The Lost Dimension*, New York: William Sloane Associates
—— Neutrality or Profession of Faith?, in *Science and Freedom*, Proceedings of the Hamburg Congress, pp. 234-42
1956 *The Young Child and the Life of Today,* Third Margaret McMillan Lecture, University of London Press.
1957 *Residential Life in the University Today*, Report of Proceedings of Home Universities Conference, Association of Universities of the British Commonwealth, p. 14
—— *Halls of Residence*, Report of UGC Sub-Committee, London: H.M.S.O.
—— A Stranger Looks at American Education Today, *University of Leeds Review*, Vol. V, December, pp. 353-60
1958 Administrators and Independence, *British Journal of Educational Studies*, Vol. 7, No. 1, November, pp. 3-11
—— *Character Training and the New Education,* National Froebel Foundation Bulletin, No. 82
—— Ideas and Realities in Teacher Training: Three Year Teacher Training. *The Joseph Payne and Sir Philip Magnus Memorial Lectures of the College of Preceptors*. London: Methuen, pp. 36-52
—— The Liberal Arts: A British View, *Current History*, Vol. 35, No. 205, pp. 147-51
—— Some Problems Facing University Education in the West, *Education Forum*, March, pp. 315-24
—— Some Notes on a Visit to the Middle East, *University of Leeds Institute of Education Bulletin*, No. 29, November, pp. 1-4
1959 English Education and the English Character, *Education Forum*, May, pp. 453-59
1960 Can Man Stay Human? Address to Institute of Handicraft Teachers, York, April
—— *Experiment and Experience,* Tenth Annual Foundation Lecture delivered at Bretton Hall, Wakefield, 11 May
—— *Religious Education in English Schools*, Council for Christian Education in Schools, Sydney, Australia
—— Teaching Without Meeting – A Comment on Crowther, *Frontier*, Vol. 3, pp. 119-22
—— *Christian Education in a Secular Society*, London: Oxford University Press, pp. 132
1961 Objectives in Secondary Education Today (Presidential Address to the 44th Annual Conference of Educational Associations), *Education Today*, April Supplement, pp. 1-12

—— A Challenge to Christian Education, Conference on Christian Education in a Changing Africa – All Africa Churches Conference, May

—— Some Objectives in Higher Education Today (W. Australia)

1962 *Christian Education in an Open Society,* First Thicknesse Memorial Lecture, Wigan

—— *The Expanding University* (ed.), London: Faber and Faber

—— Trends in Education in England Today, *Educational Forum*, Vol. 26, No. 4, Pt.1, pp. 403-14

1963 *Education in an Acquiescent Society* (Lecture delivered in the University of Natal, Pietermaritzburg, on the occasion of the first annual ceremony for the award of diplomas and certificates in the Faculty of Education), 20 April, University of Natal Press

—— *Moral Education in a Changing Society* (ed.), London: Faber and Faber, 172pp.

—— Oxbridge and Redbrick – The Debt and the Interest, *Sociological Review* Monographs: Sociological Studies in British University Education, No. 7, University of Keele, October

1964 The Education Component in the B.Ed.. Course, *University of London Institute of Education Bulletin,* No. 4, Autumn, pp. 14-18

1965 Expansion and Traditional Values, in Reeves, M. (ed.), *Eighteen Plus – Unity and Diversity in Higher Education*, London: Faber and Faber, pp. 125-34

—— *How and Why Do We Learn?*, London: Faber and Faber

1966 The Religious Education Clauses of the 1944 Act – Aims, Hopes and Fulfilment, in Wedderspoon, A. G. (ed.), *Religious Education 1944-1984*, London: Allen and Unwin, pp. 15-32

—— Keeping the Humanities Human, *Conference Speeches, 17-18 June,* Association of Head Mistresses, pp. 40-55

—— Higher Education – Personal and Impersonal, in *Christianity in Education* (Hibbert Lectures, 1965), pp. 81-96, London: George Allen and Unwin

1967 Research and Outside Pressures, *Education*, January, pp. 182-3

—— Recent Developments in Higher Education Britain, *Ontario Journal of Educational Research*, Vol. 9, No. 3, pp. 161-74

—— *Moral Education in a Changing Society* (ed.), Japanese edition inTranslation), 230pp.

1968 Autonomy in Higher Education, *Universities Quarterly*, Vol. 22, No. 3, pp. 337-43

—— Moral Education – Whose Responsibility?, *Learning for Living*, No.5, pp. 10-13

—— Some Objectives in Higher Education Today, *University of Western Australia Gazette,* Vol. 11, No. 1, pp. 1-3

1969 Classification of Results in Degree Examinations in England and the United States, *1969 World Year Book of Education*, London: Evans pp. 272-8

——— Education as a Humane Study, *British Journal of Educational Studies*, Vol. XVII, No. 3, October, pp. 243-8

——— *Higher Education – Demand and Response* (ed.), London: Tavistock Publications, 261pp.

——— Insight and Foresight in Higher Education, in Niblett, W. R. (ed.), *Higher Education – Demand and Response*, London: Tavistock Publications, Ch. 11, pp. 243-56.

——— Objectives in Higher Education, *Proceedings of the 4th Conference Organised by the University Teaching Methods Research Unit*, Department of Higher Education, University of London Institute of Education, pp. 1-5

——— Religious Education in School, *AAM Journal*, Vol. 20, No. 1, pp. 36-40

——— Students' Everlasting Unrest, *Frontier*, Vol. 12, No. 2, pp. 125-8

1970 Authority and the Curriculum, *Curriculum Innovation in Arts and Science, Report of a Canadian Universities Workshop, Higher Education Group*, University of Toronto, pp. 25-35

——— *All for the Best? An Inaugural Lecture, 28 October, 1969,* Harrap, for the University of London Institute of Education, 27pp.

——— Putting Heart into Polytechnics, *Education*, March

1971 Higher Education in a Changing World, *World Year Book of Education 1971-2* (Associate Joint Editor with Brian Holmes and David G. Scanlon), London: Evans

——— A Background for School Development, *Secondary Education*, Vol. 1, No. 3, pp. 6-8

——— Introduction (pp. 1-6) to *Residence and Student Life,* (Brothers, Joan and Hatch, Stephen) London: Tavistock Publications, 419 pp.

1972 Objectives in Higher Education, in Butcher, H. J. and Rudd, E. (eds.), *Contemporary Problems in Higher Education – An Account of Research,* London: McGraw Hill, pp. 35-44

——— The Place of Teacher Education in the Structure of Higher Education, *London Educational Review*, Vol. 1, No. 1, pp. 6-13

——— Preface to *Problems of Integrated Higher Education*, Paris: International Association of Universities

——— Universities Facing the Future – Issues and Choices, in Niblett, W. R. and Freeman Butts, R. (eds.), *The World Year Book of Education 1972-3*. London: Evans in association with University of London Institute of Education and Teachers' College, Columbia University

1973 A View from Abroad – Carnegie Commission on Higher Education, *Change – The Magazine of Higher Learning*, Vol. 5, No. 9, November, pp. 38-44

——— Jottings, *Change*, March, pp. 63-4

——— Higher Education – One System or Two? *New Society*, 28 January, pp. 177-80

1974 The Scope and Use of Research in Higher Education, (in *Methodological*

Problems in Research and Development in Higher Education, Presidential Address to the Inaugural Congress of the European Association for Research and Development in Higher Education) Amsterdam: Swets and Zeitlinger

——— *Universities Between Two Worlds*, London: University of London Press, 179pp.

1975 Higher Education in the Post-Robbins Era, in Preston, R. H. (ed.), *Theology and Change – Essays in Memory of Alan Richardson*, London: S.C.M. Press, pp. 185-203

——— *The Sciences, the Humanities and the Technological Threat* (ed.), London: University of London Press, 168pp.

——— *The University Connection – The Antecedents, Concept and Development of Institutes of Education 1922-1972.* (with Humphreys, D. and Fairhurst, John R.), Windsor: NFER Publishing, 300pp.

1976 *The Church's Colleges of Higher Education*, London: Church Information Office for the Central Board of Finance of the Church of England

1977 Recent Trends in British Higher Education, *School Review*, November, pp. 82-95

——— Excursion Twenty, *University of London Institute of Education Reporter*, June, pp. 13-14

1978 Whither Education?, *The Modern Churchman*, Vol. XXI, Nos. 2-3, pp. 31-7

——— William Hazlitt as Critic, *The Charles Lamb Bulletin*, New Series, No. 23, July, pp. 137-44

——— The Spirit As Well As the Intellect – Some Reflections on Higher Education Today, *Vesper Exchange*, 1st Quarter, pp. 1-4

1979 Christianity and Higher Education, *Perspectives* (Westhill College, Birmingham), No. 6, Spring, pp. 4-10

——— Christian Schools in the 1980s, *The Month – A Review of Christian Thought and World Affairs*, November, pp. 383-6

1980 Are Colleges Moving in the Right Direction?, *Vesper Exchange*, 3rd Quarter

1981 Robbins Revisited, *Studies in Higher Education*, Vol. 6, No. 1, pp. 1-12

1982 Christian Education – Authority and Communication, *British Journal of Religious Education*, Spring, pp. 76-80

1983 Where We Are Now, *Studies in Higher Education*, Vol. 8, No. 2, pp. 105-10

1984 Elemental Religion and Corporate Worship, *The Modern Churchman*, Vol. XXVI, No. 3, pp. 9-12

——— Outer Space or Inner Light, *New Fire*, Vol. VIII, No. 59, Summer, pp. 87-9

——— Outward and Inward Knowledge, *The Friend*, Vol. 142, No. 19, May, pp. 581-2

1986 University Characters, *University of Bristol Newsletter*, Vol. 16, No. 15, p. 10

1987 Education: The Status Quo Is Not an Option, *Audenshaw Paper*, No. AP113

1988 The Enlightenment and the Lost Dimension, *Reflections on Higher Education*, Vol. 1, No. 1, July, pp. 49-57

1989 A Hope for the Future?, *The Modern Churchman*, Vol. XXX, No. 4, pp. 6-11

—— Amber – With Red to Follow, *Education Today*, Vol. 39, No. 3, pp. 21-3

—— Walter Moberly in Retrospect, *Reflections on Higher Education*, Vol. 1, No. 3, July, pp. 39-41

1990 An Absence of Outrage – Cultural Change and Values in British Higher Education 1930-1990, *Higher Education Policy*, Vol. 3, No. 1, March, pp. 20-4

—— Secular Insufficiency, *Audenshaw Paper*, No. AP 126

—— Two Kinds of Knowledge, *Epworth Review*, Vol. 17, No. 2, May, pp. 42-8

—— A Village Childhood, *North Wansdyke Past and Present*, Keynsham: Saltford Local History Society, No. 3, pp. 3-10

1991 Knowledge Which Can't Be Awarded Marks, *Reform*, November

1992 Building on the Thirties – Some Recollections, *London Institute of Education Society Newsletter*, July, p. 4

1993 A Religious Dimension in Education?, *Values and the Curriculum – Theory and Practice*, pp. 30-1

—— Coming to Belief, *Religious Experience*, Alister Hardy Research Centre, Oxford, October pp. 2-4

—— Why Believe?, *The Modern Churchman,* New Series, Vol. XXXIV, No. 4, pp. 20-6

1994 Levels of Discord, in Barnett, R. (ed.), *Academic Community – Discourse and Discord*, London: Jessica Kingsley Publications, pp. 109-21

1996 Unbelief and Belief, *Farmington Paper,* MT4, Oxford: Farmington Institute for Christian Studies

—— Looking Back and Looking Forward, *Audenshaw Paper,* No. AP 163

1997 Churches in a Twenty First Century Britain, *Crucible*, July-September, pp. 114-19

—— Sensibility and Values, *NAVET Papers*, Vol. XV, pp. 1-3

—— Some Reminiscences, *University of London Institute of Education Alumni Association Bulletin*, pp. 10-11

1998 Higher Education and Christian Believing, *Audenshaw Paper,* No. AP 175

—— Post-Modernism and Christianity, *The Friend*, 8 May, pp. 4-5

1999 A Ferment of Ideas on Education, in Reeves, M. (ed.), *Christian Thinking and Social Order*, London: Cassell, pp. 101-13

—— Doubt Versus Belief – Now, *Audenshaw Paper*, No. AP 185
—— The Job of the Humanities, in *Village Voices*, Amberley: Millenium
Book Group, pp. 193-5
2000 A Cure for Our Superficialty?, *Crucible*, October-December, pp. 242-8
—— A Diagnosis, *European Business Review – New European*, Vol. 12, No. 5,
pp. iv-xi
—— Subjects That Civilise – Religion Too?, *Audenshaw Paper,* No. AP 190

Sources of material previously published

Part I
A Village Childhood (1990), *Keynsham and Saltford Local History Society*
publication No. 3, pp. 3-10
On Not Being Sent Empty Away (2001), *Epworth Review*, Vol. 28, No. 3, p.35
Part II
Needs of the Child (1944), *Durham University Journal* Vol. XXXVII, No. 1,
pp. 28-33 (New Series Vol. VI, No. 1)
The Training of Teachers (1951), *Report of the 79th Meeting of the Headmasters'
Conference*, held at King's College, Cambridge, 26/27 September 1951
The Job of the Humanities (1999), *Village Voices*, Millennium Book Group,
Amberley, Glos. pp. 193-5
Education as a Humane Study (1969), *British Journal of Educational Studies*,
Vol. XVII, No. 3, pp. 243-8
On Existentialism and Education (1954), *British Journal of Educational Studies*,
Vol. 11, No. 2, pp. 101-11
Education: The Status Quo Is Not an Option (1987), *Audenshaw Paper,* No. 113
The Hinksey Network, Torquay TQ2 6RX
An Absence of Outrage – Cultural Change in British Higher Education 1930-
1990 (1990) *Higher Education Policy*, Vol. 3, No. 1, March, pp. 20-4
A Diagnosis (2000), *European Business Review – New European*, Vol. 12, No. 5,
pp. iv-xi
Doubt Versus Belief – Now (1999), *Audenshaw Paper,* No. 185, The Hinksey
Network, Torquay TQ2 6RX
Religion – Can We Do Without It? (2000)
Modern Believing *(in press)*

Index